Vikings of the Pacific

*THE ADVENTURES
OF THE
EXPLORERS WHO CAME FROM THE
WEST, EASTWARD*

BERING, THE DANE; THE OUTLAW HUNTERS OF RUSSIA;
BENYOWSKY, THE POLISH PIRATE; COOK AND
VANCOUVER, THE ENGLISH NAVIGATORS; GRAY OF
BOSTON, THE DISCOVERER OF THE
COLUMBIA; DRAKE, LEDYARD, AND OTHER
SOLDIERS OF FORTUNE ON THE
WEST COAST OF AMERICA

BY
A. C. LAUT

AUTHOR OF "PATHFINDERS OF THE WEST," ETC.

New York
THE MACMILLAN COMPANY

{vii}

Foreword

At the very time the early explorers of New France were pressing from the east, westward, a tide of adventure had set across Siberia and the Pacific from the west, eastward. Carrier and Champlain of New France in the east have their counterparts and contemporaries on the Pacific coast of America in Francis Drake, the English pirate on the coast of California, and in Staduchin and Deshneff and other Cossack plunderers of the North Pacific, whose rickety keels first ploughed a furrow over the trackless sea out from Asia. Marquette, Jolliet and La Salle—backed by the prestige of the French government are not unlike the English navigators, Cook and Vancouver, sent out by the English Admiralty. Radisson, privateer and adventurer, might find counterpart on the Pacific coast in either Gray, the discoverer of the Columbia, or Ledyard, whose ill-fated, wildcat plans resulted in the Lewis and Clark expedition. Bering was contemporaneous with La Vérendrye; and so the comparison might be carried on between Benyowsky, the Polish pirate of the Pacific, or the Outlaw Hunters of Russia, and the famous buccaneers of the eastern Spanish Main. The main point is—that both tides {viii} of adventure, from the east, westward, from the west, eastward, met, and clashed, and finally coalesced in the great fur trade, that won the West.

The Spaniards of the Southwest—even when they extended their explorations into the Northwest—have not been included in this volume, for the simple reason they would require a volume by themselves. Also, their aims as explorers were always secondary to their aims as treasure hunters; and their main exploits were confined to the Southwest. Other Pacific coast explorers, like La Pérouse, are not included here because they were not, in the truest sense, discoverers, and their exploits really belong to the story of the fights among the different fur companies, who came on the ground after the first adventurers.

In every case, reference has been to first sources, to the records left by the doers of the acts themselves, or their contemporaries—some of the data in manuscript, some in print; but it may as well be frankly acknowledged that *all* first sources have *not* been exhausted. To do so in the case of a single explorer, say either Drake or Bering—would require a lifetime. For instance, there are in St. Petersburg some thirty thousand folios on the Bering expedition to America. Probably only one person—a Danish professor—has ever examined all of these; and the results of his investigations I have consulted. Also, there are in the State Department, Washington, some hundred old log-books of the Russian hunters which {ix} have—as far as I know—never been turned by a single hand, though I understand their outsides were looked at during the fur seal controversy. The data on this era of adventure I have chiefly obtained from the works of Russian archivists, published in French and English. To give a list of all authorities quoted would be impossible. On Alaska alone, the least-known section of the Pacific coast, there is a bibliographical list of four thousand. The better-known coast southward has equally voluminous records. Nor is such a list necessary. Nine-tenths of it are made up of either descriptive works or purely scientific pamphlets; and of the remaining tenth, the contents are obtained in undiluted condition by going directly to the first sources. A few of these first sources are indicated in each section.

It is somewhat remarkable that Gray—as true a naval hero as ever trod the quarter-deck, who did the same for the West as Carrier for the St. Lawrence, and Hudson for the river named after him—is the one man of the Pacific coast discoverers of whom there are scantiest records. Authentic histories are still written, that cast doubt on his achievement. Certainly a century ago Gray was lionized in Boston; but it may be his feat was overshadowed by the world-history of the new American republic and the Napoleonic wars at the opening of the nineteenth century; or the world may have taken him at his own valuation; and Gray was a hero of the non-shouting sort. The data on {x} Gray's discovery have been obtained from the descendants of the Boston men who outfitted him, and from his own great-grandchildren. Though he died a poor man, the red blood of his courage and ability seems to have come down to his descendants; for their names are among the best known in contemporary American life. To them my thanks are tendered. Since the contents of this volume appeared serially in *Leslie's Monthly*, *Outing*, and *Harper's Magazine*, fresh data have been sent to me on minor points from descendants of the explorers and from collectors. I take this opportunity to thank these contributors. Among many others, special thanks are due Dr. George Davidson, President of San Francisco Geographical Society, for facts relating to the topography of the coast, and to Dr. Leo Stejneger of the Smithsonian, Washington, for facts gathered on the very spot where Bering perished.

WASSAIC, New York,
July 15, 1905.

CONTENTS

and take Possession for England of Unclaimed Territory—The Myth of a
Northeast Passage dispelled Forever

PART III

EXPLORATION GIVES PLACE TO FUR TRADE—THE
EXPLOITATION OF THE PACIFIC COAST UNDER THE RUSSIAN
AMERICAN FUR COMPANY, AND THE RENOWNED LEADER
BARANOF

CHAPTER XI
1579-1867
THE RUSSIAN AMERICAN FUR COMPANY

CHAPTER XII
1747-1818
BARANOF, THE LITTLE CZAR OF THE PACIFIC

ILLUSTRATIONS

{1}

PART I

DEALING WITH THE RUSSIANS ON THE PACIFIC COAST OF AMERICA —BERING, THE DANE, THE SEA-OTTER HUNTERS, THE OUTLAWS, AND BENYOWSKY, THE POLISH PIRATE

{3}

Vikings of the Pacific

CHAPTER I
1700-1743
VITUS BERING, THE DANE

Peter the Great sends Bering on Two Voyages: First, to discover whether America and Asia are united;
Second, to find what lies north of New Spain—Terrible Hardships of Caravans crossing Siberia for
Seven Thousand Miles—Ships lost in the Mist—Bering's Crew cast away on a Barren Isle

We have become such slaves of shallow science in these days, such firm believers in the fatalism which declares man the creature of circumstance, that we have almost forgotten the supremest spectacle in life is when man becomes the Creator of Circumstance. We forget that man can rise to be master of his destiny, fighting, unmaking, re-creating, not only his own environment, but the environment of multitudinous lesser men. There is something titanic in such lives. They are the hero myths of every nation's legends. We {4} somehow feel that the man who flings off the handicaps of birth and station lifts the whole human race to a higher plane and has a bit of the God in him, though the hero may have feet of clay and body of beast. Such were the old Vikings of the North, who spent their lives in elemental warfare, and rode out to meet death in tempest, lashed to the spar of their craft. And such, too, were the New World Vikings of the Pacific, who coasted the seas of two continents in cockle-shell ships,—planks lashed with deer thongs, calked with moss,—rapacious in their deep-sea plunderings as beasts of prey, fearless as the very spirit of the storm itself. The adventures of the North Pacific Vikings read more like some old legend of the sea than sober truth; and the wild strain had its fountain-head in the most tempestuous hero and beastlike man that ever ascended the throne of the Russias.

Peter the Great.

[Illustration: Peter the Great.]

When Peter the Great of Russia worked as a ship's carpenter at the docks of the East India Company in Amsterdam, the sailors' tales of vast, undiscovered lands beyond the seas of Japan must have acted on his imagination like a match to gunpowder.[1] Already he was dreaming those imperial conquests which Russia still dreams: of pushing his realm to the southernmost edge of Europe, to the easternmost verge of Asia, to the doorway of the Arctic, to the very threshold of the {5} Chinese capital. Already his Cossacks had scoured the two Siberias like birds of prey, exacting tribute from the wandering tribes of Tartary, of Kamchatka, of the Pacific, of the Siberian races in the northeasternmost corner of Asia. And these Chukchee Indians of the Asiatic Pacific told the Russians of a land beyond the sea, of driftwood floating across the ocean unlike any trees growing in Asia, of dead whales washed ashore with the harpoons of strange hunters, {6} and—most comical of all in the light of our modern knowledge about the Eskimo's tail-shaped fur coats—of men wrecked on the shores of Asia who might have qualified for Darwin's missing link, inasmuch as they wore "tails."

And now the sailors added yet more fabulous things to Peter's knowledge. There was an unknown continent east of Asia, west of America, called on the maps "Gamaland." [2] Now, Peter's consuming ambition was for new worlds to conquer. What of this "Gamaland"? But, as the world knows, Peter was called home to suppress an insurrection. War, domestic broils, massacres that left a bloody stain on his glory, busied his hands for the remaining years of his life; and January of 1725 found the palaces of all the Russias hushed, for the Hercules who had scrunched all opposition like a giant lay dying, ashamed to consult a physician, vanquished of his own vices, calling on Heaven for pity with screams of pain that drove physicians and attendants from the room.

Perhaps remorse for those seven thousand wretches executed at one fell swoop after the revolt; perhaps memories of those twenty kneeling supplicants whose heads he had struck off with his own hand, drinking a bumper of quass to each stroke; perhaps reproaches {7} of the highway robbers whom he used to torture to slow death, two hundred at a time, by suspending them from hooks in their sides; perhaps the first wife, whom he repudiated, the first son whom he had done to death either by poison or convulsions of fright, came to haunt the darkness of his deathbed.

Catherine, the peasant girl, elevated to be empress of all the Russias, could avail nothing. Physicians and scientists and navigators, Dane and English and

Dutch, whom he had brought to Russia from all parts of Europe, were powerless. Vows to Heaven, in all the long hours he lay convulsed battling with Death, were useless. The sins of a lifetime could not be undone by the repentance of an hour. Then, as if the dauntless Spirit of the man must rise finally triumphant over Flesh, the dying Hercules roused himself to one last supreme effort.

Radisson, Marquette, La Salle, Vérendrye, were reaching across America to win the undiscovered regions of the Western Sea for France. New Spain was pushing her ships northward from Mexico; and now, the dying Peter of Russia with his own hand wrote instructions for an expedition to search the boundaries between Asia and America. In a word, he set in motion that forward march of the Russians across the Orient, which was to go on unchecked for two hundred years till arrested by the Japanese. The Czar's instructions were always laconic. They were written five weeks before his death. "(1) At {8} Kamchatka ... two boats are to be built. (2) With these you are to sail northward along the coast.... (3) You are to enquire where the American coast begins.... Write it down ... obtain reliable information ... then, having charted the coast, return." [3]

From the time that Peter the Great began to break down the Oriental isolation of Russia from the rest of Europe, it was his policy to draw to St. Petersburg— the city of his own creation—leaders of thought from every capital in Europe. And as his aim was to establish a navy, he especially endeavored to attract foreign navigators to his kingdom. Among these were many Norse and Danes. The acquaintance may have dated from the apprenticeship on the docks of the East India Company; but at any rate, among the foreign navigators was one Vitus Ivanovich Bering, a Dane of humble origin from Horsens,[4] who had been an East India Company sailor till he joined the Russian fleet as sub-lieutenant at the age of twenty-two, and fought his way up in the Baltic service through Peter's wars till in 1720 he was appointed captain of second rank. To Vitus Bering, the Dane, Peter gave the commission for the exploration of the waters between Asia and America. As a sailor, Bering had, of course, been on the borders of the Pacific.[5]

{9} The scientists of every city in Europe were in a fret over the mythical Straits of Anian, supposed to be between Asia and America, and over the yet more mythical Gamaland, supposed to be visible on the way to New Spain. To all this jangling of words without knowledge Peter paid no heed. "You will go and obtain some reliable information," he commands Bering. Neither did he pay any heed to the fact that the ports of Kamchatka on the Pacific were six thousand miles by river and mountain and tundra and desert through an unknown country from St. Petersburg. It would take from three to five years to transport material across two continents by caravan and flatboat and dog sled. Tribute of food and fur would be required from Kurd and Tartar and wild Siberian tribe. More than a thousand horses must be requisitioned for the caravans; more than two thousand leathern sacks made for the flour. Twenty or thirty boats must be constructed to raft down the inland rivers. There were forests to be traversed for hundreds of miles, where only the keenest vigilance could keep the wolf packs off the heels of the travellers. And when the expedition should reach the tundras of eastern Siberia, there was the double danger of the Chukchee tribes on the north, hostile as the American Indians, and of the Siberian exile population on the south, branded criminals, political malcontents, banditti of {10} the wilderness, outcasts of nameless crimes beyond the pale of law. It needed no prophet to foresee such people would thwart, not help, the expedition. And when the shores of Okhotsk were reached, a fort must be built to winter there. And a vessel for inland seas must be constructed to cross to the Kamchatka peninsula of the North Pacific. And the peninsula which sticks out from Asia as Norway projects from Europe, must be crossed with provisions—a distance of some two hundred miles by dog trains over mountains higher than the American Rockies. And once on the shores of the Pacific itself, another fort must be built on the east side of the Kamchatka peninsula. And the two double-decker vessels must be constructed to voyage over the sleepy swell of the North Pacific to that mythical realm of mist like a blanket, and strange, unearthly rumblings smoking up from the cold Arctic sea, with the red light of a flame through the gray haze, and weird voices, as if the fog wraith were luring seamen to destruction. These were mere details. Peter took no heed of impossibles. Neither did Bering; for he was in the prime of his honor, forty-four years of age. "You will go," commanded the Czar, and Bering obeyed.

Barely had the spirit of Peter the Great passed from this life, in 1725, when Bering's forces were travelling in midwinter from St. Petersburg to cross Siberia to the Pacific, on what is known as the First Expedition.[6] {11} Three years it took him to go from the west coast of Europe to the east coast of Asia, crossing from Okhotsk to Kamchatka, whence he sailed on the 9th of July, 1728, with forty-four men and three lieutenants for the Arctic seas.[7] This voyage is unimportant, except as the kernel out of which grew the most famous expedition on the Pacific coast. Martin Spanberg, another Danish navigator, huge of frame, vehement, passionate, tyrannical out dauntless, always followed by a giant hound ready to tear any one who approached to pieces, and Alexei Chirikoff, an able Russian, were seconds in command. They encountered all the difficulties to be expected transporting ships, rigging, and provisions across two continents. Spanberg and his men, winter-bound in East Siberia, were reduced to eating their dog harness and shoe-straps for food before they came to the trail of dead horses that marked Bering's path to the sea, and guided them to the fort at Okhotsk.

Bering did exactly as Czar Peter had ordered. He built the two-deckers at Kamchatka. Then he followed the coast northward past St. Lawrence Island, which he named, to a point where the shore seemed to turn back on itself northwestward at 67 degrees 18 minutes, which proved to Bering that Asia and America were *not* {12} united.[8] And they had found no "Gamaland," no new world wedged in between Asia and America, Twice they were within only forty miles of America, touching at St. Lawrence Island, but the fog hung like a blanket over the sea as they passed through the waters now known as Bering Straits. They saw no continent eastward; and Bering was compelled to return with no knowledge but that Russia did *not* extend into America. And yet, there were definite signs of land eastward of Kamchatka—driftwood, seaweed, sea-birds. Before setting out for St. Petersburg in 1729, he had again tried to sail eastward to the Gamaland of the maps, but again foul weather had driven him back.

It was the old story of the savants and Christopher Columbus in an earlier day. Bering's conclusions were different from the moonshine of the schools. There was no "Gamaland" in the sea. There was in the maps. The learned men of St. Petersburg ridiculed the Danish sailor. The fog was supposed to have concealed "Gamaland." There was nothing for Bering but to retire in ignominy or prove his conclusions. He had arrived in St. Petersburg in March, 1730. He had induced the court to undertake a second expedition by April of the same year.[9]

{13} And for this second expedition, the court, the senate the admiralty, and the academy of sciences decided to provide with a lavish profusion that would dazzle the world with the brilliancy of Russian exploits. Russia was in the mood to do things. The young savants who thronged her capital were heady with visionary theories that were to astonish the rest of mortals. Scientists, artisans, physicians, monks, Cossacks, historians, made up the motley roll of conflicting influences under Bering's command; but because Bering was a Dane, this command was not supreme. He must convene a council of the Russian officers under him, submit all his plans to their vote, then abide by their decision. Yet he alone must carry responsibility for blunders. And as the days went on, details of instructions rolling out from admiralty, senate, and academy were like an avalanche gathering impetus to destruction from its weight. He was to establish new industries in Siberia. He was to chart the whole Arctic coast line of Asia. He was to Christianize the natives. He was to provide the travelling academicians with luxurious equipment, though some of them had forty wagon-loads of instruments and carried a peripatetic library.

Early in 1733, the Second Expedition set out from St. Petersburg in detachments to cross Siberia. There were Vitus Bering, the commander, Chirikoff and Spanberg, his two seconds, eight lieutenants, sixteen mates, twelve physicians, seven priests, carpenters, {14} bakers, Cossacks, sailors,—in all, five hundred and eighty men.[10] Now, if it was difficult to transport a handful of attendants across Siberia for the first simple voyage, what was it to convoy this rabble composed of self-important scientists bent on proving impossible theories, of underling officers each of whom considered himself a czar, of wives and children unused to such travel, of priests whose piety took the extraordinary form of knouting subordinates to death, of Cossacks who drank and gambled and brawled at every stopping place till half the lieutenants in the company had crossed swords in duels, of workmen who looked on the venture as a mad banishment, and only watched for a chance to desert?

Scouts went scurrying ahead with orders for the Siberian Cossacks to prepare wintering quarters for the on-coming host, and to levy tribute on the inhabitants for provision; but in Siberia, as the Russians say, "*God is high in the Heaven, and the Czar is far away*;" and the Siberian governors raised not a finger to prepare for Bering.

Spanberg left St. Petersburg in February, 1733. Bering followed in March; and all summer the long caravans of slow-moving pack horses—as many as four thousand in a line—wound across the desert wastes of West Siberia.

{15} Only the academists dallied in St. Petersburg, kissing Majesty's hand farewell, basking in the sudden sunburst of short notoriety, driving Bering almost mad by their exorbitant demands for luxuriously appointed barges to carry them down the Volga. Winter was passed at Tobolsk; but May of 1734 witnessed a firing of cannon, a blaring of trumpets, a clinking of merry glasses among merry gentlemen; for the caravans were setting out once more to the swearing of the Cossacks, the complaining of the scientists, the brawling of the underling officers, the silent chagrin of the endlessly patient Bering. One can easily believe that the God-speed from the Siberians was sincere; for the local governors used the orders for tribute to enrich themselves; and the country-side groaned under a heavy burden of extortion. The second winter was passed at Yakutsk, where the ships that were to chart the Arctic coast of Siberia were built and launched with crews of some hundred men.

It was the end of June, 1735, before the main forces were under way again for the Pacific. From Yakutsk to Okhotsk on the Pacific, the course was down the Lena, up the Aldan River, up the Maya, up the Yudoma, across the Stanovoi Mountains, down the Urak river to the sea. A thousand Siberian exiles were compelled to convoy these boats.[11] Not a roof had been prepared to house the forces in the mountains. Men and horses were torn to pieces by the timber {16} wolves. Often, for days at a time, the only rations were carcasses of dead horses, roots, flour, and rice. Winter barracks had to be built between the rivers, for the navigable season was short. In May the rivers broke up in spring flood. Then, the course was against a boiling torrent. Thirty men could not tug a boat up the Yudoma. They stood in ice-water up to their waists lifting the barges over the turbulent places. Sores broke out on the feet of horses and men. Three years it took to transport all the supplies and ships' rigging from the Lena to the Pacific, with wintering barracks constructed at each stopping place.

At Okhotsk on the Pacific, Major-General Pissarjeff was harbor master. This old reprobate, once a favorite of Peter the Great, had been knouted, branded and exiled for conspiracy, forbidden even to conceal his brand; and now, he let loose all his seventy years of bitterness on Bering. He not only had *not* made preparation to house the explorers; but he refused to permit them inside the stockades of the miserable huts at Okhotsk, which he called his fort. When they built a fort of their own outside, he set himself to tantalize the two Danes, Bering and Spanberg, knouting their men, sending coureurs with false accusations against Bering to St. Petersburg, actually countermanding their orders for supplies from the Cossacks. Spanberg would have finished the matter neatly with a sharp sword; but Bering forbore, and Pissarjeff {17} was ultimately replaced by a better harbor master. The men set to work cutting the timber for the ships that were to cross from Okhotsk to the east shore of Kamchatka; for Bering's ships of the first voyage could now be used only as packet boats.

Not till the fourth of June, 1741, had all preparations ripened for the fulfilment of Czar Peter's dying wishes to extend his empire into America. Two vessels, the *St. Peter* and the *St. Paul*, rode at anchor at Petropaulovsk in the Bay of Avacha on the east coast of Kamchatka. On the shore was a little palisaded fort of some fifty huts, a barrack, a chapel, a powder magazine. Early that morning, solemn religious services had been held to invoke the blessing of Heaven on the voyagers. Now, the chapel bell was set ringing. Monks came singing down to the water's edge. Cannon were fired. Cheer on cheer set the echoes rolling among the white domed mountains. There was a rattling of anchor chains, a creaking of masts and yard-arms. The sails fluttered out bellying full; and with a last, long shout, the ships glided out before the wind to the lazy swell of the Pacific for the discovery of new worlds.

And why not new worlds? That was the question the officers accompanying Bering asked themselves as the white peaks of Kamchatka faded on the offing. Certainly, in the history of the world, no expedition had set out with greater prestige. Eight years had it {18} taken to cross Siberia from St. Petersburg to the Pacific. A line of forts across two continents had been built for winter quarters. Rivers had been bridged; as many as forty boats knocked together in a single year to raft down the Siberian torrents. Two hundred thousand dollars in modern money had been spent before the Pacific was reached. In all, nine ships had been built on the Pacific to freight supplies across from Okhotsk to the eastern side of Kamchatka, two to carry Bering to the new continent of "Gamaland" which the savants persisted in putting on the maps, three to explore the region between Russia and Japan. Now, Bering knew there was *no* "Gamaland" except in the ignorant, heady imaginings of the foolish geographers. So did Alexei Chirikoff, the Russian second assistant. So did Spanberg, the Dane, third in command, who had coasted the Pacific in charting Japan.

Roughly speaking, the expedition had gradually focussed to three points: (1) the charting of the Arctic coast; (2) the exploration of Japan; (3) the finding of what lay between Asia and America. Some two hundred men, of whom a score had already perished of scurvy, had gone down the Siberian rivers to the Arctic coast. Spanberg, the Dane, with a hundred others, had thoroughly charted Japan, and had seen his results vetoed by the authorities at St. Petersburg because there was no Gamaland. Bering, himself, undertook the voyage to America. All the month of {19} May, council after council had been held at Avacha Bay to determine which way Bering's two ships should sail. By the vote of this council, Bering, the commander, was compelled to abide; and the mythical Gamaland proved his evil star.

The maps of the D'Isles, the famous geographers, contained a Gamaland; and Louis la Croyére d'Isle, relative of the great map maker, who had knocked about in Canada and was thought to be an authority on American matters, was to accompany Chirikoff, Bering's first lieutenant. At the councils, these maps were hauled out. It was a matter of family pride with the D'Isles to find that Gamaland. Bering and Chirikoff may have cursed all scientists, as Cook, the great navigator, cursed savants at a later day; but they must bow to the decision of the council; and the decision was to sail south-southeast for Gamaland. And yet, there could have been no bitterness in Bering's feelings; for he knew that the truth must triumph. He would be vindicated, whatever came; and the spell of the North was upon him with its magic beckoning on—on—on to the unknown, to the unexplored, to the undreamed. All that the discoveries of Columbus gave to the world, Bering's voyage might give to Russia; for he did *not* know that the La Vérendryes of New France had already penetrated west as far as the Rockies; and he did know that half a continent yet lay unexplored, unclaimed, on the other side of the Pacific.

{20}

Map of Course followed by Bering.

[Illustration: Map of Course followed by Bering.]

But with boats that carried only one hundred casks of water, and provisions for but five months, the decision to sail south-southeast was a deplorable waste of precious time. It would lead to the Spanish possessions, not to the unknown North. On Bering's boat, the *St. Peter*, was a crew of seventy-seven, Lieutenant Waxel, second in command, George William Steller, the famous scientist, Bering's friend, on board. On the *St. Paul*, under the stanch, level-headed Russian lieutenant, Alexei Chirikoff, were seventy-six men, with La Croyére d'Isle as astronomer. Not the least {21} complicating feature of the case was the personnel of the crews. For the most part, they were branded criminals and malcontents. From the first they had regarded the Bering expedition with horror. They had joined it under compulsion for only six years; and the exploration was now in its eleventh year. Spanberg, the other Dane, with his brutal tongue and constant recourse to the knout, who had gone to St. Petersburg to report on Japan, they cordially hated. Chirikoff, the Russian, was a universal favorite, and Bering, the supreme commander, was loved for his {22} kindness; but Bering's commands were subject to veto by the Russian underlings; and the Russian underling officers kept up a constant brawl of duels and gaming and drink. No wonder the bluff Dane sailed out from the snow-rimmed peaks of Avacha Bay with dark forebodings. He had carried a load of petty instructions issued by ignoramus savants for eight years. He had borne eight years of nagging from court and senate and academy. He had been criticised for blunders of others' making. He had been set to accomplish a Herculean task with tied hands. He had been threatened with fines and court martial for the delay caused by the quarrels of his under officers to whom he was subject. He had been deprived of salary for three years and accused of pilfering from public funds. His wife, who had by this time returned with the wives of the other officers to Russia, had actually been searched for hidden booty.[12] And now, after toils and hardships untold, only five months' provisions were left for the ships sailing from Kamchatka; and the blockhead underlings were compelling a waste of those provisions by sailing in the wrong direction. If the worst came, could Bering hold his men with those tied hands of his?

The commander shrugged his shoulders and signalled Chirikoff, the Russian, on the *St. Paul*, to lead the way. They must find out there was no Gamaland {23} for themselves, those obstinate Russians! The long swell of the Pacific meets them as they sheer out from the mountain-girt harbor. A dip of the sails to the swell of the rising wind, and the snowy heights of Avacha Bay are left on the offing. The thunder of the surf against the rocky caves of Kamchatka coast fades fainter. The myriad birds become fewer. Steller, the scientist, leans over the rail to listen if the huge sperm whale, there, "hums" as it "blows." The white rollers come from the north, rolling—rolling down to the tropics. A gray thing hangs over the northern offing, a grayish brown thing called "fog" of which they will know more anon. The grayish brown thing means storm; and the "porps" tumbling, floundering, somerseting round the ships in circles, mean storm; and Chirikoff, far ahead there, signals back doubtfully to know if they shouldn't keep together to avoid being lost in the gathering fog. The Dane shrugs his shoulders and looks to the north. The grayish brown thing has darkened, thickened, spread out impalpably, and by the third day, a northling wind is whistling through the riggings with a rip. Sails are furled. The white rollers roll no longer. They lash with chopped-off tops flying backward; and the *St. Peter* is churning about, shipping sea after sea with the crash of thunder. That was what the fog meant; and it is all about them, in a hurricane now, stinging cold, thick to the touch, washing out every outline but sea—sea!

{24} Never mind! They are nine days out. It is the twelfth of June. They are down to 46 degrees and no Gamaland! The blockheads have stopped spreading their maps in the captain's cabin. One can see a smile wreathing in the whiskers of the Dane. Six hundred miles south of Kamchatka and no Gamaland! The council convenes again. It is decided to turn about, head north, and say no more of Gamaland. But when the fog, that has turned hurricane, lifts, the consort ship, the *St. Paul*, is lost. Chirikoff's vessel has disappeared. Up to 49 degrees, they go; but still no Chirikoff, and no Gamaland! Then the blunder-makers, as usual, blunder more. It is dangerous to go on without the sister ship. The council convenes. Bering must hark back to 46 degrees and hunt for Chirikoff. So passes the whole month of June. Out of five months' provisions, one wasted, the odium on Bering, the Dane.

It was noticed that after the ship turned south, the commander looked ill and depressed. He became intolerant of opposition or approach. Possibly to avoid irritation, he kept to his cabin; but he issued peremptory orders for the *St. Peter* to head back north.

In a few days, Bering was confined to bed with that overwhelming physical depression and fear, that precede the scourge most dreaded by seamen—scurvy. Lieutenant Waxel now took command. Waxel had all a sailor's contempt for the bookful blockheads, who wrench fact to fit theory; and deadly enmity arose {25} between him and Steller, the scientist. By the middle of July, the fetid drinking water was so reduced that the crew was put on half allowance; but on the sleepy, fog-blanketed swell of the Pacific slipping past Bering's wearied eyes, there were so many signs of land—birds, driftwood, seaweed—that the commander ordered the ship hove to each night for fear of grounding.

On the thirteenth of July, the council of underlings had so far relinquished all idea of a Gamaland, that it was decided to steer continuously north. Sometime between the 16th and 20th, the fog lifted like a curtain. Such a vision met the gaze of the stolid seamen as stirred the blood of those phlegmatic Russians. It was the consummation of all their labor, what they had toiled across Siberia to see, what they had hoped against hope in spite of the learned jargon of the geographers. There loomed above the far horizon of the north sea what might have been an immense opal dome suspended in mid-heaven. One can guess how the lookout strained keen eyes at this grand, crumpled apex of snow jagged through the clouds like the celestial tent peak of some giant race; how the shout of "land" went up, how officers and underlings flocked round Bering with cries and congratulations. "We knew it was land beyond a doubt on the sixteenth," says Steller. "Though I have been in Kamchatka, I have never seen more lofty mountains." The shore was broken everywhere, showing inlets and harbors. {26} Everybody congratulated the commander, but he only shrugged shoulders, saying: "We think we've done big things, eh? but who knows? Nobody realizes where this is, or the distance we must sail back. Winds may be contrary. We don't know this land; and we haven't provisions to winter."

The truth is—the maps having failed, Bering was good enough seaman to know these uncharted signs of a continent indicated that the *St. Peter* was hopelessly lost. Sixteen years of nagging care, harder to face than a line of cannon, had sucked Bering's capacity of resistance like a vampire. That buoyancy, which lifts man above Anxious Fright, had been sapped. The shadowy elemental powers—physical weakness, disease, despair—were closing round the explorer like the waves of an eternal sea.

The boat found itself in a wonder world, that beggared romance. The great peak, which they named St. Elias, hung above a snowy row of lesser ridges in a dome of alabaster. Icebergs, like floating palaces, came washing down from the long line of precipitous shore. As they neared anchorage at an island now known as Kyak, they could see billows of ferns, grasses, lady's slippers, rhododendrons, bluebells, forget-me-nots, rippling in the wind. Perhaps they saw those palisades of ice, that stretch like a rampart northward along the main shore west of St. Elias.

The *St. Peter* moved slowly landward against a head wind. Khitroff and Steller put off in the small {27} boats with fifteen men to reconnoitre. Both found traces of inhabitants—timbered huts, fire holes, shells, smoked fish, footprints in the grass. Steller left some kettles, knives, glass beads, and trinkets in the huts to replace the possessions of the natives, which the Russians took. Many years later, another voyager met an old Indian, who told of seeing Bering's ship anchor at Kyak Island when he was a boy; but the terrified Indians had fled, only returning to find the presents in the huts, when the Russians had gone.[13] Steller was as wild as a child out of school, and accompanied by only one Cossack went bounding over the island collecting specimens and botanizing. Khitroff, meanwhile, filled water-casks; but on July 21, the day after the anchorage, a storm-wind began whistling through the rigging. The rollers came washing down from the ice wall of the coast and the far offing showed the dirty fog that portended storm. Only half the water-casks had been filled; but there was a brisk seaward breeze. Without warning, contrary to his custom of consulting the other officers, Bering appeared on deck pallid and ashen from disease, and peremptorily ordered anchors up.

In vain Steller stormed and swore, accusing the chief of pusillanimous homesickness, "of reducing his explorations to a six hours' anchorage on an island shore," "of coming from Asia to carry home American water." The commander had had enough of {28} vacillation, delay, interference. One-third of the crew was ailing. Provisions for only three months were in the hold. The ship was off any known course more than two thousand miles from any known port; and contrary winds might cause delay or drive the vessel on the countless reefs that lined this strange coast, like a ploughed field.

Dense clouds and a sleety rain settled over the sea, washing out every outline, as the *St. Peter* began her westward course. But what baffled both Bering and the officers was the fact that the coast trended, not north, but south. They were coasting that long peninsula of Alaska that projects an arm for a thousand miles southwestward into the Pacific.

The roar of the rollers came from the reefs. Through the blanketing fog they could discern, on the north, island after island, ghostlike through the mist, rocky, towering, majestic, with a thunder of surf among the caves, a dim outline of mountains above, like Loki, Spirit of Evil, smiling stonily at the dark forces closing round these puny men. All along Kadiak, the roily waters told of reefs. The air was heavy with fogs thick to the touch; and violent winds constantly threatened a sudden shift that might drive the vessel on the rocks. At midnight on August 1, they suddenly found themselves with only three feet of water below the keel. Fortunately there was no wind, but the fog was like ink. By swinging into a current, that ran a mill-race, they were carried out to eighteen fathoms {29} of water, where they anchored till daybreak. They called this place Foggy Island. To-day it is known as Ukamok.

The St. Peter and St. Paul, from a rough sketch by Bering's comrade, Steller, the scientist.

[Illustration: The *St. Peter* and *St. Paul*, from a rough sketch by Bering's comrade, Steller, the scientist.]

The underlings now came sharply to their senses and, at the repeatedly convened and distracted councils between July 25 and August 10, decided that there was only one thing to do—sail at once for the home port of Kamchatka. The *St. Peter* was tossing about in frightful winds among reefs and hurricane fog like a cork. Half the crew lay ill and helpless of scurvy, {30} and only two months' provisions remained for a voyage of two thousand miles. The whole crew signed the resolution to go home.

Only twenty-five casks of water remained. On August 30 the *St. Peter* anchored off a group of thirteen bald, bare, treeless rocks. It was thought that if some of the scurvy-stricken sailors could be carried ashore, they might recover. One, Shumagin, died as he was lifted ashore. This was the first death, and his name was given to the islands. Bering himself was so ill he could not stand. Twenty emaciated men were laid along the shore. Steller hurried off to hunt anti-scorbutic plants, while Waxel, who had taken command, and Khitroff ordered the water-casks filled. Unfortunately the only pool they could find was connected with an arm of the sea. The water was brackish, and this afterward increased disease.

A fatality seemed to hang over the wonder world where they wandered. Voices were heard in the storm, rumblings from the sea. Fire could be seen through the fog. Was this fire from volcanoes or Indians? And such a tide-rip thundered along the rocks as shook the earth and set the ship trembling. Waxel knew they must not risk delay by going to explore, but by applying to Bering, who lay in his berth unconscious of the dangers on this coast, Khitroff gained permission to go from the vessel on a yawl with five sailors; but by the time he had rowed against head winds to the scene of the fire, the Indians had {31} fled, and such beach combers were crashing ashore, Khitroff dare not risk going back to the ship. In vain Waxel ground his teeth with rage, signalled, and waited. "The wind seemed to issue from a flue," says Steller, "with such a whistling and roaring and rumbling that we expected to lose mast and rudder, or be crushed among the breakers. The dashings of the sea sounded like a cannon."

The fact was, Khitroff's yawl had been smashed to kindling wood against the rocks; and the six half-drowned Russians were huddling together waiting for help when Waxel took the other small boat and went to the rescue. Barely had this been effected at the cost of four days' delay, in which the ship might have made five hundred miles toward home, when natives were seen paddling out in canoes, gesticulating for the white men to come ashore. Waxel lowered away in the small boat with nine armed men to pay the savages a visit. Close ashore, he beckoned the Indians to wade out; but they signalled him in turn to land, and he ordered three men out to moor the boat to a rock. All went well between Russians and Indians, presents being exchanged, till a chief screwed up his courage to paddle out to Waxel in the boat. With characteristic hospitality, Waxel at once proffered some Russian brandy, which, by courtesy among all Western sailors, is always known as "chain lightning." The chief took but one gulp of the liquid fire, when with a wild yell he spat it out, shouted that he had been poisoned, and dashed ashore.

{32} The three Russians succeeded in gaining Waxel's boat, but the Indians grabbed the mooring ropes and seized the Chukchee interpreter, whom Waxel had brought from Siberia. Waxel ordered the rope cut, but the Chukchee interpreter called out pitifully to be saved. Quick as flash, the Russians fired two muskets in midair. At the crash that echoed among the cliffs, the Indians fell prostrate with fear, and the interpreter escaped; but six days had been wasted in this futile visit to the natives.

Scarcely had they escaped this island, when such a hurricane broke over the *St. Peter* for seventeen days that the ship could only scud under bare poles before a tornado wind that seemed to be driving north-northwest. The ship was a chip in a maelstrom. There were only fifteen casks of water fit to drink. All food was exhausted but mouldy sea-biscuits. One sailor a day was now dying of scurvy, and those left were so weak that they had no power to man the ship. The sailors were so emaciated they had to be carried back and forward to the rudder, and the underling officers were quarrelling among themselves. The crew dared not hoist sails, because not a man of the *St. Peter* had the physical strength to climb and lower canvas.[14]

{33} The rain turned to sleet. The sleet froze to the rotting sails, to the ice-logged hull, to the wan yardarms frost-white like ghosts. At every lurch of the sea slush slithered down from the rigging on the shivering seamen. The roar of the breakers told of a shallow sea, yet mist veiled the sky, and they were above waters whose shallows drop to sudden abysmal depths of three thousand fathoms. Sheets of smoking vapor rose from the sea, sheets of flame-tinged smoke from the crevasses of land volcanoes which the fogs hid. Out of the sea came the hoarse, strident cry of the sea-lion, and the walrus, and the hairy seal. It was as if the poor Russians had sailed into some under-world. The decks were slippery as glass, the vessel shrouded in ice. Over all settled that unspeakable dread of impending disaster, which is a symptom of scurvy, and saps the fight that makes a man fit to survive.

Waxel, alone, held the vessel up to the wind. Where were they? Why did this coasting along unknown northern islands not lead to Kamchatka?

The councils were no longer the orderly conferences of savants over cut-and-dried maps. They were bedlam. Panic was in the marrow of every man, even the passionate Steller, who thought all the while they were on the coast of Kamchatka and made loud complaint that the expedition had been misled by "unscrupulous leaders."

At eight o'clock on the morning of October 30 it was seen that the ice-clogged ropes on the starboard {34} side had been snapped by the wind like dry sticks. Offerings, vows, prayers went up from the stricken crew. Piety became a very real thing. The men prayed aloud and conferred on ways to win the favor of God. The colder weather brought one relief. The fog lifted and the air was clear. The wind veered northeast, and on November 4, to their inexpressible joy, a dim outline sharpened to hard, clear horizon; and the gazing crew gradually saw a high, mountainous coast become clear beyond doubt directly ahead sixteen miles. Surely, this was Kamchatka? Surely, God had heard their vows? The sick crawled on hands and knees above the hatchway to see land once more, and with streaming eyes thanked Heaven for the escape from doom. Grief became joy; gruff, happy, hilarious laughter; for a few hidden casks of brandy were brought out to celebrate the end of their miseries, and each man began pointing out certain headlands that he thought he recognized. But this ecstasy was fool joy born of desperation. As the ship rounded northeastward, a strangeness came over the scene; a chill over the good cheer—a numbing, silent, unspeakable dread over the crew. These turbulent waters running a mill-race between reefs looked more like a channel between two islands than open coast. The men could not utter a word. They hoped against hope. They dare not voice their fears. That night, the *St. Peter* stood off from land in case of storm. Topsails were furled, and the wind had ripped the other {35} sails to tatters, that flared and beat dismally all night against the cordage. One can imagine the anxiety of that long night with the roar of the breakers echoing angrily from shore, the whistle of the wind through the rotten rigging, the creaking of the timbers to the crash and growl and rebound of the tide. Clear, refulgent with sunshine like the light of creation's first day, the sting of ozone in the air, and the freshness of a scene never before witnessed by human eyes—dawned the morning of November 5.

The shore was of black, adamant rock rising sheer from the sea in a rampart wall. Reefs, serried, rank on rank, like sentinels, guarded approach to the coast in jagged masses, that would rip the bottom from any keel like the teeth of a saw; and over these rolled the roaring breakers with a clutch to the back-wash that bade the gazing sailors beware. Birds, birds in myriads upon myriads, screamed and circled over the eerie heights of the beetling cliffs. This did not look like Kamchatka. These birds were not birds of the Asiatic home port. These cliffs were not like the snow-rimmed mountains of Avacha Bay.

Waxel called a council.

Officers and men dragged themselves to Bering's cabin. Waxel had already canvassed all hands to vote for a landing to winter on these shores. This, the dying Bering opposed with all his might. "We roust be almost home," he said. "We still have six casks of water, and the *foremast*. Having risked so {36} much, let us risk three days more, let us risk everything to reach Avacha Bay." Poor Bering! Had his advice been followed, the saddest disaster of northern seas might have been averted; for they were less than ten days' run from the home harbor; but inspired by fool hopes born of fear, like the old marsh lights that used to lure men to the quicksands—Waxel and Khitroff actually persuaded themselves this *was* Kamchatka, and when one lieutenant, Ofzyn, who knew the north well from charting the Arctic coast, would have spoken in favor of Bering's view, he was actually clubbed and thrown from the cabin. The crew voted as a man to land and winter on this coast. Little did they know that vote was their own death warrant.

[1] See *Life of Peter the Great*, by Orlando Williams, 1859; *Peter the Great*, by John Lothrop Motley, 1877; *History of Peter I*, by John Mottley, 1740; *Journal of Peter the Great*, 1698; Voltaire's *Pierre le Grand*; Ségur's *Histoire de Russie et de Pierre le Grand*.

[2] Who this man *Gama*, supposed to have seen the unknown continent of Gamaland, was, no one knew. The Portuguese followed the myth blindly; and the other geographers followed the Portuguese. Texeira, court geographer in Portugal, in 1649 issued a map with a vague coast marked at latitude 45 degrees north, with the words "Land seen by John de Gama, Indian, going from China to New Spain."

[3] These instructions were handed to Peter's admiral—Count Apraxin.

[4] Born 1681, son of Jonas and Anna Bering, whom a petition describes, in 1719, as "old, miserable, decrepit people, no way able to help ourselves."

[5] He fought in Black Sea wars of 1711; and from lieutenant-captain became captain of the second rank by 1717, when Russians, jealous of the foreigner, blocked his promotion. He demanded promotion or discharge, and withdrew to Finland, where the Czar's Kamchatkan expedition called him from retirement.

[6] The expedition left St. Petersburg February 5th.

[7] The midshipman of this voyage was Peter Chaplin, whose journal was deposited in the Naval College of the Admiralty, St. Petersburg. Berg gives a summary of this journal. A translation by Dall is to be found in *Appendix 19, Coast Survey, Washington, 1890*.

[8] A great dispute has waged among the finical academists, where the Serdze Kamen of this trip really was; the Russian observations varying greatly owing to fog and rude instruments. *Lauridsen* quarrels with *Müller* on this score. *Müller* was one of the theorists whose wrongheadedness misled Bering.

[9] It was in 1730 that Gvozdef's report of a strange land between 65 degrees and 66 degrees became current. Whether this land was America, Gamaland, or Asia, the savants could not know.

[10] It is from the works of *Gmelin, Müller,* and *Steller,* scientists named to accompany the expedition, that the most connected accounts are obtained. The "menagerie," some one has called this collection of scientists.

[11] Many of the workmen died of their hardships at this stage of the journey.

[12] Berg says Bering's two sons, Thomas and Unos, were also with him in Siberia.

[13] *Sauer* relates this incident.

[14] See *Müller*, p. 93, 1764 edition: "The men, notwithstanding want, misery, sickness, were obliged to work continually in the cold and wet, and the sickness was so dreadful that the sailors who governed the rudder were obliged to be led to it by others, who could hardly walk. They durst not carry much sail, because there was nobody to lower them in case of need, and they were so thin a violent wind would have torn them to pieces. The rain now changed to hail and snow."

{37}

CHAPTER II
1741-1743
CONTINUATION OF BERING, THE DANE

Frightful Sufferings of the Castaways on the Commander Islands—The Vessel smashed in a Winter Gale, the Sick are dragged for Refuge into Pits of Sand—Here, Bering perishes, and the Crew Winter—The Consort Ship under Chirikoff Ambushed—How the Castaways reach Home

Without pilot or captain, the *St. Peter* drifted to the swirling current of the sea along a high, rocky, forbidding coast where beetling precipices towered sheer two thousand feet above a white fret of reefs, that gave the ocean the appearance of a ploughed field. The sick crawled mutely back to their berths. Bering was past caring what came and only semiconscious. Waxel, who had compelled the crew to vote for landing here under the impression born of his own despair,— that this was the coast of Avacha Bay, Kamchatka,—saw with dismay in the shores gliding past the keel momentary proofs that he was wrong. Poor Waxel had fought desperately against the depression that precedes scurvy; but now, with a dumb hopelessness settling over the ship, the invisible hand of the scourge {38} was laid on him, too. He went below decks completely fordone.

The underling officers still upon their feet, whose false theories had led Bering into all this disaster, were now quarrelling furiously among themselves, blaming one another. Only Ofzyn, the lieutenant, who had opposed the landing, and Steller, the scientist, remained on the lookout with eyes alert for the impending destruction threatened from the white fret of the endless reefs. Rocks rose in wild, jagged masses out of the sea. Deep V-shaped ravines, shadowy in the rising moonlight, seemed to recede into the rock wall of the coast, and only where a river poured out from one of these ravines did there appear to be any gap through the long lines of reefs where the surf boomed like thunder. The coast seemed to trend from northwest to southeast, and might have been from thirty to fifty miles long, with strange bizarre arches of rock overhanging endless fields of kelp and seaweed. The land was absolutely treeless except for willow brushwood the size of one's finger. Lichens, moss, sphagnum, coated the rocks. Inland appeared nothing but billowing reaches of sedges and shingle and grass.

Steller's Arch on Bering Island, named after the scientist Steller, of Bering's Expedition.

[Illustration: **Steller's Arch on Bering Island, named after the scientist Steller, of Bering's Expedition.**]

Suddenly Steller noticed that the ebb-tide was causing huge combing rollers that might dash the ship against the rocks. Rushing below decks he besought Bering's permission to sound and anchor. The early darkness of those northern latitudes had been followed by moon-light bright as day. Within a mile of the east shore, {39} Steller ordered the anchor dropped, but by this time, the rollers were smashing over decks with a quaking that seemed to tear the ship asunder. The sick were hurled from their berths. Officers rushed on deck to be swept from their feet by blasts of salt spray, and just ahead, through the moonlight, could be seen the sharp edge of a long reef where the beach combers ran with the tide-rip of a whirlpool. There is something inexpressibly terrifying even from a point of safety in these beach combers, clutching their long arms hungrily for prey. The confusion of orders and {40} counter-orders, which no man had strength to carry out, of terrified cries and prayers and oaths—was indescribable. The numb hopelessness was succeeded by sheer panic terror. Ofzyn threw out a second anchor that raked bottom. Then, another mountain roller thundering over the ship with a crash—and the first cable snapped like a pistol shot. The ship rebounded; then drove before the back-wash of the angry sea. With no fate possible but the wall of rocks ahead, the terrorized crew began heaving the dead overboard in the moonlight; but another roaring billow smashed the *St. Peter* squarely broadside. The second hawser ripped back with the whistling rebound of a whip-lash, and Ofzyn was in the very act of dropping the third and last anchor, when straight as a bullet to the mark, as if hag-ridden by the northern demons of sailor fear, hurled the *St. Peter* for the reef! A third time the beach combers crashed down like a falling mountain. When the booming sheets of blinding spray had cleared and the panic-stricken sailors could again see, the *St. Peter* was staggering stern foremost, shore ahead, like a drunken ship. Quick as shot, Ofzyn and Steller between them heaved over the last anchor. The flukes gripped—raked—then caught—and held.

The ship lay rocking inside a reef in the very centre of a sheltered cove not six hundred yards from land. The beach comber had either swept her through a gap in the reef, or hurled her clear above the reefs into shelter.

{41} For seven hours the ship had battled against tide and counter-current. Now, at midnight, with the air clear as day, Steller had the small boat lowered and with another—some say Waxel, others Pleneser, the artist, or Ofzyn, of the Arctic expedition—rowed ashore to reconnoitre. Sometime between the evening of November 5 and the morning of November 6, their eyes met such a view as might have been witnessed by an Alexander Selkirk, or Robinson Crusoe. The exact landing was four or five miles north of what is now known as Cape Khitroff, below the centre of the east coast of Bering Island.[1] Poor Waxel would have it, they were on the coast of Kamchatka, and spoke of sending messengers for help to Petropaulovsk on Avacha Bay; but, as they were to learn soon enough, the nearest point in Kamchatka was one hundred miles across the sea. Avacha Bay was two hundred miles away. And the Spanish possessions of America, three thousand. They found the landing place literally swarming with animal life unknown to the world before. An enormous mammal, more than three tons in weight, with hind quarters like a whale, snout and fore fins resembling a cow, grazed in herds on the fields of sea-kelp and gazed languidly without fear on the newcomer—Man. This was the famous sea-cow described by the enthusiastic Steller, but long since extinct. Blue foxes swarmed round the very feet of the {42} men with such hungry boldness that half a dozen could be clubbed to death before the others scampered. Later, Steller was to see the seal rookeries, that were to bring so much wealth to the world, the sea-lions that roared along the rocks till the surf shook, the sea-otter whose rare pelt, more priceless than beaver or sable, was to cause the exploration and devastation of the northern half of the Pacific coast.

The land was as it had appeared to the ship—utterly treeless except for trailing willows. The brooks were not yet frozen, and snow had barely powdered the mountains; but where the coves ran in back between the mountains from the sea were gullies or ditches of sand and sedge. When Steller presently found a broken window casing of Kamchatka half buried in the sand, it gave Waxel some confidence about being on the mainland of Asia; but before Steller had finished his two days' reconnoitre, there was no mistaking the fact—this was an island, and a barren one at the best, without tree or shelter; and here the castaways must winter.

The only provisions now remaining to the crew were grease and mouldy flour. Steller at once went to work. Digging pits in the narrow gullies of sand, he covered these over with driftwood, the rotten sail-cloth, moss, mud, and foxskins. Cracks were then chinked up with clay and more foxskins. By the 8th of November he was ready to have the crew landed; but the ship rolled helpless as a log to the tide, and the few well {43} men of the staff, without distinction of officers from sailors, had to stand waist-deep in ice-slush to steady the stretchers made of mast poles and sail-cloth, that received the sick lowered over decks. Many of the scurvy stricken had not been out of their berths for six weeks. The fearful depression and weakness, that forewarn scurvy, had been followed by the pains, the swollen limbs, the blue spots that presage death. A spongy excrescence covered the gums. The teeth loosened. The slightest noise was enough to throw the patient into a paroxysm of anguished fright; and some died on the decks immediately on contact with the cuttingly cold air. Others expired as they were lowered to the stretchers; others, as they were laid along the strip of sandy shore, where the bold foxes were already devouring the dead and could scarcely be driven off by the dying. In this way perished nine of the *St. Peter's* crew during the week of the landing.

By November 10, all was in readiness for Bering's removal from the ship. As the end approached, his irritability subsided to a quieted cheerfulness; and he could be heard mumbling over thanks to God for the great success of his early life. Wrapped in furs, fastened to a stretcher, the Dane was lowered over the ship, carried ashore, and laid in a sand pit. All that day it had been dull and leaden; and just as Bering was being carried, it began to snow heavily. Steller occupied the sand pit next to the commander; and in {44} addition to acting as cook and physician to the entire crew, became Bering's devoted attendant.

By the 13th of November, a long sand pit had been roofed over as a sort of hospital with rug floor; and here Steller had the stricken sailors carried in from the shore. Poor Waxel, who had fought so bravely, was himself carried ashore on November 21.

Daily, officers tramped inland exploring; and daily, the different reconnoitring parties returned with word that not a trace of human habitation, of wood, or the way to Kamchatka had been discovered. Another island there was to the east—now known as Copper Island—and two little islets of rock; but beyond these, nothing could be descried from the highest mountains but sea—sea. Bering Island, itself, is some fifty miles long by ten wide, very high at the south, very swampy at the north; but the Commander Group is as completely cut off from both Asia and America as if it were in another world. The climate was not intensely cold; but it was so damp, the very clothing rotted; and the gales were so terrific that the men could only leave the mud huts or *yurts* by crawling on all fours; and for the first three weeks after the landing, blast on blast of northern hurricane swept over the islands.

The poor old ship rode her best at anchor through the violent storms; but on November 28 she was seen to snap her cable and go staggering drunkenly to open sea. The terror of the castaways at this spectacle {45} was unspeakable. Their one chance of escape in spring seemed lost; but the beach combers began rolling landward through the howling storm; and when next the spectators looked, the *St. Peter* was driving ashore like a hurricane ship, and rushed full force, nine feet deep with her prow into the sands not a pistol shot away from the crew. The next beach comber could not budge her. Wind and tide left her high and dry, fast in the sand.

But what had become of Chirikoff, on board the *St. Paul*, from the 20th of June, when the vessels were separated by storm? Would it have been any easier for Bering if he had known that the consort ship had been zigzagging all the while less than a week's cruise from the *St. Peter*? When the storm, which had separated the vessels, subsided, Chirikoff let the *St. Paul* drift in the hope that Bering might sight the missing vessel. Then he steered southeast to latitude 48 degrees in search of the commander; but on June 23 a council of officers decided it was a waste of time to search longer, and ordered the vessel to be headed northeastward. The wind was light; the water, clear; and Chirikoff knew, from the pilot-birds following the vessel, from the water-logged trees churning past, from the herds of seal floundering in the sea, that land must lie in this direction. A bright lookout was kept for the first two weeks of July. Two hundred and forty miles were traversed; and on a calm, {46} clear night between the 13th and 15th of July, there loomed above the horizon the dusky heights of a wooded mountainous land in latitude 55 degrees 21 minutes. Chirikoff was in the Alexander Archipelago. Daybreak came with the *St. Paul* only four miles off the conspicuous heights of Cape Addington. Chirikoff had discovered land some thirty-six hours before Bering. The new world of mountains and forests roused the wildest enthusiasm among the Russians. A small boat was lowered; but it failed to find a landing. A light wind sprang up, and the vessel stood out under shortened sails for the night. By morning the wind had increased, and fog had blurred out all outlines of the new-found land. Here the ocean currents ran northward; and by morning of the 17th, when the sun pierced the washed air and the mountains began to appear again through jagged rifts of cloud-wraith, Chirikoff found himself at the entrance of a great bay, girt by forested mountains to the water's edge, beneath the high cone of what is now known as Mount Edgecumbe, {47} in Sitka Sound. Sitka Sound is an indentation about fifteen miles from north to south, with such depths of water that there is no anchorage except south and southwestward of Mount Edgecumbe. Impenetrable woods lined the mountains to the very shore. Great trunks of uprooted trees swept past the ship continually. Even as the clouds cleared, leaving vast forests and mountain torrents and snowy peaks visible, a hazy film of intangible gloom seemed to settle over the shadowy harbor.[2]

A Glacier

[Illustration: A Glacier]

Chirikoff wished to refill his water-casks. Also, he was ambitious to do what the scientists cursed Bering for not doing off St. Elias—explore thoroughly the land newly found. The long-boat was lowered with Abraham Dementieff and ten armed men. The crew was supplied with muskets, a brass cannon, and provisions for several days. Chirikoff arranged a simple code of signals with the men— probably a column of smoke, or sunlight thrown back by a tin mirror—by which he could know if all went well. Then, with a cheer, the first Russians to put foot on the soil of America bent to the oar and paddled swiftly away from the *St. Paul* for the shadow of the forested mountains etched from the inland shore. The long-boat seemed smaller as the distance from the *St. Paul* increased. Then men and boat disappeared behind an {48} elbow of land. A flash of reflected light from the hidden shore; and Chirikoff knew the little band of explorers had safely landed. The rest of the crew went to work putting things shipshape on the *St. Paul*. The day passed with more safety signals from the shore. The crew of the *St. Paul* slept sound out in mid-harbor unsuspicious of danger. Another day passed, and another night. Not so many signals! Had the little band of Russians gone far inland for water, and the signals been hidden by the forest gloom? A wind was singing in the rigging—threatening a landward gale that might carry the *St. Paul* somewhat nearer those rocky shores than the Russians could wish. Chirikoff sent a sailor spying from the lookout of the highest yard-arm. No signals at all this day; nor the next day; nor the next! The *St. Paul* had only one other small boat. Fearing the jolly-boat had come to grief among the rocks and counter-currents, Chirikoff bade Sidor Savelief, the bo'swain, and six armed sailors, including carpenters to repair damages, take the remaining boat and go to Dementieff's rescue. The strictest orders were given that both boats return at once. Barely had the second boat rounded the elbow of shore where the first boat had disappeared when a great column of smoke burst from the tree-tops of the hidden shore. To Chirikoff's amazement, the second crew made no signal. The night passed uneasily. Sailors were on the watch. Ship's rigging was put in shape. Dawn was witnessed {49} by eager eyes gazing shoreward. The relief was inexpressible when two boats—a long and a short one like those used by the two crews—were seen rounding the elbow of land. The landward breeze was now straining the *St. Paul's* hawsers. Glad to put for open sea to weather the coming gale, Chirikoff ordered all hands on deck and anchors up. The small boats came on with a bounce over the ocean swell; but suddenly one of Chirikoff's Russians pointed to the approaching crafts. There was a pause in the rattle of anchor chains. There was a pause in the bouncing of the small boats, too. They were *not* the Russian jolly-boats. They were canoes; and the canoes were filled with savages as dumb with astonishment at the apparition of the *St. Paul* as the Russians were at the canoes. Before the Russians had come to their senses, or Chirikoff had time to display presents to allure the savages on board as hostages, the Indians rose in their places, uttered a war-whoop that set the rocks echoing, and beating their paddles on the gun'els, scudded for shore. Gradually the meaning dawned on Chirikoff. His two crews had been destroyed. His small boats were lost. His supply of fresh water was running low. The fire that he had observed had been a fire of orgies over mutilated men. The *St. Paul* was on a hostile shore with such a gale blowing as threatened destruction on the rocks. There Was nothing to do but scud for open sea. When the gale abated, Chirikoff returned to Sitka and cruised {50} the shore for some sign of the sailors: but not a trace of the lost men could be descried. By this time water was so scarce, the men were wringing rain moisture out of the sails and distilling sea-water. A council was called. All agreed it would be worse than folly to risk the entire crew for the twelve men, who were probably already dead. There was no small boat to land for more water; and the *St. Paul* was headed about with all speed for

Slant rain settled over the sea. The wind increased and grew more violent. The *St. Paul* drove ahead like a ghost form pursued through a realm of mist. Toward the end of July, when the weather cleared, stupendous mountains covered with snow were seen on the northwestward horizon like walls of ice with the base awash in thundering sea. Thousands of cataracts, clear as crystal, flashed against the mountain sides; and in places the rock wall rose sheer two thousand feet from the roaring tide. Inlets, gloomy with forested mountain walls where impetuous streams laden with the milky silt of countless glaciers tore their way through the rocks to the sea, could be seen receding inland through the fog. Then the foul weather settled over the sea again; and by the first {51} week of August, with baffling winds and choppy sea, the *St. Paul* was veering southwestward where Alaska projects a long arm into the Pacific. Chirikoff had passed the line where forests dwarf to willows, and willows to sedges, and sedges to endless leagues of rolling tundras. Somewhere near Kadiak, land was again sighted. When the fog lifted, the vapor of far volcanoes could be seen hanging lurid over the mountain tops.

Wind was followed by dead calm, when the sails literally fell to pieces with rain-rot in the fog; and on the evening of September 8 the becalmed crew were suddenly aroused by the tide-rip of roaring breakers. Heaving out all anchors at once, Chirikoff with difficulty made fast to rocky bottom. In the morning, when the fog lifted, he found himself in the centre of a shallow bay surrounded by the towering cliffs of what is now known as Adakh Island. While waiting for a breeze, he saw seven canoe loads of savages put out from shore chanting some invocation. The Russians threw out presents, but the savages took no notice, gradually surrounding the *St. Paul*. All this time Chirikoff had been without any water but the stale casks brought from Kamchatka; and he now signalled his desperate need to the Indians. They responded by bringing bladders full of fresh water; but they refused to mount the decks. And by evening fourteen canoe loads of the taciturn savages were circling threateningly round the Russians. Luckily, {52} at nightfall a wind sprang up. Chirikoff at once slipped anchor and put to sea.

By the third week of August, the rations of rye meal had been reduced to once a day instead of twice in order to economize water. Only twelve casks of water remained; and Chirikoff was fifteen hundred miles from Kamchatka. Cold, hunger, thirst, then did the rest. Chirikoff himself was stricken with scurvy by the middle of September, and one sailor died of the scourge. From the 26th, one death a day followed in succession. Though down, Chirikoff was not beaten. Discipline was maintained among the hungry crew; and each day Chirikoff issued exact orders. Without any attempt at steering, the ship drifted westward. No more land was seen by the crew; but on the 2d of October, the weather clearing, an observation was taken of the sun that showed them they were nearing Kamchatka. On the 8th, land was sighted; but one man alone, the pilot, Yelagin, had strength to stay at the helm till Avacha Bay was approached, when distress signals were fired from the ship's cannon to bring help from land. Poor Croyére de l'Isle, kinsman to the map makers whose mistakes had caused disaster, sick unto death of the scurvy, had kept himself alive with liquor and now insisted on being carried ashore. The first breath of clear air above decks was enough. The scientist fell dead within the home harbor. Chirikoff was landed the same day, all unaware that at times in the mist and {53} rain he had been within from fifteen to forty miles of poor Bering, zigzagging across the very trail of the afflicted sister ship.

[Illustration: Sea Cows.]

By December the entire crew of Bering's castaways, prisoners on the sea-girt islands of the North Pacific, were lodged in five underground huts on the bank of a stream. In 1885, when these mud huts or *yurts* were examined, they were seen to have walls of peat three feet thick. To each man was given a pound of flour. For the rest, their food must be what they caught or clubbed—mainly, at first, the sea-otter, whose flesh was unpalatable to the taste and tough as leather. Later, Steller discovered that the huge sea-cow—often thirty-five feet long—seen pasturing on the fields of sea-kelp at low tide, afforded food of almost the same quality as the land cow. Seaweed grew in miniature forests on the island; and on this pastured the monster bovine of the sea—true fish in its hind quarters but oxlike in its head and its habits—herding together like cattle, snorting like a horse, moving the neck from side to side as it grazed, with the hind leg a fin, the fore fin a leg, udder between the fore legs, and in place of teeth, plates. Nine hundred or more sea-otter—whose pelts afterward brought a fortune to the crew —were killed for food by Steller and his companions; but two sea-cows provided the castaways with food for six weeks. On November 22d died the old mate, who had weathered northern seas for fifty {54} years. In all, out of a crew of seventy-seven, there had perished by January 6, 1742, when the last death occurred, thirty-one men.

Steller's hut was next to Bering's. From that November day when he was carried from the ship through the snow to the sand pit, the commander sank without rallying. Foxskins had been spread on the ground as a bed; but the sand loosened from the sides of the pit and kept rolling down on the dying man. Toward the last he begged Steller to let the sand rest, as it kept in the warmth; so that he was soon covered with sand to his waist. White billows and a gray sky followed the hurricane gale that had hurled the ship in on the beach. All night between the evening of the 7th and the morning of the 8th of December, the moaning of the south wind could be heard through the tattered rigging of the wrecked ship; and all night the dying Dane was communing with his God. He was now over sixty years of age. To a constitution already broken by the nagging cares of eight years and by hardships indescribable, by scurvy and by exposure, was added an acute inflammation. Bering's power of resistance was sapped. Two hours before daybreak on December 8, 1741, the brave Dane breathed his last. He was interred on the 9th of December between the graves of the mate and the steward on the hillside; and the bearded Russians came down from the new-made grave that day bowed and hopeless. A plain Greek cross was placed above {55} his grave; and a copy of that cross marks the same grave to-day.

The question arises—where does Bering stand among the world heroes? The world loves success better than defeat; and spectacular success better than duty plainly done. If success means accomplishing what one sets out to do in spite of almost insuperable difficulties—Bering won success. He set out to discover the northwest coast of America; and he perished doing it. But if heroism means a something more than tangible success; if it means that divine quality of fighting for the truth independent of reward, whether one is to be beaten or not; if it means setting to one's self the task of perishing for a truth, without the slightest hope of establishing that truth—then, Bering stands very high indeed among the world's heroes. Steller, who had cursed him for not remaining longer at Mount St. Elias, bore the highest testimony to his integrity and worth. It may be said that a stronger type of hero would have scrunched into nothingness the vampire blunderers who misled the ship; but it must be remembered that stronger types of heroes usually save their own skins and let the underlings suffer. While Bering *might* have averted the disaster that attended the expedition, it must not be forgotten that when he perished, there perished the very soul of the great enterprise, which at once crumbled to pieces.

On a purely material plane, what did Bering accomplish?

{56} He dispelled forever the myth of the Northeast Passage if the world would have but accepted his conclusions. The coast of Japan was charted under his direction. The Arctic coast of Asia was charted under his direction. A country as large as from Maine to Florida, or Baltimore to Texas, with a river comparable only to the Mississippi, was discovered by him. The furs of this country for a single year more than paid all that Russia spent to discover it; all that the United States later paid to Russia for it.

A dead whale thrown up on the shore proved a godsend to the weak and famishing castaways. As their bodies grew stronger, the spirit of merriment that gilds life's darkest clouds began to come back, and the whale was jocularly known among the Russians as "our magazine of provisions."

Then parties of hunters began going out for the sea-otter, which hid its head during storm under the kelp of the sea fields. Steller knew the Chinese would pay what in modern money is from one hundred to one hundred and fifty dollars for each of these sea-otter skins; and between nine hundred and one thousand were taken by the wrecked crew. The same skin of prime quality sells in a London auction room to-day for one thousand dollars. And in spring, when the sea-otter disappeared, there came herds—herds in millions upon millions—of another visitant to the shores of the Commander Islands—the fur seal, {57} which afforded new hunting to the crew, and new wealth to the world.

Seals in a Rookery on Bering Island.

[Illustration: Seals in a Rookery on Bering Island.]

The terrible danger now was not from starvation, but mutiny, murder, or massacre among the branded criminals of the discontented crew. Waxel, as he recovered, was afraid of tempting revolt with orders, and convened the crew by vote to determine all that should be done. Officers and men—there was no distinction. By March of 1742 the ground had cleared of snow. Waxel called a meeting to suggest breaking up the packet vessel to build a smaller craft. A vote {58} was asked. The resolution was called, written out, and signed by every survivor, but afterward, when officers and men set themselves to the well-nigh impossible task of untackling the ship without implements of iron, revolt appeared among the workers. Again Waxel avoided mutiny. A meeting was called, another vote taken, the recalcitrants shamed down. The crew lacked more than tools. There was no ship's carpenter. Finally a Cossack, who was afterward raised to the nobility for his work, consented to act as director of the building, and on the 6th of May a vessel forty feet long, thirteen beam, and six deep, was on the stocks. All June, the noise of the planking went on till the mast raised its yard-arms, and an eight-oared single-master, such as the old Vikings of the North Sea used, was well under way.

The difficulties of such shipbuilding can hardly be realized. There was no wood but the wood of the old ship, no rigging but the old hemp, no tar but such as could be melted out of the old hemp in earth pits; and very few axes. The upper part was calked with tallow of the sea-cow, the under with tar from the old hull. The men also constructed a second small boat or canoe.

On the 10th of August, with such cheers as the island never heard before or since, the single-master was launched from the skids and named the *St. Peter*. Cannon balls and cartridges were thrown in bottom as ballast. Luckily, eight hundred pounds of {59} meal had been reserved for the return voyage, and Steller had salted down steaks of whale meat and sea-cow. On the evening of August 16, after solemn prayer and devotions, with one last look to the lonely crosses on the hillside where lay the dead, the castaways went on board. A sharp breeze was blowing from the north. Hoisting sail, they glided out to sea. The old jolly-boat bobbled behind in tow. Late at night, when the wind fell, the eager mariners bent to the oar. By noon next day they had rounded the southeast corner of the island. Two days afterward, rough weather set the old jolly-boat bumping her nose so violently on the heels of the *St. Peter*, that the cable had to be cut and the small boat set adrift. That night the poor tallow-calked planks leaked so badly, pumps and buckets were worked at fever heat, and all the ballast was thrown overboard. Sometime during the 25th, there shone above the silver rim where sea and sky met, the opal dome of far mountains, Kamchatka!

The bearded men could control themselves no longer. Shout on shout made the welkin ring. Tears streamed down the rough, unwashed faces. The Cossacks wept like children. Men vied with each other to seize the oars and row like mad. The tide-rip bounding—lifting—falling—racing over seas for the shores of Kamchatka never ran so mad and swift a course as the crazy craft there bouncing forward over the waves. And when they saw the home harbor {60} of Petropaulovsk, Avacha Bay, on August 27, exultation knew no bounds. The men fired off guns, beat oars on the deck rail, shouted—shouted—shouted till the mountains echoed and every living soul of Avacha dashed to the waterside scarcely believing the evidence of his eyes—that the castaways of Bering's ship had returned. Then one may well believe that the monks set the chapel bells ringing and the cannon roared a welcome from Avacha Bay.

Chirikoff had in May sailed in search of Bering, passing close to the island where the castaways were prisoners of the sea, but he did not see the Commander Islands; and all hope had been given up for any word of the *St. Peter*. Waxel wintered that year at Avacha Bay, crossing the mainland in the spring of 1743. In September of the same year, an imperial decree put an end to the Northern Expedition, and Waxel set out across Siberia to take the crew back to St. Petersburg. Poor Steller died on the way from exposure.

So ended the greatest naval exploration known to the world. Beside it, other expeditions to explore America pale to insignificance. La Salle and La Vérendrye ascended the St. Lawrence, crossed inland plains, rafted down the mighty tide of the great inland rivers; but La Salle stopped at the mouth of the Mississippi, and La Vérendrye was checked by the barrier of the Rockies. Lewis and Clark accomplished yet more. After ascending the Missouri and crossing the plains, they traversed the Rockies; but they were {61} stopped at the Pacific. When Bering had crossed the rivers and mountains of the two continents—first Europe, then Asia—and reached the Pacific, his expedition had *only begun*. Little remains to Russia of what he accomplished but the group of rocky islets where he perished. But judged by the difficulties which he overcame; by the duties desperately impossible, done plainly and doggedly, by death heroic in defeat—Bering's expedition to northwestern America is without a peer in the annals of the New World discovery.[4]

[1] I adopt the views of Dr. Stejneger, of the National Museum, Washington, on this point, as he has personally gone over every foot of the ground.

[2] Dr. George Davidson, President of the Geographical Society of the Pacific, has written an irrefutable pamphlet on why Kyak Island and Sitka Sound must be accepted as the landfalls of Bering and Chirikoff.

[3] Thus the terrible Sitkan massacre of a later day was preceded by the slaughter of the first Russians to reach America. The Russian government of a later day originated a comical claim to more territory on the ground that descendants of these lost Russians had formed settlements farther down the coast, alleging in proof that subsequent explorers had found red-headed and light-complexioned people as far south as the Chinook tribes. To such means will statecraft stoop.

[4] Coxe's *Discoveries of the Russians between Asia and America* (Paris, 1781) supplies local data on Siberia in the time of Bering. *Voyages from Asia to America*, by S. Müller of the Royal Academy, St. Petersburg, 1764, is simply excellent in that part of the voyage dealing with the wreck. *Peter Lauridsen's Vitus Bering translated from the Danish by Olson* covers all three aims of the expedition, Japanese and Arctic voyages as well as American.

{62}

CHAPTER III
1741-1760

THE SEA-OTTER HUNTERS

How the Sea-otter Pelts brought back by Bering's Crew led to the Exploitation of the Northwest Coast of America—Difference of Sea-otter from Other Fur-bearing Animals of the West—Perils of the Hunt

When the castaway crew of Vitus Bering looked about for means to exist on the barren islands where they were wrecked, they found the kelp beds and seaweed fields of the North Pacific literally alive with a little animal, which the Russians called "the sea-beaver." Sailors of Kamchatka and eastern Siberia knew the sea-beaver well, for it had been found on the Asiatic side of the Pacific, and its pelt was regarded as priceless by Chinese and Tartar merchants. But where did this strange denizen of northern waters live? Only in rare seasons did the herds assemble on the rocky islets of Kamchatka and Japan. And when spring came, the sea-beaver disappeared. Asia was not its home. Where did it go?

Russian adventurers who rafted the coast of Siberia {63} in crazy skiffs, related that the sea-beaver always disappeared northeastward, whence the spruce driftwood and dead whales with harpoons of strange hunters and occasionally wrecks of walrus-skin boats came washing from an unknown land.

It was only when Bering's crew were left prisoners of the sea on an island barren as a billiard ball that the hunger-desperate men found the habitat of the sea-beaver to be the kelp beds of the Aleutian Islands and northwestern America. But what use were priceless pelts where neither money nor merchant was, and men mad with hunger were thrown back on the primal necessities without thought of gain?

The hungry Russian sailors fell on the kelp beds, clubbing right and left regardless of pelts. What matter if the flesh was tough as leather and rank as musk? It filled the empty stomachs of fifty desperate men; and the skins were used on the treeless isle as rugs, as coats, as walls, as stuff to chink the cracks of earth pits, where the sailors huddled like animals in underground caves with no ceiling but the tattered sails. So passed a year—the most desolate year in the annals of ocean voyaging, and when the castaways rafted back to Asia on a skiff made of their wrecked ship, they were clad in the raw skins of the sea-otter, which they had eaten. In all, nearly a thousand skins were carried back; and for those skins, which the Russian sailors had scarcely valued, Chinese merchants paid what in modern money would be from {64} one hundred and fifty to two hundred dollars a pelt.[1]

After that, the Russians of Siberia needed no incentive to hunt the sea-beaver. Its habitat was known, and all the riffraff adventurers of Siberian exile, Tartars, Kamchatkans, Russians, criminals, and officers of royal lineage, engaged in the fur trade of western America. Danger made no difference. All that was needed was a boat; and the boat was usually rough-hewn out of the green timbers of Kamchatka. If iron bolts were lacking so far from Europe as the width of two continents, the boat builders used deer sinew, or thongs of walrus hide. Tallow took the place of tar, deerskin the place of hemp, and courage the place of caution. A Siberian merchant then chanced an outfit of supplies for half what the returns might be. The commander—officer or exile—then enlisted sailors among landsmen. Landsmen were preferable for this kind of voyaging. Either in the sublime courage of ignorance, or with the audacity of desperation, the poor landsmen dared dangers which no sailors would risk on such crazy craft, two thousand miles from a home port on an outrageous sea.

England and the United States became involved in the exploitation of the Pacific coast in almost the same way. When Captain Cook was at Nootka Sound thirty years after Bering's death, his crews traded {65} trinkets over the taffrail netting for any kind of furs the natives of the west coast chose to exchange. In the long voyaging to Arctic waters afterward, these furs went to waste with rain-rot. More than two-thirds were thrown or given away. The remaining third sold in China on the home voyage of the ships for what would be more than ten thousand dollars of modern money. News of that fact was enough. Boston, New York, London, rubbed their eyes to possibilities of fur trade on the Pacific coast. As the world knows, Boston's efforts resulted in the chance discovery of the Columbia; New York's efforts, in the foundation of the Astor fortunes. East India, France, England, Spain, the United States, vied with each other for the prize of America's west coast.

Just as the beaver led French voyagers westward from Quebec to the Rocky Mountains, south to Texas, north to the Athabasca, so the hunt of the sea-beaver led to the exploration of the North Pacific coast.

"Sea-beaver" the Russians called the owner of the rare pelt. "Sea-otter" it was known to the English and American hunters. But it is like neither the otter nor beaver, though its habits are akin to both. Its nearest relative is probably the fur seal. Like the seal, its pelt has an ebony shimmer, showing silver when blown open, soft black tipped with white, when examined hair by hair. Six feet, the full-grown sea-otter measures from nose to stumpy tail, with a {66} beaver-shaped face, teeth like a cat, and short webbed feet. Some hunters say the sea-otter is literally born on the tumbling waves—a single pup at a time; others, that the sea-otter retire to some solitary rocky islet to bring forth their young. Certain it is they are rocked on the deep from their birth, "cradled" in the sea, sleeping on their backs in the water, clasping the young in their arms like a human being, tossing up seaweed in play by the hour like mischievous monkeys, or crawling out on some safe, sea-girt rocklet, where they shake the water from their fur and make their toilet, stretching and arranging and rearranging hair like a cat. Only the fiercest gales drive the sea-otter ashore, for it must come above water to breathe; and it must come ashore to sleep where it *can* breathe; for the ocean wash in a storm would smother the sleeper. And its favorite sleeping grounds are in the forests of kelp and seaweed, where it can bury its head, and like the ostrich think itself hidden. A sound, a whiff—the faintest tinge—of smoke from miles away is enough to frighten the sleeper, who leaps up with a fierce courage unequalled in the animal world, and makes for sea in lightning-flash bounds.

When Bering found the northwest coast of America, the sea-otter frequented all the way from what is now California to the Commander Islands, the last link of the chain from America to Asia. Sea-otter were found and taken in thousands at Sitka Sound, in Yakutat Bay, Prince William Sound, Cook's Inlet, and all {67} along the chain of eleven hundred Aleutian Islands to the Commander Group, off Kamchatka. Where they were found in thousands then, they are seen only in tens and hundreds to-day. Where they are in hundreds one year, they may not come at all the next, having been too hard hunted. This explains why there used to be returns of five thousand in a single year at Kadiak or Oonalaska or Cook's Inlet; and the next year, less than a hundred from the same places. Japan long ago moved for laws to protect the sea-otter as vigorously as the seal; but Japan was only snubbed by England and the United States for her pains, and to-day the only adequate protection afforded the diminishing sea-otter is in the tiny remnant of Russia's once vast American possessions—on the Commander Islands where by law only two hundred sea-otter may be taken a year, and the sea-otter rookeries are more jealously guarded than diamond mines. The decreasing hunt has brought back primitive methods. Instead of firearms, the primitive club and net and spear are again used, giving the sea-otter a fair chance against his antagonist—Man. Except that the hunters are few and now dress in San

Francisco clothes, they go to the hunt in the same old way as when Baranof, head of the Russian Fur Company, led his battalions out in companies of a thousand and two thousand "bidarkies"—walrus-skin skiffs taut as a drumhead, with seams tallowed and an oilskin wound round each of the manholes, so that the boat {68} could turn a somerset in the water, or be pitched off a rock into the surf, and come right side up without taking water, paddler erect.

The first thing the hunter had to look to was boat and hunting gear. Westward of Cook's Inlet and Kadiak was no timber but driftwood, and the tide wash of wrecks; so the hunter, who set out on the trail of the pathless sea, framed his boat on the bones of the whale. There were two kinds of boats—the long ones, for from twelve to twenty men, the little skiffs which Eskimos of the Atlantic call kyacks—with two or three, seldom more, manholes. Over the whalebone frame was stretched the wet elastic hide of walrus or sea-lion. The big boat was open on top like a Newfoundland fisherman's dory or Frenchman's bateau, the little boat covered over the top except for the manholes round which were wound oilskins to keep the water out when the paddler had seated himself inside. Then the wet skin was allowed to dry in sunshine and wind. Hot seal oil and tallow poured over the seams and cracks, calked the leaks. More sunshine and wind, double-bladed paddles for the little boats, strong oars and a sail for the big ones, and the skiffs were ready for water. Eastward of Kadiak, particularly south of Sitka, the boats might be hollowed trees, carved wooden canoes, or dugouts— not half so light to ride shallow, tempestuous seas as the skin skiff of the Aleut hunter.

We supercilious civilized folk laugh at the odd dress {69} of the savage; but it was exactly adapted to the need. The otter hunter wore the fur in, because that was warmer; and the skin out, because cured in oil, that was waterproof; and the chimney-pot capote, because that tied tight enough around his neck kept the ice-water from going down his back when the bidarka turned heels up; and the skin boots, because they, too, were waterproof; and the sedge grass padding in place of stockings, because it protected the feet from the jar of rocks in wild runs through surf and kelp after the game. On land, the skin side of the coats could be turned in and the fur out.

Oonalaska, westward of the Aleutian chain of islands and Kadiak, just south of the great Alaskan peninsula, were the two main points whence radiated the hunting flotillas for the sea-otter grounds. Formerly, a single Russian schooner or packet boat would lead the way with a procession of a thousand bidarkas. Later, schooners, thirty or forty of them, gathered the hunters at some main fur post, stowed the light skin kyacks in piles on the decks, and carried the Aleuts to the otter grounds. This might be at Atka, where the finest otter hunters in the world lived, or on the south shore of Oonalaska, or in Cook's Inlet where the rip of the tide runs a mill-race, or just off Kadiak on the Saanach coast, where twenty miles of beach boulders and surf waters and little islets of sea-kelp provide ideal fields for the sea-otter. Here the sweeping tides and {70} booming back-wash keep up such a roar of tumbling seas, the shy, wary otter, alert as an eagle, do not easily get scent or sound of human intruder. Surf washes out the scent of the man track. Surf out-sounds noise of the man killer; and no fires are lighted, be it winter or summer, unless the wind is straight from the southward; for the sea-otter always frequent the south shores. The only provisions on the carrying schooner are hams, rancid butter or grease, some rye bread and flour; the only clothing, what the Aleut hunters wear.

No sooner has the schooner sheered off the hunting-grounds, than the Aleuts are over decks with the agility of performing monkeys, the schooner captain wishing each good luck, the eager hunters leaping into their bidarkas following the lead of a chief. The schooner then returns to the home harbor, leaving the hunters on islands bare as a planed board for two, three, four months. On the Commander Group, otter hunters are now restricted to the use of the net alone, but formerly the nature of the hunting was determined entirely by the weather. If a tide ran with heavy surf and wind landward to conceal sound and sight, the hunters lined alongshore of the kelp beds and engaged in the hunt known as surf-shooting. Their rifles would carry a thousand yards. Whoever saw the little round black head bob above the surface of the water, shot, and the surf wash carried in the dead body. If the weather was dead calm, fog or clear, bands of twenty {71} and thirty men deployed in a circle to spear their quarry. This was the spearing-surround. Or if such a hurricane gale was churning the sea so that gusty spray and sleet storm washed out every outline, sweeping the kelp beds naked one minute, inundating them with mountainous rollers that thundered up the rocks the next, the Aleut hunters risked life, scudded out on the back of the raging storm, now riding the rollers, now dipping to the trough of the sea, now scooting with lightning paddle-strokes right through the blasts of spray athwart wave wash and trough—straight for the kelp beds or rocky boulders, where the sea-otter must have been driven for refuge by the storm. This hunting is the very incarnation of the storm spirit itself, for the wilder the gale, the more sea-otter have come ashore; the less likely they will be to see or hear or smell the hunter. Gaff or paddle in hand, the Aleut leaps from rock to rock, or dashes among the tumbling beds of tossed kelp. A quick blow of the bludgeon; the otter never knows how death came. This is the club hunt. But where the shore is honeycombed with caves and narrow inlets of kelp fields, is a safer kind of hunting. Huge nets now made of twine, formerly of sinew, with wooden floaters above, iron sinkers below, are spread athwart the kelp fields. The tide sweeps in, washing the net flat. And the sea-otter swim in with the tide. The tide sweeps out, washing the net up, but the otter are enmeshed in a tangle that holds neck and feet. This is, perhaps, the {72} best kind of otter hunting, for the females and young can be thrown back in the sea.

Barely has the supply schooner dipped over the offing, when the cockle-shell bidarkas skimming over the sea make for the shore of the hunting-grounds. Camping is a simple matter, for no fires are to be lighted, and the tenting place is chosen if possible on the north side of some knoll. If it is warm weather, the Aleut will turn his skin skiff upside down, crawl into the hole head first and sleep there. Or he may erect the V-shaped tent such as the prairie tepee. But if it is cold, he has a better plan yet. He will dig a hole in the ground and cover over the top with sail-cloth. Let the wind roar above and the ice bang the shore rocks, the Aleut swathed in furs sleeps sound close to earth. If driftwood lines the shore, he is in luck; for he props up the poles, covers them with furs, and has what might be mistaken for a wigwam, except that these Indians construct their tents round-topped and always turn the skin side of the fur out.

For provisions, he has brought very little from the ship. He will depend on the winds driving in a dead whale, or on the fish of the shore, or on the eggs of the sea-birds that nest on these rocks millions upon millions—such myriads of birds they seem to crowd each other for foot room, and the noise of their wings is like a great wind.[2] The Aleut himself is what any race of men {73} would become in generations of such a life. His skin is more like bronze than leather. His chest is like a bellows, but his legs are ill developed from the cramped posture of knees in the manhole. Indeed, more than knees go under the manhole. When pressed for room, the Aleut has been known to crawl head foremost, body whole, right under the manhole and lie there prone between the feet of the paddlers with nothing between him and the abysmal depths of a hissing sea but the parchment keel of the bidarka, thin as paper.

How do these thin skin boats escape wreckage on a sea where tide-rip washes over the reefs all summer and ice hummocks sweep out from the shore in winter tempest? To begin with, the frost that creates the ice clears the air of fog, and the steel-shod pole either sheers the bidarka off from the ice, or the ice off from the bidarka. Then, when the fog lies knife-thick over the dangerous rocks in summer time, there is a certain signal to these deep-sea plunderers. The huge Pacific walrus—the largest species of walrus in the world—lie in herds of hundreds on these danger rocks, and the walrus snorts through the gray mist like a continual fog-horn. No better danger signal exists among the rocks of the North Pacific than this same snorting walrus, who for all his noise and size is a floundering coward. The great danger to the nutshell skin's is from becoming ice-logged when the sleet storms fall and freeze; and for the rest, the sea makes small matter of a hunter more or less.

{74} No landsman's still-hunt affords the thrilling excitement of the otter hunter's spearing-surrounds. Fifteen or twenty-five little skin skiffs, with two or three men in each, paddle out under a chief elected by common consent. Whether fog or clear, the spearing is done only in calm weather. The long line of bidarkas circles silently over the silver sea. Not a word is spoken, not a paddle blade allowed to click against the bone gun'els of the skiff. Double-bladed paddles are frequently used, so shift of paddle is made from side to side of the canoe without a change of hands. The skin shallops take to the water as noiselessly as the glide of a duck. Yonder, where the boulders lie mile on mile awash in the surf, kelp rafts—forests of seaweed—lift and fall with the rhythmical wash of the tide. Hither the otter hunters steer, silent as shadows. The circle widens, deploys, forms a cordon round the outermost rim of the kelp fields. Suddenly a black object is seen floating on the surface of the waters—a sea-otter asleep. Quick as flash, the steersman lifts his paddle. Not a word is spoken, but so keen is the hearing of the sleeping otter, the drip of the lifted paddle has not splashed into the sea before the otter has awakened, looked and dived like lightning to the bottom of the sea before one of the Aleut hunters can hurl his spear. Silently, not a whisper, the steersman signals again. The hunters deploy in a circle half a mile broad round the place where the sea-otter disappeared; for they know that in fifteen or twenty {75} minutes the animal must come up for breath, and it cannot run farther than half a mile under sea before it reappears.

Suddenly somebody sees a round black-red head poke above water, perhaps close to the line of watchers. With a wild shout, the nearest bidarkas dart forward. Whether the spear-throw has hit or missed, the shout has done enough.

The terrified otter dives before it has breath. Over the second diving spot a hunter is stationed, and the circle narrows, for the otter must come up quicker this time. It must have breath. Again and again, the little round head peeps up. Again the shout greets it. Again the lightning dive. Sometimes only a bubble gurgling to the top of the water guides the watchers. Presently the body is so full of gases from suppressed breathing, it can no longer sink, and a quick spear-throw secures the quarry. One animal against, perhaps, sixty men. Is the quest fair? Yonder thunders the surf below beetling precipices. Then the tide wash comes in with a rip like a whirlpool, or the ebb sets the beach combers rolling—lashing billows of tumbling waters that crash together and set the sheets of blinding spray shattering. Or the fog comes down over a choppy sea with a whizzing wind that sets the whitecaps flying backward like a horse's mane. The chase may have led farther and farther from land. As long as the little black head comes up, as long as the gurgling bubble tells of a struggling breather below, the hunters follow, be it {76} near or far, till, at the end of two or three hours, the exhausted sea-otter is taken. Perhaps forty men have risked their lives for a single pelt for which the trader cannot pay more than forty dollars; for he must have his profit, and the skin must be dressed, and the middlemen must have their profit; so that if it sells even for eleven hundred dollars in London—though the average is nearer one hundred and fifty dollars—the Aleut is lucky to receive forty or fifty dollars. Day after day, three months at a time, warm or cold, not daring to light fires on the island, the Aleut hunters go out to the spearing-surround, till the schooner returns for them from the main post; and whether the hunt is harder on man or beast may be judged from the fact that where the hunting battalions used to rally out in companies of thousands, they to-day go forth only in twenties and forties. True, the sea-otter has decreased and is almost extinct in places; but then, where game laws protect it, as in the Commander Islands, it is on the increase, and as for the Aleut hunters—their thousands lie in the bottom of the sea; and of the thousands who rallied forth long ago, often only a few hundred returned.

But while the spearing-surround was chiefly followed in battalions under the direction of a trading company, the clubbing was done by the individuals—the dauntless hunters, who scudded out in twos and threes in the wake of the blast, lost themselves in the shattering sheets of spray, with the wind screaming mad riot in their ears {77} and the roily rollers running a mill-race against tide and wind. How did they steer their cockle-shell skiffs—these Vikings of the North Pacific; or did they steer at all, or only fly before the gale on the wings of the mad north winds? Who can tell? The feet of man leave earth sometimes when the spirit rides out reckless of land or sea, or heaven or hell, and these plunderers of the deep took no reckoning of life or death when they rode out on the gale, where the beach combers shattered up the rocks, and the creatures of the sea came huddling landward to take refuge among the kelp rafts.

Tossing the skin skiffs high and dry on some rock, with perhaps the weight of a boulder to keep them from blowing away, the hunters rushed off to the surf wash armed only with a stout stick.

The otters must be approached away from the wind, and the noise of the surf will deaden the hunter's approach; so beating their way against hurricane gales—winds that throw them from their feet at times—scrambling over rocks slippery as glass with ice, running out on long reefs where the crash of spray confuses earth and air, wading waist-deep in ice slush, the hunters dash out for the kelp beds and rocks where the otter are asleep. Clubbing sounds brutal, but this kind of hunting is, perhaps, the most merciful of all—to the animal, not the man. The otter is asleep. The gale conceals the approaching danger. One blow of the gaff, and the otter never awakes. In this way have three hunters killed as many as a hundred otter {78} in two hours; and in this way have the thousands of Aleutian otter hunters, who used to throng the inlets of the northern islands, perished and dwindled to a population of poverty stricken, scattered men.

What were the rewards for all this risk of life? A glance at the records of the old fur companies tells why the Russian and American and English traders preferred sea-otter to the gold mines of the Spaniards in Mexico. Less than ten years after Cook's crew had sold their sea-otter for ten thousand dollars, the East India Company sold six hundred sea-otter for from sixty to one hundred dollars each. Two years later, Portlock and Dixon sold their cargo for fifty-five thousand dollars; and when it is remembered that two hundred sea-otter—twelve thousand dollars' worth at the lowest average—were sometimes got from the Nootka tribes for a few dollars' worth of old chisel iron—the profit can be estimated.

In 1785 five thousand sea-otter were sold in China for one hundred and sixty thousand dollars. A capital of fifty thousand usually yielded three hundred thousand dollars; that is—if the ships escaped the dangers of hostile Indians and treacherous seas. What the Russians made from sea-otter will probably never be known; for so many different companies were engaged in the trade; and a hundred years ago, as many as fifteen thousand Indian hunters went out for the Russians yearly. One ship, the year after Bering's wreck, {79} is known to have made half a million dollars from its cargo. By definite figures—not including returns not tabulated in the fur companies—two hundred thousand sea-otter were taken for the Russians in half a century. Just before the United States took over Alaska, Russia was content with four hundred sea-otter a year; but by 1875 the Americans were getting three thousand a year. Those gathered at Kadiak have totalled as many as six thousand in a year during the heyday of the hunt, at Oonalaska three thousand, on the Prybilofs now noted for their seal, five thousand. In 1785 Cook's Inlet yielded three thousand; in 1812, only one hundred. Yakutat gave two thousand in 1794, only three hundred, six years later. Fifteen thousand were gathered at Sitka in 1804, only one hundred and fifty thirty years later. Of course the Russians obtained such results only by a system of musket, bludgeon, and outrage, that are repellent to the modern mind. Women were seized as hostages for a big hunt. Women were even murdered as a punishment for small returns. Men were sacrificed like dogs by the "promyshleniki"—riffraff blackguard Russian hunters from the Siberian exile population; but this is a story of outrageous wrong followed by its own terrible and unshunnable Nemesis which shall be told by itself.

[1] The price of the sea-otter varied, falling in seasons when the market was glutted to $40 a pelt, selling as high, in cases of rare beauty, as $1000 a pelt.

[2] See John Burroughs's account of birds observed during the Harriman Expedition. Elliott and Stejenger have remarked on the same phenomenon.

{80}

CHAPTER IV
1760-1770
THE OUTLAW HUNTERS

The American Coast becomes the Great Rendezvous for Siberian Criminals and Political Exiles—Beyond Reach of Law, Cossacks and Criminals perpetrate Outrages on the Indians—The Indians' Revenge

"God was high in the Heavens, and the Czar was far away," as the Russians say, and the Siberian exiles—coureurs of the sea—who flocked to the west coast of America to hunt the sea-otter after Bering's discoveries in 1741 took small thought and recked no consequences of God or the Czar.

They timbered their crazy craft from green wood in Kamchatka, or on the Okhotsk Sea, or among the forests of Siberian rivers. They lashed the rude planks together, hoisted a sail of deer hide above a deck of, perhaps, sixty feet, and steering by instinct across seas as chartless as the forests where French coureurs ran, struck out from Asia for America with wilder {81} dreams of plunder than ever Spanish galleon or English freebooter hoped coasting the high seas.

The crews were criminals with the brands of their crimes worn uncovered, banded together by some Siberian merchant who had provided goods for trade, and set adrift under charge of half a dozen Cossacks supposed to keep order and collect tribute of one-tenth as homage from American Indians for the Czar. English buccaneers didn't scruple as to blood when they sacked Spanish cities for Spanish gold. These Russian outlaws scrupled less, when their only hope of bettering a desperate exile was the booty of precious furs plundered, or bludgeoned, or exacted as tribute from the Indians of Northwest America. The plunder, when successful, or trade, if the crazy planks did not go to pieces above some of the reefs that cut up the North Pacific, was halved between outfitter and crew. If the cargo amounted to half a million dollars in modern money—as one of Drusenin's first trips did—then a quarter of a million was a tidy sum to be divided among a crew of, say, thirty or forty. Often as not, the long-planked single-master fell to pieces in a gale, when the Russians went to the bottom of the sea, or stranded among the Aleutian Islands westward of Alaska, when the castaways took up comfortable quarters among the Indians, who knew no other code of existence than the *rights of the strong*; and the Russians with their firearms seemed strong, indeed, to the Aleuts. As long as the newcomer demanded only furs, {82} on his own terms of trade—the Indians acquiesced. Their one hope was to become strong as the Russians by getting iron in "toes"— bands two inches thick, two feet long. It was that ideal state, which finical philosophers describe as the "survival of the fit," and it worked well till the other party to the arrangement resolved he would play the same game and become fit, too, when there resulted a cataclysm of bloodshed. The Indians bowed the neck submissively before oppression. Abuse, cruelty, outrage, accumulated on the heads of the poor Aleuts. They had reached the fine point where it is better for the weak to die trying to overthrow strength, than to live under the iron heel of brute oppression.

The immediate cause of revolt is a type of all that preceded it.[1] Running out for a thousand miles from the coast of Alaska is the long chain of Aleutian Islands linking across the Pacific toward Asia. Oonalaska, the most important and middle of these, is as far from Oregon as Oregon is from New York. Near Oonalaska were the finest sea-otter fields in the world; and the Aleutians numbered twenty thousand hunters—men, women, children—born to the light skin boat as plainsmen were born to the saddle. On Oonalaska and its next-door neighbor westward were at least ten thousand of these Indian otter hunters, when Russia first sent her ships to America. Bassof came soonest after Bering's discovery; and he carried back {83} on each of three trips to the Commander Islands a cargo of furs worth from seventy-five thousand to one hundred thousand dollars in modern money. The effect on the Siberian mind was the same as a gold find. All the riffraff adventurers of Siberia swarmed to the west coast of America.

We have only the Russian version of the story—not the Indians'—and may infer that we have the side most favorable to Russia. When booty of half a million was to be had for the taking, what Siberian exiles would permit an Indian village to stand between them and wealth? At first only children were seized as hostages of good conduct on the part of the Indians while the white hunters coasted the islands. Then daughters and wives were lured and held on the ships, only to be returned when the husbands and fathers came back with a big hunt for the white masters. Then the men were shot down; safer dead, thought the Russians; no fear of ambush or surprise; and the women were held as slaves to be knouted and done to death at their masters' pleasure.

In 1745—four years after Russia's discovery of western America—a whole village in Attoo was destroyed so that the Russians could seize the women and children fleeing for hiding to the hills. The next year Russians were caught putting poison in the food of another village: the men ate first among the Indians. The women would be left as slaves to the Russians; and these same Russians carried a pagan boy home to {84} be baptized in the Christian faith; for the little convert could come back to the Aleutian Islands as interpreter. It was as thorough a scheme of subjugation as the wolf code of existence could have entailed.

The culmination came with the crew of Betshevin, a Siberian merchant, in 1760. There were forty Russians, including Cossacks, and twenty other Asiatic hunters and sailors. Four of the merchant's agents went along to enforce honest returns. Sergeant Pushkareff of the Cossacks was there to collect tribute from Russia's Indian subjects on the west coast of America. The ship was evidently better than the general run, with ample room in the hold for cargo, and wide deck room where the crew slept in hammocks without cover—usually a gruff, bearded, ragged, vermin-infested horde. The vessel touched at Oomnak, after having met a sister ship, perhaps with an increase of aggressiveness toward the natives owing to the presence of these other Russians under Alixei Drusenin; and passed on eastward to the next otter resort, Oonalaska Island.

Oonalaska is like a human hand spread out, with the fingers northeast, the arm end down seventy miles long toward Oomnak Island. The entire broken coast probably reaches a circuit of over two hundred miles. Down the centre and out each spur are high volcanic mountains, two of them smoking volcanoes, all pitted with caves and hot springs whose course can be traced in winter by the runnels of steam {85} down the mountain side. On the south side, reefs line all approach. North, east, and west are countless abrupt inlets opening directly into the heart of the mountains down whose black cliffs shatter plumes of spray and cataract. Not a tree grows on the island. From base to summit the hills are a velvet sward, willow shrubs the size of one's finger, grass waist high, and such a wealth of flowers—poppy fields, anemones, snowdrops, rhododendrons—that one might be in a southern climate instead of close proximity to frozen zones. Fogs wreathe the island three-quarters of the time; and though snow lies five feet deep in winter, and such blizzards riot in from the north as would tear trees up by the roots, and drive all human beings to their underground dwellings, it is never cold, never below zero, and the harbors are always open. Whaling, fishing, fur hunting—those were the occupations of the islanders then, as now.

Here, then, came Pushkareff in 1762 after two years' cruising about the Aleutian Islands. The natives are friendly, thinking to obtain iron, and knives, and firearms like the other islanders who have traded with the Russians. Children are given as hostages of good conduct for the Oonalaskan men, who lead the Russians off to the hunt, coasting from point to point. Pushkareff, the

Cossack, himself goes off with twenty men to explore; but somehow things go wrong at the native villages on this trip. The hostages find they are not guests, but slaves. Anyway, Betshevin's {86} agent is set upon and murdered. Two more Russians are speared to death under Pushkareff's eyes, two wounded, and the Cossack himself, with his fourteen men, forced to beat a hasty retreat back to ships and huts on the coast. Here, strange enough, things have gone wrong, too! More women and children objecting to their masters' pleasure—slavery, the knout, the branding iron, death by starvation and abuse. Two Russians have been slain bathing in the hot springs near Makushin Volcano, four murdered at the huts, four wounded; and the barrack is burned to the ground. Promptly the Cossack wreaks vengeance by slaughtering seven of the hostages on the spot; but he deems it wise to take refuge on his ship, weigh anchor and slip out to sea carrying with him by way of a lesson to the natives, two interpreters, three boys, and twenty-five women, two of whom die of cruelty before the ship is well out of Oonalaskan waters.

He may have intended dropping the captives at some near island on his way westward; for only blind rage could have rendered him so indifferent to their fate as to carry such a cargo of human beings back to the home harbor of Kamchatka. Meanwhile a hurricane caught Pushkareff's ship, chopping the wave tops off and driving her ahead under bare poles. When the gale abated, the ship was off Kamchatka's shore and the Cossack in a quandary about entering the home port with proofs of his cruelty in the cowering group of Indian women huddled above the deck. {87} On pretence of gathering berries, six sailors were landed with fourteen women. Two watched their chance and dashed for liberty in the hills. On the way back to the ship, one woman was brained to death by a sailor, Gorelin; seeing which, the others on board the jolly-boat took advantage of the confusion, sprang overboard, and suicided. But there were still a dozen hostages on the ship. These might relate the crime of their companions' murder. It was an old trick out of an ugly predicament—destroy the victim in order to dodge retribution, or torture it so it would destroy itself. Fourteen had been tortured into suicide. The rest Pushkareff seized, bound, and threw into the sea.

To be sure, on official investigation, Betshevin, the Siberian merchant, was subjected to penal tortures for this crime on his ship; and an imperial decree put an end to free trade among the fur hunters to America. Henceforth a government permit must be obtained; but that did not undo the wrong to the Aleutian Islanders. Primal instincts, unhampered by law, have a swift, sure, short-cut to justice; to the fine equipoise between weak and strong. It was two years before punishment was meted out by the Russian government for this crime. What did the Aleut Indian care for the law's slow jargon? His only law was self-preservation. His furs had been plundered from him; his hunting-fields overrun by brigands from he knew not where; his home outraged; his warriors poisoned, bludgeoned, done to death; his women and children {88} kidnapped to lifelong slavery; the very basic, brute instincts of his nature tantalized, baited, tortured to dare!

It was from January to September of 1762, that Pushkareff had run his mad course of outrage on Oonalaska Island. It was in September of the same year, that four other Russian ships, all unconscious of the reception Pushkareff's evil doings had prepared for them, left Kamchatka for the Aleutian Islands. Each of the ships was under a commander who had been to the islands before and dealt fairly by the Indians.

Betshevin's ship with Pushkareff, the Cossack, reached Kamchatka September 25. On the 6th there had come to winter at the harbor a ship under the same Alexei Drusenin, who had met Pushkareff the year before on the way to Oonalaska. Drusenin was outward bound and must have heard the tales told of Pushkareff's crew; but the latter had brought back in all nearly two thousand otter,—half sent by Drusenin, half brought by himself,—and Oonalaska became the lodestar of the otter hunters. The spring of '63 found Drusenin coasting the Aleutians. Sure enough, others had heard news of the great find of the new hunting-grounds. Three other Russian vessels were on the grounds before him, Glottoff and Medvedeff at Oomnak, Korovin halfway up Oonalaska. No time for Drusenin to lose! A spy sent out came back with the report that every part of Oomnak and {89} Oonalaska was being thoroughly hunted except the extreme northeast, where the mountain spurs of Oonalaska stretch out in the sea like a hand. Up to the northeast end, then, where the tide-rip thunders up the rock wall like an inverted cataract, posts Drusenin where he anchors his ship in Captain Harbor, and has winter quarters built before snow-fall of '63.

An odd thing was—the Indian chiefs became so very friendly they voluntarily brought hostages of good conduct to Drusenin. Surely Drusenin was in luck! The best otter-hunting grounds in the world! A harbor as smooth as glass, mountain-girt, sheltered as a hole in a wall, right in the centre of the hunting-grounds, yet shut off from the rioting north winds that shook the rickety vessels to pieces! And best of all, along the sandy shore between the ship and the mountains that receded inland tier on tier into the clouds—the dome-roofed, underground dwellings of two or three thousand native hunters ready to risk the surf of the otter hunt at Drusenin's beck! Just to make sure of safety after Pushkareff's losses of ten men on this island, Drusenin exchanges a letter or two with the commanders of those other three Russian vessels. Then he laid his plans for the winter's hunt. But so did the Aleut Indians; and their plans were for a man-hunt of every Russian within the limits of Oonalaska.

A curious story is told of how the Aleuts arranged to have the uprising simultaneous and certain. A bunch of sticks was carried to the chief of every tribe. {90} These were burned one a day, like the skin wick in the seal oil of the Aleut's stone lamp. When the last stick had burned, the Aleuts were to rise.

Now, the northeast coast was like the fingers of a hand. Drusenin had anchored between two mountain spurs like fingers. Eastward, across the next mountain spur was another village—Kalekhta, of some forty houses; eastward of Kalekhta, again, ten miles across, another village of seventy families on the island of Inalook. Drusenin decided to divide his crew into three hunting parties: one of nine men to guard the ship and trade with the main village of Captain Harbor; a second of eleven, to cross to the native huts at Kalekhta; a third of eleven, to cross the hills, and paddle out to the little island of Inalook. To the island ten miles off shore, Drusenin went himself, with Korelin, a wrecked Russian whom he had picked up on the voyage. On the way they must have passed all three mountains, that guard the harbor of Oonalaska, the waterfalls that pour over the cliffs near Kalekhta, and the little village itself where eleven men remained to build huts for the winter. From the village to the easternmost point was over quaking moss ankle-deep, or through long, rank grass, waist-high and water-rotted with sea-fog. Here they launched their boat of sea-lion skin on a bone frame, and pulled across a bay of ten miles to the farthermost hunting-grounds. Again, the natives overwhelm Drusenin with kindness. The Russian keeps his sentinels as {91} vigilant as ever pacing before the doors of the hut; but he goes unguarded and unharmed among the native dwellings. Perhaps, poor Drusenin was not above swaggering a little, belted in the gay uniform Russian officers loved to wear, to the confounding of the poor Aleut who looked on the pistols in belt, the cutlass dangling at heel, the bright shoulder straps and colored cuffs, as insignia of a power almighty. Anyway, after Drusenin had sent five hunters out in the fields to lay fox-traps, early in the morning of December 4, he set out with a couple of Cossack friends to visit a native house. Korelin, the rescued castaway, and two other men kept guard at the huts.[2]

At that time, and until very recently, the Aleuts' winter dwelling was a domed, thatched roof over a cellar excavation three or four feet deep, circular and big enough to lodge a dozen families. The entrance to this was a low-roofed, hall-like annex, dark as night, leading with a sudden pitch downward into the main circle. Now, whether the Aleut had counted burning fagots, or kept tally some other way, the count was up. Barely had Drusenin stepped into the dark of the inner circle, when a blow clubbed down on his skull that felled him to earth. The Cossack, coming second, had stumbled over the prostrate body before either had any suspicion of danger; and in a {92} second, both were cut to pieces by knives traded to the Indians the day before for otter skins.

Shevyrin, the third man, happened to be carrying an axe. One against a score, he yet kept his face to the enemy, beat a retreat backward striking right and left with the axe, then turned and fled for very life, with a shower of arrows and lances falling about him, that drenched him in his own blood. Already a crash of muskets told of battle at the huts. More dead than alive, the pursued Russian turned but to strike his assailants back. Then, he was at the huts almost stumbling over the man who had probably been doing sentinel duty but was now under the spears of the crowd—when the hut door opened; and Korelin, the Russian, dashed out flourishing a yard-long bear knife under protection of the other guard's musket fire from the window, slashed to death two of the nearest Indians, cut a swath that sent the others scattering, seized the two wounded men, dragged them inside the hut, and slammed the door to the enraged yells of the baffled warriors.

Some one has said that Oonalaska and Oomnak are the smelting furnaces of America. Certainly, the volcanic caves supplied sulphur that the natives knew how to use as match lighters. The savages were without firearms, but might have burned out the Russians had it not been for the constant fusillade of musketry from door and roof and parchment windows of the hut. Two of the Russians were wounded and weak {93} from loss of blood. The other two never remitted their guard day or night for four days, neither sleeping nor eating, till the wounded pair, having recovered somewhat, seized pistols and cutlasses, waited till a quelling of the musketry tempted the Indians near, then sallied out with a flare of their pistols, that dropped three Aleuts on the spot, wounded others, and drove the rest to a distance. But in the sortie, there had been flaunted in their very faces, the coats and caps and daggers of the five hunters Drusenin had sent fox trapping. Plainly, the fox hunters had been massacred. The four men were alone surrounded by hundreds of hostiles, ten miles from the shores of

Oonalaska, twenty from the other hunting detachments and the ship. But water was becoming a desperate need. To stay cooped up in the hut was to be forced into surrender. Their only chance was to risk all by a dash from the island. Dark was gathering. Through the shadowy dusk watched the Aleuts; but the pointed muskets of the two wounded men kept hostiles beyond distance of spear-tossing, while the other two Russians destroyed what they could not carry away, hauled down their skin boat to the water loaded with provisions, ammunition, and firearms, then under guard of levelled pistols, pulled off in the darkness across the sea, heaving and thundering to the night tide.

But the sea was the lesser danger. Once away from the enemy, the four fugitives pulled for dear life {94} across the tumbling waves—ten miles the way they went, one account says—to the main shore of Oonalaska. It was pitch dark. When they reached the shore, they could neither hear nor see a sign of life; but the moss trail through the snows had probably become well beaten to the ship by this time—four months from Drusenin's landing—or else the fugitives found their way by a kind of desperation; for before daybreak they had run within shouting distance of the second detachment of hunters stationed at Kalekhta. Not a sound! Not a light! Perhaps they had missed their way! Perhaps the Indians on the main island are still friendly! Shevyrin or Korelin utters a shout, followed by the signal of a musket shot for that second party of hunters to come out and help. Scarcely had the crash died over the snows, when out of the dark leaped a hundred lances, a hundred faces, a hundred shrieking, bloodthirsty savages. Now they realize the mistake of having landed, of having abandoned the skin boat back on the beach there! But no time to retrace steps! Only a wild dash through the dark, catching by each other to keep together, up to a high precipitous rock they know is somewhere here, with the sea behind, sheer drop on each side, and but one narrow approach! Here they make their stand, muskets and sword in hand, beating the assailants back, wherever a stealthy form comes climbing up the rock to hurl spear or lance! Presently, a well-directed fusillade drives the savages off! While night still hid {95} them, the four fugitives scrambled down the side of the rock farthest from the savages, and ran for the roadstead where the ship had anchored.

As dawn comes up over the harbor something catches the attention of the runners. It is the main hatch, the planking, the mast poles of the ship, drawn up and scattered on the beach. Drusenin's ship has been destroyed. The crew is massacred; they, alone, have escaped; and the nearest help is one of those three other Russian ships anchored somewhere seventy miles west. Without waiting to look more, the three men ran for the mountains of the interior, found hiding in one of the deep-grassed ravines, scooped out a hole in the sand, covered this with a sail white as snow, and crawled under in hiding for the day.

The next night they came down to the shore, in the hope, perhaps, of finding refugees like themselves. They discovered only the mangled bodies of their comrades, literally hacked to pieces. A saint's image and a book of prayers lay along the sand. Scattered everywhere were flour sacks, provisions, ships' planking. These they carried back as well as they could three miles in the mountains. A pretty legend is told of a native hunter following their tracks to this retreat, and not only refusing to betray them but secretly carrying provisions; and some such explanation is needed to know how the four men lived hidden in the mountains from December 9 to February 2, 1764.

If they had known where those other Russian ships {96} were anchored, they might have struck across country to them, or followed the coast by night; but rival hunters did not tell each other where they anchored, and tracks across country could have been followed. The trackless sea was safer.

There is another story of how the men hid in mountain caves all those weeks, kept alive by the warmth of hot springs, feeding on clams and shell-fish gathered at night. This, too, may be true; for the mountains inland of Oonalaska Harbor are honeycombed with caves, and there are well-known hot springs.

By February they had succeeded in making a skin skiff of the leather sacks. They launched this on the harbor and, stealing away unseen, rounded the northwest coast of Oonalaska's hand projecting into the sea, travelling at night southwestward, seeking the ships of Korovin, or Medvedeff, or Glottoff. Now the majority of voyagers don't care to coast this part of Oonalaska at night during the winter in a safe ship; and these men had nothing between them and the abyss of the sea but the thickness of a leather sack badly oiled to keep out water. Their one hope was—a trader's vessel.

All night, for a week, they coasted within the shadow of the shore rocks, hiding by day, passing three Indian villages undiscovered. Distance gave them courage. They now paddled by day, and just as they rounded Makushin Volcano, lying like a great white corpse five thousand feet above Bering Sea, they came on five {97} Indians, who at once landed and running alongshore gave the alarm. The refugees for the second time sought safety on a rock; but the rising tide drove them off. Seizing the light boat, they ran for shelter in a famous cave of the volcanic mountain. Here, for five weeks, they resisted constant siege, not a Russian of the four daring to appear within twenty yards of the cave entrance before a shower of arrows fell inside. Their only food now was the shell-fish gathered at night; their only water, snow scooped from gutters of the cave. Each night one watched by turn while the others slept; and each night one must make a dash to gather the shell-fish. Five weeks at last tired the Indians' vigilance out. One dark night the Russians succeeded in launching out undetected. That day they hid, but daybreak of the next long pull showed them a ship in the folds of the mountain coast—Korovin's vessel. They reached the ship on the 30th of March. Poor Shevyrin soon after died from his wounds in the underground hut, but Korovin's troubles had only begun.

Ivan Korovin's vessel had sailed out of Avacha Bay, Kamchatka, just two weeks before Pushkareff's crew of criminals came home. It had become customary for the hunting vessels to sail to the Commander Islands—Bering and Copper—nearest Kamchatka, and winter there, laying up a store of sea-cow meat, the huge bovine of the sea, which was soon to be exterminated by the hunters. Here Korovin met Denis Medvedeff's {98} crew, also securing a year's supply of meat for the hunt of the sea-otter. The two leaders must have had some inkling of trouble ahead, for Medvedeff gave Korovin ten more sailors, and the two signed a written contract to help each other in time of need.

In spring (1763) both sailed for the best sea-otter fields then known—Oonalaska and Oomnak, Korovin with thirty-seven men, Medvedeff, forty-nine. In order not to interfere with each other's hunt, Medvedeff stopped at Oomnak, Korovin went on to Oonalaska. Anchoring sixty yards from shore, not very far from the volcano caves, where Drusenin's four fugitives were to fight for their lives the following spring, Korovin landed with fourteen men to reconnoitre. Deserted houses he saw, but never a living soul. Going back to the ship for more men, he set out again and went inland five miles where he found a village of three hundred souls. Three chiefs welcomed him, showed receipts for tribute of furs given by the Cossack collector of a previous ship, and gave over three boys as hostages of good conduct—one, called Alexis, the son of a chief. Meanwhile, letters were exchanged with Medvedeff down a hundred miles at Oomnak. All was well. The time had not come. It was only September—about the same time that Drusenin up north was sending out his hunters in three detachments.

Korovin was so thoroughly satisfied all was safe, that he landed his entire cargo and crew, and while the carpenters were building wintering huts out of {99} driftwood, set out himself, with two skin boats, to coast northeast. For four days he followed the very shore that the four escaping men were to cruise in an opposite direction. About forty miles from the anchorage he met Drusenin himself, leading twenty-five Russian hunters out from Captain Harbor. Surely, if ever hunters were safe, Korovin's were, with Medvedeff's forty-nine men southwest a hundred miles, and Drusenin's thirty sailors forty miles northeast. Korovin decided to hunt midway between Drusenin's crew and Medvedeff's. It is likely that the letters exchanged among the different commanders from September to December were arranging that Drusenin should keep to the east of Oonalaska, Korovin to the west of the island, while Medvedeff hunted exclusively on the other island—Oomnak.

By December Korovin had scattered twenty-three hunters southwest, keeping a guard of only sixteen for the huts and boat. Among the sixteen was little Alexis, the hostage Indian boy. The warning of danger was from the mother of the little Aleut, who reported that sixty hostiles were advancing on the ship under pretence of trading sea-otter. Between the barracks and the sea front flowed a stream. Here the Cossack guard took their stand, armed head to foot, permitting only ten Indians at a time to enter the huts for trade. The Aleuts exchanged their sea-otter for what iron they could get, and departed without any sign. Korovin had almost concluded it was a false {100} alarm, when three Indian servants of Drusenin's ship came dashing breathless across country with news that the ship and all the Russians on the east end of Oonalaska had been destroyed.

Including the three newcomers, Korovin had only nineteen men; and his hostages numbered almost as strong. The panic-stricken sailors were for burning huts and ship, and escaping overland to the twenty-three hunters somewhere southwest.

It was the 10th of December—the very night when Drusenin's fugitives had taken to hiding in the north mountains. While Korovin was still debating what to do, an alarm came from beneath the keel of the ship. In the darkness, the sea was suddenly alive with hundreds of skin skiffs each carrying from eight to twenty Indian warriors. One can well believe that lanterns swinging from bow and stern, and lights behind the talc windows of the huts, were put suddenly out to avoid giving targets for the hurricane of lances and darts and javelins that came hurtling through the air. Two Russians fell dead, reducing Korovin's defence to fourteen; but a quick swing of musketry exacted five Indian lives for the two dead whites. At the end of four days, the Russians were completely exhausted. The besiegers withdrew to a cave on the mountain side, perhaps to tempt Korovin on land.

Quick as thought, Korovin buried his iron deep under the barracks, set fire to the huts, and concentrated all his forces on the vessel, where he wisely carried the {101} hostages with him and sheered fifty yards farther off shore. Had the riot of winter winds not been driving mountain billows along the outer coast, he might have put to sea; but he had no proof the twenty-three men gone inland hunting to the south might not be yet alive, and a winter gale would have dashed his ship to kindling wood outside the sheltered harbor.

Food was short, water was short, and the ship over-crowded with hostages. To make matters worse, scurvy broke out among the crew; and the hostiles renewed the attack, surrounding the Russian ship in forty canoes with ten to twenty warriors in each. An ocean vessel of the time, or even a pirate ship, could have scattered the assailants in a few minutes; but the Russian hunting vessels were long, low, flat-bottomed, rickety-planked craft, of perhaps sixty feet in length, with no living accommodation below decks, and very poor hammock space above. Hostages and scurvy-stricken Russians were packed in the hold with the meat stores and furs like dying rats in a garbage barrel. It was as much as a Russian's life was worth, to show his head above the hatchway; and the siege lasted from the middle of December to the 30th of March, when Drusenin's four refugees, led by Korelin, made a final dash from Makushin Volcano, and gained Korovin's ship.

With the addition of the fugitives, Korovin now had eighteen Russians. The Indian father of the hostage, {102} Alexis, had come to demand back his son. Korovin freed the boy at once. By the end of April, the spring gales had subsided, and though half his men were prostrate with scurvy, there was nothing for Korovin to do but dare the sea. They sailed out from Oonalaska on April 26 heading back toward Oomnak, where Medvedeff had anchored.

In the straits between the different Aleutian Islands runs a terrific tide-rip. Crossing from Oonalaska to Oomnak, Korovin's ship was caught by the counter-currents and cross winds. Not more than five men were well enough to stand upon their feet. The ship drifted without pilot or oarsmen, and driving the full force of wind and tide foundered on the end of Oomnak Island. Ammunition, sails, and skins for fresh rowboats were all that could be saved of the wreck. One scurvy-stricken sailor was drowned trying to reach land; another died on being lifted from the stiflingly close hold to fresh air. Eight hostages sprang overboard and escaped. Of the sixteen white men and four hostages left, three were powerless from scurvy. This last blow on top of a winter's siege was too much for the Russians. Their enfeebled bodies were totally exhausted. Stretching sails round as a tent and stationing ten men at a time as sentinels, they slept the first unbroken sleep they had known in five months. The tired-out sentinels must have fallen asleep at their places; for just as day dawned came a hundred savages, stealthy and silent, seeking the ship that had slipped {103} out from Oonalaska. Landing without a sound, they crept up within ten yards of the tents, stabbed the sleeping sentinels to death, and let go such a whiz of arrows and lances at the tent walls, that three of the Indian hostages inside were killed and every Russian wounded.

Korovin had not even time to seize his firearms. Cutlass in hand, followed by four men—all wounded and bleeding like himself—he dashed out, slashed two savages to death, and scattered the rest at the sword point. A shower of spears was the Indians' answer to this. Wounded anew, the five Russians could scarcely drag themselves back to the tent where by this time the others had seized the firearms.

All that day and night, a tempest lashed the shore. The stranded ship fell to pieces like a boat of paper; and the attacking islanders strewed the provisions to the winds with shrieks of laughter. On the 30th of April, the assailants began firing muskets, which they had captured from Korovin's massacred hunters; but the shots fell wide of the mark. Then they brought sulphur from the volcanic caves, and set fire to the long grass on the windward side of the tents. Again, Korovin sallied out, drove them off, and extinguished the fire. May, June, and half July he lay stranded here, waiting for his men to recover, and when they recovered, setting them to build a boat of skin and driftwood.

Toward the third week of July, a skin boat twenty-four feet long was finished. In this were laid the wounded; and the well men took to the paddles. All {104} night they paddled westward and still westward, night after night, seeking the third vessel—that of Denis Medvedeff, who had come with them the year before from Bering Island. On the tenth day, Russian huts and a stone bath-house were seen on the shore of a broad inlet. Not a soul was stirring. As Korovin's boat approached, bits of sail, ships' wreckage, and provisions were seen scattered on the shore. Fearing the worst, Korovin landed. Signs of a struggle were on every hand; and in the bath-house, still clothed but with thongs round their necks as if they had been strangled to death, lay twenty of Medvedeff's crew. Closer examination showed Medvedeff himself among the slain. Not a soul was left to tell the story of the massacre, not a word ever heard about the fate of the others in the crew. Korovin's last hope was gone. There was no third ship to carry him home. He was in the very act of ordering his men to construct winter quarters, when Stephen Glottoff, a famous hunter on the way back from Kadiak westward, appeared marching across the sands followed by eight men. Glottoff had heard of the massacres from natives on the north shore with whom he was friendly; and had sent out rescue parties to seek the survivors on the south coast of whom the Indian spies told.

The poor fugitives embraced Glottoff, and went almost mad with joy. But like the prospector, who suffers untold hardships seeking the wealth of gold, these seekers of wealth in furs could not relinquish the {105} wild freedom of the perilous life. They signed contracts to hunt with Glottoff for the year.

It is no part of this story to tell how the Cossack, Solovieff, entered on a campaign of punishment for the Aleuts when he came. Whole villages were blown up by mines of powder in birch bark. Fugitives dashing from the conflagration were sabred by the Russians, as many as a hundred Aleuts butchered at a time, villages of three hundred scattered to the winds, warriors bound hand and foot in line, and shot down.

Suffice it to say, scurvy slaked Solovieff's vengeance. Both Aleuts and Russians had learned the one all-important lesson—the Christian's doctrine of retribution, the scientist's law of equilibrium—that brute force met by brute force ends only in mutual destruction, in anarchy, in death. Thirty years later, Vancouver visiting the Russians could report that their influence on the Indians was of the sort that springs from deep-rooted kindness and identity of interests. Both sides had learned there was a better way than the wolf code.[3]

[1] See Coxe's *Discoveries of the Russians.*

[2] Some of the old records spell the name of this wrecked Russian "Korelin," as if it were "Gorelin," the sailor, of Pushkareff's crew, who brained the Indian girl; I am unable to determine whether "Korelin" and "Gorelin" are the same man or not. If so, then the punishment came home indeed.

[3] It would be almost impossible to quote all the authorities on this massacre of the Russians, and every one who has written on Russian fur trade in America gives different scraps of the tragedy; but nearly all can be traced back to the detailed account in Coxe's *Discoveries of the Russians between Asia and America*, and on this I have relied, the French edition of 1781. The Census Report, Vol. VIII, 1880, by Ivan Petroff, is invaluable for topography and ethnology of this period and region. It was from Korelin, one of the four refugees, that the Russian archivists took the first account of the massacre; and Coxe's narrative is based on Korelin's story, though the tradition of the massacre has been handed down from father to child among Oonalaskans to this day, so that certain caves near Captain Harbor, and Makushin Volcano are still pointed out as the refuge of the four pursued Russians.

CHAPTER V
1768-1772
COUNT MAURITIUS BENYOWSKY, THE POLISH PIRATE

Siberian Exiles under Polish Soldier of Fortune plot to overthrow Garrison of Kamchatka and escape to West Coast of America as Fur Traders—A Bloody Melodrama enacted at Bolcheresk—The Count and his Criminal Crew sail to America

Fur hunters, world over, live much the same life. It was the beaver led French voyageurs westward to the Rocky Mountains. It was the sea-otter brought Russian coasters cruising southward from Alaska to California; and it was the little sable set the mad pace of the Cossacks' wild rush clear across Siberia to the shores of the Pacific. The tribute that the riotous Cossacks collected, whether from Siberia or America, was tribute in furs.

The farther the hunters wandered, the harder it was to obtain supplies from the cities. In each case—in New France, on the Missouri, in Siberia—this compelled resort to the same plan; a grand rallying place, a yearly rendezvous, a stamping-ground for hunters and traders. Here merchants brought their goods; {107} hunters, their furs; light-fingered gentry, offscourings from everywhere, horses to sell, or smuggled whiskey, or plunder that had been picked up in ways untold.

The great meeting place for Russian fur traders was on a plain east of the Lena River, not far from Yakutsk, a thousand miles in a crow line from the Pacific. In the fall of 1770 there had gathered here as lawless birds of a feather as ever scoured earth for prey. Merchants from the inland cities had floated down supplies to the plain on white and black and lemon-painted river barges. Long caravans of pack horses and mules and tented wagons came rumbling dust-covered across the fields, bells ajingle, driven by Cossacks all the way from St. Petersburg, six thousand miles. Through snow-padded forests, over wind-swept plains, across the heaving mountains of two continents, along deserts and Siberian rivers, almost a year had the caravans travelled. These, for the most part, carried ship supplies—cordage, tackling, iron—for vessels to be built on the Pacific to sail for America.

Then there rode in at furious pace, from the northern steppes of Siberia, the Cossack tribute collectors—four hundred of them centred here—who gathered one-tenth of the furs for the Czar, nine-tenths for themselves: drunken brawlers they were, lawless as Arabs; and the only law they knew was the law they wielded. Tartar hordes came with horses to sell, freebooters of the boundless desert, banditti in league with the Cossacks to smuggle across the {108} borders of the Chinese. And Chinese smugglers, splendid in silk attire, hobnobbed with exiles, who included every class from courtiers banished for political offences to criminals with ears cut off and faces slit open. What with drink and play and free fights—if the Czar did not hear, it was because he was far away.

On this August night half a dozen new exiles had come in with the St. Petersburg cavalcade. The prisoners were set free on parole to see the sights, while their Cossack guard went on a spree. The new-comers seemed above the common run of criminals sent to Siberia, better clothed, of the air born to command, and in possession of money. The leading spirit among them was a young Pole, twenty-eight years or thereabouts, of noble rank, Mauritius Benyowsky, very lame from a battle wound, but plainly a soldier of fortune who could trump every trick fate played him, and give as good knocks as he got. Four others were officers of the army in St. Petersburg, exiled for political reasons. Only one, Hippolite Stephanow, was a criminal in the sense of having broken law.

Hoffman, a German surgeon, welcomed them to his quarters at Yakutsk. Where were they going?—To the Pacific?—"Ah; a long journey from St. Petersburg; seven thousand miles!" That was where he was to go when he had finished surgical duties on the Lena. By that they knew he, too, was an exile, practising his profession on parole. He would advise {109} them—cautiously feeling his ground—to get transferred as soon as they could from the Pacific coast to the Peninsula of Kamchatka; that was safer for an exile—fewer guards, farther from the Cossacks of the mainland; in fact, nearer America, where exiles might make a fortune in the fur trade. Had they heard of schemes in the air among Russians for ships to plunder furs in America "with powder and hatchets and the help of God," as the Russians say?

Mauritius Augustus, Count Benyowsky.

[Illustration: Mauritius Augustus, Count Benyowsky.]

Benyowsky, the Pole, jumped to the bait like a trout to the fly. If "powder and hatchets and the help of God"—*and an exile crew*—could capture wealth in the fur trade of western America, why not a break for freedom?

They didn't scruple as to means, these men. Why should they? They had been penned in festering dungeons, where the dead lay, corrupting the air till living and dead became a diseased mass. They had been knouted for differences of political opinion. They {110} had been whisked off at midnight from St. Petersburg—mile after mile, week after week, month after month, across the snows, with never a word of explanation, knowing only from the jingle of many bells that other prisoners were in the long procession. Now their hopes took fire from Hoffman's tales of Russian plans for fur trade. The path of the trackless sea seems always to lead to a boundless freedom.

In a word, before they had left Hoffman, they had bound themselves by oath to try to seize a fur-trading ship to escape across the Pacific. Stephanow, the common convict, was the one danger. He might play spy and obtain freedom by betraying all. To prevent this, each man was required to sign his name to an avowal of the conspirators' aim. Hoffman was to follow as soon as he could. Meanwhile he kept the documents, which were written in German; and Benyowsky, the Pole, was elected chief.

The Cossack guards came sulkily back from their gambling bout. The exiles were placed in elk-team sleds, and the remaining thousand miles to the Pacific resumed. But the spree had left the soldiers with sore heads. At the first camping place they were gambling again. On the sixth day out luck turned so heavily against one soldier that he lost his entire belongings to the captain of the troops, flew in a towering rage, and called his officer some blackguard name. The officer nonchalantly took over the {111} gains, swallowed the insult, and commanded the other Cossacks to tie the fellow up and give him a hundred lashes.

For a moment consternation reigned. There are some unwritten laws even among the Cossacks. To play the equal, when there was money to win, then act the despot when offended, was not according to the laws of good fellows among Cossacks. Before the officer knew where he was, he had been seized, bundled out of the tent, stripped naked and flogged on the bare back three hundred strokes.

He was still roaring with rage and pain and fear when a coureur came thundering over the path from Yakutsk with word that Hoffman had died suddenly, leaving certain papers suspected of conspiracy, which were being forwarded for examination to the commander on the Pacific. The coureur handed the paper to the officer of the guards. Not a man of the Cossacks could read German. What the papers were the terrified exiles knew. If word of the plot reached the Pacific, they might expect knouting, perhaps mutilation, or lifelong, hopeless servitude in the chain-gangs of the mines.

One chance of frustrating detection remained—the Cossack officer looked to the exiles for protection against his men. For a week the cavalcade moved sullenly on, the soldiers jeering in open revolt at the officer, the officer in terror for his life, the exiles quaking with fear. The road led to a swift, somewhat {112} dangerous river. The Cossacks were ordered to swim the elk teams across. The officer went on the raft to guard the prisoners, on whose safe delivery his own life depended. With hoots of laughter, that could not be reported as disobedience, the Cossacks hustled the snorting elk teams against the raft. A deft hoist from the pole of some unseen diver below, and the raft load was turned helter-skelter upside down in the middle of the river, the commander going under heels up! When officer and exiles came scrambling up the bank wet as water-rats, they were welcomed with shouts by the Cossacks. Officer and prisoners lighted a fire to dry clothes. Soldiers rummaged out the brandy casks, and were presently so deep in drunken sleep not a man of the guard was on his feet. Benyowsky waited till the commander, too, slept. Then the Pole limped, careful as a cat over cut glass, to the coat drying before the fire, drew out the packet of documents, and found what the exiles had feared—Hoffman's papers in German, with orders to the commander on the Pacific to keep the conspirators fettered till instructions came the next year from St. Petersburg.

The prisoners realized that all must be risked in one desperate cast of the dice. "I and time against all men," says the proverb. No fresh caravan would be likely to come till spring. Meanwhile they must play against time. Burning the packet to ashes, they replaced it with a forged order instructing the commander on the Pacific to treat the exiles with all {113} freedom and liberality, and to forward them by the first boat outward bound for Kamchatka.

The governor at Okhotsk did precisely as the packet instructed. He allowed them out on parole. He supplied them with clothing and money. He forwarded them to Kamchatka on the first boat outward bound, the *St. Peter and Paul*, with forty-three of a crew and ten cannon, which had just come back from punishing American Indians for massacring the Russians.

A year less two days from the night they had been whisked out of St. Petersburg, the exiles reached their destination—the little log fort or *ostrog* of Bolcheresk, about twenty miles up from the sea on the inner side of Kamchatka, one hundred and fifty miles overland from the Pacific. The rowboat conducting the exiles up-stream met rafts of workmen gliding down the current. Rafts and rowboat paused within call. The raftsmen wanted news from Europe.

Benyowsky answered that exiles had no news. "Who are you?" an officer demanded bluntly. Always and unconsciously playing the hero part of melodrama, Benyowsky replied—"Once a soldier and a general, now a slave." Shouts of laughter broke from the raftsmen. The enraged Pole was for leaping overboard and thrashing them to a man for their mockery; but they called out, "no offence had been meant": they, too, were exiles; their laughter was welcome; they had suffered enough in Kamchatka to know that when men must laugh or weep, better, much better, laugh! Even as they {114} laughed came the tears. With a rear sweep, the rafts headed about and escorted the newcomers to the fortress, where they were locked for the night. After all, a welcome to exile was a sardonic sort of mirth.

Kamchatka occupies very much the same position on the Pacific as Italy to the Mediterranean, or Norway to the North Sea. Its people were nomads, wild as American Indians, but Russia had established garrisons of Cossacks—collectors of tribute in furs—all over the peninsula, of whom four hundred were usually moving from place to place, three hundred stationed at Bolcheresk, the seat of government, on the inner coast of the peninsula.

The capital itself was a curious conglomeration of log huts stuck away at the back of beyond, with all the gold lace and court satins and regimental formalities of St. Petersburg in miniature. On one side of a deep ravine, was the fort or *ostrog*—a palisaded courtyard of some two or three hundred houses, joined together like the face of a street, with assembly rooms, living apartments, and mess rooms on one side of a passageway, kitchens, servants' quarters, and barracks for the Cossacks on the other side of the aisle. Two or three streets of these double-rowed houses made up the fort. Few of the houses contained more than three rooms, but the rooms were large as halls, one hundred by eighty feet, some of them, with whip-sawed floors, clay-chinked log walls, parchment {115} windows, and furniture hewed out of the green fir trees of the mountains. But the luxurious living made up for the bareness of furnishings. Shining samovars sung in every room. Rugs of priceless fur concealed the rough flooring. Chinese silks, Japanese damasks,—Oriental tapestries smuggled in by the fur traders,—covered the walls; and richest of silk attired the Russian officers and their ladies, compelled to beguile time here, where the only break in monotony was the arrival of fresh ships from America, or exiles from St. Petersburg, or gambling or drinking or dancing or feasting the long winter nights through, with, perhaps, a duel in the morning to settle midnight debts. Just across a deep ravine from the fort was another kind of settlement—ten or a dozen *yurts*, thatch-roofed, circular houses half underground like cellars, grouped about a square hall or barracks in the centre. In this village dwelt the exiles, earning their living by hunting or acting as servants for the officers of the Cossacks.

Here, then, came Benyowsky and his companions, well received because of forged letters sent on, but with no time to lose; for the first spring packet overland might reveal their conspiracy. The raftsmen, who had welcomed them, now turned hosts and housed the newcomers. The Pole was assigned to an educated Russian, who had been eight years in exile.

"How can you stand it? Do you fear death too much to dare one blow for liberty?" Benyowsky asked the other, as they sat over their tea that first night.

{116} But a spy might ask the same question. The Russian evaded answer, and a few hours later showed the Pole books of travel, among which were maps of the Philippines, where twenty or thirty exiles might go *if they had a leader*.

Leader? Benyowsky leaped to his feet with hands on pistol and cutlass with which he had been armed that morning when Governor Nilow liberated them to hunt on parole. Leader? Were they men? Was this settlement, too, ready to rise if they had a leader?

No time to lose! Within a month, cautious as a man living over a volcano, the Polish nobleman had enlisted twenty recruits from the exile settlement, bound to secrecy by oath, and a score more from a crew of sailor exiles back from America, mutinous over brutal treatment by their captain. In addition to secrecy, each conspirator bound himself to implicit and instant obedience to Benyowsky, their chief, and to slay each with his own hand any member of the band found guilty of betrayal. But what gave the Pole his greatest power was his relation to the governor. The coming of the young nobleman had caused a flutter in the social life of the dull little fort. He had been appointed secretary to Governor Nilow, and tutor to his children. The governor's lady was the widow of a Swedish exile; and it took the Pole but a few interviews to discover that wife and family favored the exiles rather than their Russian lord. In fact, the good woman suggested to the Pole that he {117} should prevent her sixteen-year-old daughter becoming wife to a Cossack by marrying her himself.

The Pole's first move was to ask the governor's permission to establish a colony of exile farmers in the south of the peninsula. The request was granted. This created a good excuse for the gathering of the provisions that would be needed for the voyage on the Pacific; but when the exiles further requested a fur-trading vessel to transport the provisions to the new colony, their design was balked by the unsuspecting governor granting them half a hundred row boats, too frail to go a mile from the coast. There seemed no other course but to seize a vessel by force and escape, but Benyowsky again played for time. The governor's daughter discovered his plot through her servant planning to follow one of the exiles to sea; but instead of betraying him to her Russian father, she promised to send him red clippings of thread as danger signals if the governor or his chancellor got wind of the treason.

Their one aim was to get away from Asia before fresh orders could come overland from Yakutsk. Ice still blocked the harbor in April, but the *St. Peter and Paul*, the armed vessel that had brought the exiles across the sea from the mainland, lay in port and was already enlisting a crew for the summer voyage to America. The Pole sent twelve of his men to enlist among the crew, and nightly store provisions in the hold. The rest of the band were set to manufacturing cartridges, and buying or borrowing all the firearms {118} they could obtain on the pretence of hunting. Word was secretly carried from man to man that, when a light was hoisted on the end of a flagstaff above the Benyowsky hut, all were to rally for the settlement across the ravine from the fort.

The crisis came before the harbor had opened. Benyowsky was on a sled journey inland with the governor, when an exile came to him by night with word that one of the conspirators had lost his nerve and determined to save his own neck by confessing all to the governor.

The traitor was even now hard on the trail to overtake the governor. Without a moment's wavering, Benyowsky sent the messenger with a flask of poisoned brandy back to meet the man.

The Pole had scarcely returned to his hut in the exile village, when the governor's daughter came to him in tears. Ismyloff, a young Russian trader, who had all winter tried to join the conspirators as a spy, had been on the trail when the traitor was poisoned and was even now closeted with Governor Nilow.

It was the night of April 23. No sooner had the daughter gone than the light was run up on the flagstaff, the bridge across the ravine broken down, arms dragged from hiding in the cellars, windows and doors barricaded, sentinels placed in hiding along the ditch between village and fort. For a whole day, no word came. Governor and chancellor were still busy examining witnesses. In the morning came a maid {119} from the governor's daughter with a red thread of warning, and none too soon, for at ten o'clock, a Cossack sergeant brought a polite invitation from the governor for the pleasure of M. Benyowsky's company at breakfast.

M. Benyowsky returns polite regrets that he is slightly indisposed, but hopes to give himself the pleasure later.

The sergeant winked his eyes and opined it was wiser to go by fair means than to be dragged by main force.

The Pole advised the sergeant to make his will before repeating that threat.

Noon saw two Cossacks and an officer thundering at the Pole's door. The door opened wide. In marched the soldiers, armed to the teeth; but before their clicking heels had ceased to mark time, the door was shut again. Benyowsky had whistled. A dozen exiles rose out of the floor. Cossacks and captors rolled in a heap. The soldiers were bound head to feet, and bundled into the cellar. Meanwhile the sentinels hidden in the ravine had captured Ismyloff, the nephew of the chancellor, and two other Russians, who were added to the captives in the cellar; and the governor changed his tactics. A letter was received from the governor's daughter pleading with her lover to come and be reconciled with her father, who had now no prejudice against the exiles; but in the letter were two or three tiny red threads such as might have {120} been pulled out of a dress sleeve. The letter had been written under force.

Benyowsky's answer was to marshal his fifty-seven men in three divisions round the village; one round the house, the largest hidden in the dark on the fort side of the ravine, a decoy group stationed in the ditch to draw an attack.

By midnight, the sentinels sent word that the main guard of Cossacks had reached the ravine. The decoy had made a feint of resistance. The Cossacks sent back to the fort for reinforcements. The Pole waited only till nearly all the Cossacks were on the ditch bank, then instructing the little band of decoys to keep up a sham fight, poured his main forces through the dark, across the plain at a run, for the fort. Palisades were scaled, gates broken down, guards stabbed where they stood! Benyowsky's men had the fort and the gates barricaded again before the governor could collect his senses. As Benyowsky entered the main rooms, the enraged commander seized a pistol, which missed fire, and sprang at the Pole's throat, roaring out he would see the exiles dead before he would surrender. The Pole, being lame, had swayed back under the onslaught, when the circular slash of a cutlass in the hand of an exile officer severed the governor's head from his body.

Twenty-eight Cossacks were put to the sword inside the fort; but the exiles were not yet out of their troubles. Though they had seized the armed vessel at once and {121} transferred to the hold the entire loot of the fort,—furs, silks, supplies, gold,—it would be two weeks before the ice would leave the port. Meanwhile the two hundred defeated Cossacks had retreated to a hill, and sent coureurs scurrying for help to the other forts of Kamchatka. Within two weeks seven hundred Cossacks would be on the hills; and the exiles, whose supplies were on board the vessel, would be cut off in the fort and starved into surrender.

No time to waste, Benyowsky! Not a woman or child was harmed, but every family in the fort was quickly rounded up in the chapel. Round this, outside, were piled chairs, furniture, pitch, tar, powder, whale-oil. Promptly at nine in the morning, three women and twelve young girls—wives and daughters of the Cossack officers—were despatched to the Cossack besiegers on the hill with word that unless the Cossacks surrendered their arms to the exiles and sent down fifty soldiers as hostages of safety for the exiles till the ship could sail— precisely at ten o'clock the church would be set on fire.

The women were seen to ascend the hill. No signal came from the Cossacks. At a quarter past nine Benyowsky kindled fires at each of the four angles of the church. As the flames began to mount a forest of handkerchiefs and white sheets waved above the hill, and a host of men came spurring to the fort with all the Cossacks' arms and fifty-two hostages.

{122} The exiles now togged themselves out in all the gay regimentals of the Russian officers. Salutes of triumph were fired from the cannon. A *Te Deum* was sung. Feast and mad wassail filled both day and night till the harbor cleared. Even the Cossacks caught the madcap spirit of the escapade, and helped to load ammunition on the *St. Peter and Paul*. Nor were old wrongs forgiven. Ismyloff was bundled on the vessel in irons. The chancellor's secretary was seized and compelled to act as cook. Men, who had played the spy and tyrant, now felt the merciless knout. Witnesses, who had tried to pry into the exiles' plot, were hanged at the yard-arm. Nine women, relatives of exiles, who had been compelled to become the wives of Cossacks, now threw off the yoke of slavery, donned the costly Chinese silks, and joined the pirates. Among these was the governor's daughter, who was to have married a Cossack.

On May 11, 1771, the Polish flag was run up on the *St. Peter and Paul.* The fort fired a God-speed—a heartily sincere one, no doubt—of twenty-one guns. Again the *Te Deum* was chanted; again, the oath of obedience taken by kissing Benyowsky's sword; and at five o'clock in the evening the ship dropped down the river for the sea, with ninety-six exiles on board, of whom nine were women; one, an archdeacon; half a dozen, officers of the imperial army; one, a gentleman in waiting to the Empress; at least a dozen, convicts of the blackest dye.

{123} The rest of Benyowsky's adventures read more like a page from some pirate romance than sober record of events on the west coast of America. Barely had the vessel rounded the southern cape of the peninsula into the Pacific, when Ismyloff, the young Russian trader, who had been carried on board in irons, rallied round Benyowsky such a clamor of mutineers, duels were fought on the quarter-deck, the malcontents clapped in handcuffs again, and the ringleaders tied to the masts, where knouting enough was laid on to make them sue for peace.

The middle of May saw the vessel anchoring on the west coast of Bering Island, where a sharp lookout was kept for Russian fur traders, and armed men must go ashore to reconnoitre before Benyowsky dared venture from the ship. The Pole's position was chancy enough to satisfy even his melodramatic soul. Apart from four or five Swedes, the entire crew of ninety-six was Russian. Benyowsky was for sailing south at once to take up quarters on some South Sea island, or to claim the protection of some European power. The Russian exiles, of whom half were criminals, were for coasting the Pacific on pirate venture, and compelled the Pole to steer his vessel for the fur hunters' islands of Alaska.

The men sent to reconnoitre Bering Island came back with word that while they were gathering driftwood on the south shore, they had heard shots and met five Russians belonging to a Saxon exile, who had {124} turned fur hunter, deposed the master of his ships, gathered one hundred exiles around him, and become a trader on his own account. The Saxon requested an interview with

Benyowsky. What was the Pole to do? Was this a decoy to test his strength? Was the Saxon planning to scuttle the Pole's vessel, too? Benyowsky's answer was that he would be pleased to meet his Saxon comrade in arms on the south shore, each side to approach with four men only, laying down arms instantly on sight of each other. The two exile pirates met. Each side laid down arms as agreed. Ochotyn, the Saxon, was a man of thirty-six years, who had come an exile on fur trading vessels, gathered a crew of one hundred and thirty-four around him, and, like the Pole, become a pirate. His plan in meeting Benyowsky was to propose vengeance on Russia: let the two ships unite, go back to Siberia, and sack the Russian ports on the Pacific. But the Pole had had enough of Russia. He contented himself with presenting his brother pirate with one hundred pounds of ammunition; and the two exiles sat round a campfire of driftwood far into the night, spinning yarns of blasted hopes back in Europe, and desperate venture here on the Pacific. The Saxon's headquarters were on Kadiak, where he had formed alliance with the Indians. Hither he advised the Pole to sail for a cargo of furs.

Ismyloff, the mutineer, was marooned on Bering Island. Ice-drift had seemed to bar the way {125} northward through Bering Straits. June saw Benyowsky far eastward at Kadiak on the south shore of Alaska, gathering in a cargo of furs; and from the sea-otter fields of Kadiak and Oonalaska, Benyowsky sailed southwest, past the smoking volcanoes of the Aleutians, vaguely heading for some of those South Sea islands of which he used to read in the exile village of Kamchatka.

Not a man of the crew knew as much about navigation as a schoolboy. They had no idea where they were going, or where the ship was. As day after day slipped past with no sight but the heaving sea, the Russian landsmen became restive. Provisions had dwindled to one fish a day; and scarcely a pint of water for each man was left in the hold. In flying from Siberian exile, were they courting a worse fate? Stephanow, the criminal convict, who had crossed Siberia with the Pole, dashed on deck demanding a better allowance of water as the ship entered warmer and warmer zones. The next thing the Pole knew, Stephanow had burst open the barrel hoops of the water kegs to quench his thirst. By the time the guard had gone down the main hatch to intercept him, Stephanow and a band of Russian mutineers had trundled the brandy casks to the deck and were in a wild debauch. The main hatch was clapped down, leaving the mutineers in possession of the deck, till all fell in drunken torpor, when Benyowsky rushed his soldiers up the fore scuttle, snapped handcuffs on {126} the rebels, and tied them to the masts. In the midst of this disorder, such a hurricane broke over the ocean that the tossing yard-arms alternately touched water.

To be sure, Benyowsky had escaped exile; but his ship was a hornets' nest. After the storm all hands were busy sewing new sails. The old sails were distributed as trousers for the ragamuffin crew. For ten days no food was tasted but soup made from sea-otter skins. Then birds were seen, and seaweed drifted past the vessel; and a wild hope mounted every heart of reaching some part of Japan.

On sunset of July 15, the Pole's watch-dog was noticed standing at the bow, sniffing and barking. Two or three of the ship's hands dashed up to the masthead, vowing they would not come down till they saw land. Suddenly the lookout shouted, Land! The exiles forgot their woes. Even the mutineers tied to the masts cheered. Darker and darker grew the cloud on the horizon. By daybreak the cloud had resolved itself to a shore before the eager eyes of the watching crew. The ship had scarcely anchored before every man was overboard in a wild rush for the fresh water to be found on land. Tents were pitched on the island; and the wanderers of the sea rested.

It is no part of this narrative to tell of Benyowsky's adventures on Luzon of the Philippines, or the Ladrones,—whichever it was,—how he scuttled {127} Japanese sampans of gold and pearls, fought a campaign in Formosa, and wound up at Macao, China, where all the rich cargo of sea-otter brought from America was found to be water rotted; and Stephanow, the criminal convict, left the Pole destitute by stealing and selling all the Japanese loot.

This part of the story does not concern America; and the Pole's whole life has been told by Jokai, the Hungarian novelist, and Kotzebue, the Russian dramatist.

Benyowsky got passage to Europe from China on one of the East India Company ships, whose captain was uneasy enough at having so many pirates on board. In France he obtained an appointment to look after French forts in Madagascar; but this was too tame an undertaking for the adventure-loving Pole. He threw up his appointment, returned to Europe, interested English merchants in a new venture, sailed to Baltimore in the *Robert Anne* of twenty cannon and four hundred and fifty tons, interested merchants there in his schemes, and departed from Baltimore October 25, 1784, to conquer Madagascar and set up an independent commercial government. Here he was slain by the French troops on the 23d of May, 1786—to the ruin of those Baltimore and London merchants who had advanced him capital. His own account of his adventures is full of gross exaggerations; but even the Russians were so impressed with the prowess of his valor that a few years later, when Cook sailed to Alaska, Ismyloff could not be brought to mention his name; {128} and when the English ships went on to Kamchatka, they found the inhabitants hidden in the cellars, for fear the Polish pirate had returned. But like many heroes of misfortune, Benyowsky could not stand success. It turned his head. He entered Macao with the airs of an emperor, that at once discredited him with the solid people. If he had returned to the west coast of America, as a fur trader, he might have wrested more honors from Russia; but his scheme to capture an island of which he was to be king, ended in ruin for himself and his friends.[1]

[1] It may as well be acknowledged that Mauritius Augustus, Count Benyowsky (pronounced by himself Be-nyov-sky), is a liar without a peer among the adventurers of early American history. If it were not that his life was known to the famous men of his time, his entire memoirs from 1741 to 1771 might be rejected as fiction of the yellow order; but the comical thing is, the mendacious fellow cut a tremendous swath in his day. The garrisons of Kamchatka trembled at his name twenty-five years after his escapades. Ismyloff, who became a famous trader in the Russian Fur Company, could not be induced to open his mouth about the Pole to Cook, and actually made use of the universal fear of Benyowsky among Russians, to keep Cook from learning Russian fur trade secrets, when the Englishman went to Kamchatka, by representing that Cook was a pirate, too. The *Gentleman's Magazine* for June, 1772, contained a letter from Canton, dated November 19, 1771, giving a full account of the pirate's arrival there with his mutineers and women refugees. The Bishop Le Bon of Macao writes, September 24, 1771: "Out of his equipage, there remain no more than eight men in health. All the rest are confined to their beds. For two months they suffered hunger and thirst." Captain King of Cook's staff writes of Kamchatka: "We were informed that an exiled Polish officer named Beniowski had seized upon a galliott, lying at the entrance of the harbor, and had forced on board a number of Russian sailors, sufficient to navigate her; that he had put on shore a part of the crew … among the rest, Ismyloff." In Paris he met and interested Benjamin Franklin. Hyacinth de Magellan, a descendant of the great discoverer, advanced Benyowsky money for the Madagascar filibustering expedition. So did certain merchants of Baltimore in 1785. On leaving England, Benyowsky gave his memoirs to Magellan, who passed their editing over to William Nicholson of the Royal Society, by {129} whom they were given to the world in 1790. German, French, and Russian translations followed. This called forth Russia's account of the matter, written by Ivan Ryumin, edited by Berg, St. Petersburg, 1822. These accounts, with the facts as cited from contemporaries, enable one to check the preposterous exaggerations of the Pole. Of late years, between drama and novels, quite a Benyowsky literature has sprung up about this Cagliostro of the sea. His record in the continental armies preceding his exile would fill a book by itself; and throughout all, Benyowsky appears in the same light, an unscrupulous braggart lying gloriously, but withal as courageous as he was mendacious.

[Transcriber's note: the "e" and "o" in the above "Be-nyov-sky" are actually emacron (Unicode U+0113) and o-macron (Unicode U+014D).]

{131}

PART II

AMERICAN AND ENGLISH ADVENTURERS ON THE WEST COAST OF
AMERICA—FRANCIS DRAKE IN CALIFORNIA—COOK, FROM BRITISH
COLUMBIA TO ALASKA—LEDYARD, THE FORERUNNER OF LEWIS
AND CLARK—GRAY, THE DISCOVERER OF THE COLUMBIA—
VANCOUVER, THE LAST OF THE WEST COAST NAVIGATORS

{133}

CHAPTER VI
1562-1595
FRANCIS DRAKE IN CALIFORNIA

How the Sea Rover was attacked and ruined as a Boy on the Spanish Main off Mexico—His Revenge in
sacking Spanish Treasure Houses and crossing Panama—The Richest Man in England, he sails to the
Forbidden Sea, scuttles all the Spanish Ports up the West Coast of South America and takes Possession
of New Albion (California) for England

If a region were discovered where gold was valued less than cartloads of clay,
and ropes of pearls could be obtained in barter for strings of glass beads, the
modern mind would have some idea of the frenzy that prevailed in Spain after
the discovery of America by Columbus. Native temples were found in Chile, in
Peru, in Central America, in Mexico, where gold literally lined the walls, silver
paved the floors, and handfuls of pearls were as thoughtlessly thrown in the laps
of the conquerors as shells might be tossed at a modern clam-bake.

Within half a century from the time Spain first learned of America, Cortés not only penetrated Mexico, but sent his corsairs up the west coast of the {134} continent. Pizarro conquered Peru. Spanish ships plied a trade rich beyond dreams of avarice between the gold realms of Peru and the spice islands of the Philippines. The chivalry of the Spanish nobility suddenly became a chivalry of the high seas. Religious zeal burned to a flame against those gold-lined pagan temples. It was easy to believe that the transfer of wedges of pure gold from heathen hands to Spain was a veritable despoiling of the devil's treasure boxes, glorious in the sight of God. The trackless sea became the path to fortune. Balboa had deeper motives than loyalty, when, in 1513, on his march across Panama and discovery of the Pacific, he rushed mid-deep into the water, shouting out in swelling words that he took possession of earth, air, and water for Spain "for all time, past, present, or to come, without contradiction, ... north and south, with all the seas from the Pole Arctic to the Pole Antarctic, ... both now, and as long as the world endures, until the final day of judgment." [1]

Shorn of noise, the motive was simply to shut out the rest of the world from Spain's treasure box. The Monroe Doctrine was not yet born. *The whole Pacific was to be a closed sea*! To be sure, Vasco da Gama had found the way round the Cape of Good Hope to the Indian Ocean; and Magellan soon after passed through the strait of his name below South America {135} right into the Pacific Ocean; but round the world by the Indian Ocean was a far cry for tiny craft of a few hundred tons; and the Straits of Magellan were so storm-bound, it soon became a common saying that they were a closed door. Spain sent her sailors across Panama to build ships for the Pacific. The sea that bore her treasure craft —millions upon millions of pounds sterling in pure gold, silver, emeralds, pearls —was as closed to the rest of the world as if walled round with only one chain-gate; and that at Panama, where Spain kept the key.

That is, the sea *was* shut till Drake came coursing round the world; and his coming was so utterly impossible to the Spanish mind that half the treasure ships scuttled by the English pirate mistook him for a visiting Spaniard till the rallying cry, "God and Saint George!" wakened them from their dream.

It was by accident the English first found themselves in the waters of the Spanish Main. John Hawkins had been cruising the West Indies exchanging slaves for gold, when an ominous stillness fell on the sea. The palm trees took on the hard glister of metal leaves. The sunless sky turned yellow, the sea to brass; and before the six English ships could find shelter, a hurricane broke that flailed the fleet under sails torn to tatters clear across the Gulf of Mexico to Vera Cruz, the stronghold of Spanish power.

Sir John Hawkins.

[Illustration: Sir John Hawkins.]

But Hawkins feared neither man nor devil. He {136} reefed his storm-torn sails, had the stoppers pulled out of his cannon in readiness, his gunners alert, ran up the English ensign, and boldly towed his fleet into port directly under Spanish guns. Sending a messenger ashore, he explained that he was sorry to intrude on forbidden waters, but that he needed to careen his ships for the repair of leakages, and now asked permission from the viceroy to refit. Perhaps, in his heart, the English adventurer wasn't sorry to get an inner glimpse of Mexico's defences. As he waited for permission, there sailed into the harbor the Spanish fleet itself, twelve merchantmen rigged as frigates, loaded with treasure to the value of one million eight hundred thousand pounds. The viceroy of Mexico, Don Martin Henriquez himself, commanded the fleet. English and Spanish ships dipped colors to each other as courteous hidalgoes might have doffed hats; and the guns roared each other salutes, that set the seas churning. Master John Hawkins quaffed mug after mug of foaming beer with a boisterous boast that if the Spaniards thought to frighten *him* with a waste of powder and smoke, he could play the same game, and "singe the don's beard."

Came a messenger, then, clad in mail to his teeth, very pompous, very gracious, very profuse of welcome, with a guarantee in writing from the viceroy of security for Hawkins while dismantling the English ships. In order to avoid clashes among the common soldiers, the fortified island was assigned for the English to {137} disembark. It was the 12th of August, 1568. Darkness fell with the warm velvet caress of a tropic sea. Half the crew had landed, half the cannon been trundled ashore for the vessels to be beached next day, when Hawkins noticed torches—a thousand torches—glistening above the mailed armor of a thousand Spanish soldiers marching down from the fort and being swiftly transferred to the frigates. A blare of Spanish trumpets blew to arms! The waters were suddenly alight with the flare of five fire-rafts drifting straight where the disarmed English fleet lay moored. Hawkins had just called his page to hand round mugs of beer, when a cannon-shot splintering through the mast arms overhead ripped the tankard out of his hand.[2]

"God and Saint George," thundered the enraged Englishman, "down with the traitorous devils!"

No time to save sailors ashore! The blazing rafts had already bumped keels with the moored fleet. No chance to raise anchors! The Spanish frigates were already abreast in a life-and-death grapple, soldiers boarding the English decks, sabring the crews, hurling hand grenades down the hatches to blow up the powder magazines. Hawkins roared "to cut the cables." It was a hand-to-hand slaughter on decks slippery with blood. No light but the musketry fire and glare of burning masts! The little English company were fighting like a wild beast trapped, when with a {138} thunderclap that tore bottom out of hull—Hawkins's ship flew into mid-air, a flaring, fiery wreck—then sank in the heaving trough of the sea, carrying down five hundred Spaniards to a watery grave. Cutlass in hand, head over heels went Hawkins into the sea. The hell of smoke, of flaming mast poles, of blazing musketry, of churning waters—hid him. Then a rope's end flung out by some friend gave handhold. He was up the sides of a ship, that had cut hawsers and off before the fire-rafts came! Sails were hoisted to the seaward breeze. In the carnage of fire and blood, the Spaniards did not see the two smallest English vessels scudding before the wind as if fiend-chased. Every light on the decks was put out. Then the dark of the tropic night hid them. Without food, without arms, with scarcely a remnant of their crews—the two ships drifted to sea.

Not a man of the sailors ashore escaped. All were butchered, or taken prisoners for a fate worse than butchery—to be torn apart in the market-place of Vera Cruz, baited in the streets to the yells of on-lookers, hung by the arms to out-of-doors scaffolding to die by inches, or be torn by vultures. The two ships at sea were in terrible plight. North, west, south was the Spanish foe. Food there was none. The crews ate the dogs, monkeys, parrots on board. Then they set traps for the rats of the hold. The starving seamen begged to be marooned. They would risk Spanish cruelty to escape starvation. Hawkins landed {139} three-quarters of the remnant crews either in Yucatan or Florida. Then he crept lamely back to England, where he moored in January, 1569.

Of the six splendid ships that had spread their sails from Plymouth, only the *Minion* and *Judith* came back; and those two had been under command of a thick-set, stocky, red-haired English boy about twenty-four years of age—

Francis Drake of Devon, one of twelve sons of a poor clergyman, who eked out a living by reading prayers for the Queen's Navy Sundays, playing sailor week days. Francis, the eldest son, was born in the hull of an old vessel where the family had taken refuge in time of religious persecution. In spite of his humble origin, Sir Francis Russell had stood his godfather at baptism. The Earl of Bedford had been his patron. John Hawkins, a relative, supplied money for his education. Apprenticed before the mast from his twelfth year, Drake became purser to Biscay at eighteen; and so faithfully had he worked his way, when the master of the sloop died, it was bequeathed to young Drake. Emulous of becoming a great sailor like Hawkins, Drake sold the sloop and invested everything he owned in Hawkins's venture to the West Indies. He was ruined to his last penny by Spanish treachery. It was almost a religion for England to hate Spain at that time. Drake hated tenfold more now. Spain had taught the world to keep off her treasure box. Would Drake accept the lesson, or challenge it?

{140} Men who master destiny rise, like the Phenix, from the ashes of their own ruin. In the language of the street, when they fall—these men of destiny—they make a point of falling *up*stairs. Amid the ruin of massacre in Mexico, Drake brought away one fact—memory of Spanish gold to the value of one million eight hundred thousand pounds. Where did it come from? Was the secret of that gold the true reason for Spain's resentment against all intruders? Drake had coasted Florida and the West Indies. He knew they yielded no such harvest. Then it must come from one of three other regions—South America, Central America, Mexico.

For two years Drake prospected for the sources of that golden wealth. In the *Dragon* and *Swan*, he cruised the Spanish Main during 1570. In 1571 he was out again in the *Swan*. By 1572 he knew the secret of that gold—gold in ship-loads, in caravans of one thousand mules, in masses that filled from cellar to attic of the King's Treasure House, where tribute of one-fifth was collected for royalty. It came from the subjugated Kingdom of Peru, by boat up the Pacific to the Port of Panama, by pack-train across the isthmus—mountainous, rugged, forests of mangroves tangled with vines, bogs that were bottomless—to Nombre de Dios, the Spanish fort on the Atlantic side, which had become the storehouse of all New Spain. Drake took counsel of no one.

Next year he was back on the Spanish Main, in the {141} *Pacha*, forty-seven men; his brother John commanding the *Swan* with twenty-six of a crew, only one man older than fifty, the rest mere boys with hate in their hearts for Spanish blood, love in their hearts for Spanish gold. Touching at a hidden cove for provisions left the year before, Drake found this warning from a former comrade, stuck to the bark of a tree by a hunting knife:—

"*Captain Drake—if you do fortune into this port, haste away; for the Spaniards have betrayed this place, and taken all away that you left here—your loving friend—John Garret.*"

Heeding the warning, Drake hastened away to the Isle of Pinos, off the isthmus, left the ships at a concealed cove here, armed fifty-three of his boldest fellows with muskets, crossbows, pikes, and spontoons. Then he called for drummers and trumpeters, and rowed in a small boat for Nombre de Dios, the treasure house of New Spain. The small boat kept on the offing till dark, then sent ashore for some Indians—half-breeds whom Spanish cruelty had driven to revolt. This increased Drake's force to one hundred and fifty men. Silently, just as the moon emerged from clouds lighting up harbor and town, the long-boat glided into Nombre de Dios. A high platform, mounted with brass cannon, fronted the water. Behind were thirty houses, thatch-roofed, whitewashed, palisaded, surrounded by courtyards with an almost European pomp. The King's Treasure House stood at one end of the market. Near it was a chapel with high wooden steeple.

{142} A Spanish ship lay furled in port. From this glided out a punt poled like mad by a Spaniard racing to reach the platform first. Drake got athwart the fellow's path, knocked him over, gagged his yells, and was up the platform before the sleepy gunner on guard was well awake. The sentry only paused to make sure that the men scrambling up the fort were not ghosts. Then he tore at the top of his speed for the alarm-bell of the chapel and, clapping down the hatch door of the steeple stairs in the faces of the pursuing Englishmen, rang the bells like a demon possessed.

Leaving twelve men to hold the platform as a retreat, Drake sent sixteen to attack the King's Treasure just at the moment he himself, with his hundred men, should succeed in drawing the entire Spanish garrison to a sham battle on the market-place. The cannon on the platform were spiked and overturned. Drums beating, trumpets blowing, torches aflare, the English freebooter marched straight to the market. Up at the Treasure House, John Drake and Oxenham had burst open the doors of the store-room just as the saddled mules came galloping to carry the booty beyond danger. A lighted candle on the cellar stair showed silver piled bar on bar to the value of one million pounds. Down on the market, the English trumpeter lay dead. Drake had fallen from a sword slash and, snatched up by comrades, the wound stanched by a scarf, was carried back to the boat, where the raiders made good their escape, richer by a million pounds with the loss of only one man.

{143} Drake cruised the Spanish Main for six more months. From the Indians he learned that the mule trains with the yearly output of Peruvian gold would leave the Pacific in midwinter to cross overland to Nombre de Dios. No use trying to raid the fort again! Spain would not be caught napping a second time. But Pedro, a Panama Indian, had volunteered to guide a small band of lightly equipped English inland behind Nombre de Dios, to the halfway house where the gold caravans stopped. The audacity of the project is unparalleled. Eighteen boys led by a man not yet in his thirtieth year accompanied by Indians were to invade a tangled thicket of hostile country, cut off from retreat, the forts of the enemy—the cruelest enemy in Christendom—on each side, no provisions but what each carried in his haversack!

Led by the Indian Pedro, the freebooters struck across country, picked up the trail behind Nombre de Dios, marched by night, hid by day, Indian scouts sending back word when a Spaniard was seen, the English scudding to ambush in the tangled woods. Twelve days and nights they marched. At ten in the morning of February 11, they were on the Great Divide. Pedro led Drake to the top of the hill. Up the trunk of an enormous tree, the Indians had cut steps to a kind of bower, or lookout. Up clambered Francis Drake. Then he looked westward.

Mountains, hills, forested valleys, rolled from his feet westward. Beyond— what? The shining {144} expanse of the fabled South Sea! The Pacific silver in the morning light! A New World of Waters, where the sun's track seemed to pave a new path, a path of gold, to the mystic Orient! Never before had English eyes seen these waters! Never yet English prow cut these waves! Where did they lead —the endlessly rolling billows? For Drake, they seemed to lead to a New World of Dreams—dreams of gold, of glory, of immortal fame. He came down from the lookout so overcome with a great inspiration that he could not speak. Then, as with Balboa, the fire of a splendid enthusiasm lighted up the mean purposes of the adventurer to a higher manhood. Before his followers, he fell on his knees and prayed Almighty God to grant him the supreme honor of sailing an English ship on that sea!

That night the Indian came back with word that the mule train laden with gold was close on the trail. Drake scattered his men on each side of the road flat on their faces in high grass. Wealth was almost in their grasp. Hope beat riotous in the young bloods. No sound but the whir of wings as great tropic insects flitted through the dark with flashes of fire; or the clank of a soldier unstrapping haversack to steel courage by a drink of grog! An hour passed! Two hours before the eager ears pressed to earth detected a padded hoof-beat over grass. Then a bell tinkled, as the leader of the pack came in sight. Drunk with the glory of the day, or too much grog, some fool sailor leaped in {145} mid-air with an exultant yell! In a second the mule train had stampeded.

By the time Drake came to the halfway house,[3] the gold was hidden in the woods, and the Spaniards fleeing for their lives; though an old chronicle declares "the general" went from house to house assuring the Spanish ladies they were safe. The Spaniards of Tierra Firme were simply paralyzed with fright at the apparition of pirates in the centre of the kingdom. Then scouts brought word of double danger: on the Atlantic side, Spanish frigates were searching for Drake's ships; from the Pacific, two hundred horsemen were advancing in hot pursuit. Between the two—was he trapped?—Not he! Overland went a scout to the ships —Drake's own gold toothpick as token—bidding them keep offshore; he would find means to come out to them. Then he retreated over the trail at lightning pace, sleeping only in ambush, eating in snatches, coming out on the coast far distant from Nombre de Dios and Spanish frigates. Binding driftwood into a raft, Drake hoisted sail of flour sacks. Saying good-by to the Indian, the freebooter noticed Pedro's eyes wander to the gold-embossed Turkish cimeter in his own hand, and at once presented scabbard and blade to the astonished savage. In gratitude the Indian tossed three wedges of gold to the raft now sheering out with the tide to sea. These Drake gave {146} to his men. Six hours the raft was drifting to the sails on the offing, and such seas were slopping across the water-logged driftwood, the men were to their waists in water when the sail-boats came to the rescue.

On Sunday morning, August 9, 1573, the ships were once more in Plymouth. Whispers ran through the assembled congregations of the churches that Drake, the bold sea-rover, was entering port loaded with foreign treasure; and out rushed every man, woman, and child, leaving the scandalized preachers thundering to empty pews.

Drake was now one of the richest men in England. At his own cost he equipped three frigates for service under Essex in Ireland, and through the young Earl was introduced to the circle of Elizabeth's advisers. To the Queen he told his plans for sailing an English ship on the South Sea. To her, no doubt, he related the tales of Spanish gold freighting that sea, closed to the rest of the world. Good reason for England—Spain's enemy—to prove that the ocean, like air, was free to all nations! The Pope's Bull dividing off the southern hemisphere between Portugal and Spain mattered little to a nation belligerently Protestant, and less to a seaman whose dauntless daring had raised him from a wharf-rat to Queen's adviser. Elizabeth could not yet wound Spain openly; but she received Drake in audience, and presented him a magnificent sword with the words—"Who striketh thee, Drake, striketh us!"

Queen Elizabeth knighting Drake.

[Illustration: Queen Elizabeth knighting Drake.]

{147} Five ships, this time, he led out from Plymouth in November of 1577. Gales drove him back. It was December before his fleet was at sea—the *Pelican* of one hundred tons and twenty or thirty cannon under Drake, Thomas Doughty, a courtier second to Drake, the *Elizabeth* of eighty tons, the *Swan*, *Christopher*, and *Marygold* no larger than fishing schooners; manned in all by one hundred and sixty sailors, mostly boys.

Outward bound for trade in Egypt, the world was told, but as merchantmen, the ships were regally equipped—Drake in velvets and gold braid, served by ten young gentlemen of noble birth, who never sat or covered in his presence without permission; service of gold plate at the mess table, where Drake dined alone like a king to the music of viols and harps; military drill at every port, and provisions enough aboard to go round the world, not just to Egypt.

January saw the fleet far enough from Egypt, at the islands off the west coast of Africa, where three vessels were scuttled, the crews all put ashore but one Portuguese pilot carried along to Brazil as guide. Thomas Doughty now fell in disfavor by openly acting as equal in command with Drake. Not in Egypt, but at Port St. Julian—a southern harbor of South America—anchored Drake's fleet. The scaffold where Magellan had executed mutineers half a century before still stood in the sands.

The *Christopher* had already been sent adrift as useless. The *Swan* was now broken up as unseaworthy, {148} leaving only the *Pelican*, the *Elizabeth*, and the *Marygold*. One thing more remained to be done—the greatest blot across the glory of Drake. Doughty was defiant, a party growing in his favor. When sent as prisoner to the *Marygold*, he had angered every man of the crew by high-handed authority. Drake dared not go on to unknown, hostile seas with a mutiny, or the chance of a mutiny brewing. Whether justly or unjustly, Doughty was tried at Port St. Julian under the shadow of Magellan's old scaffold, for disrespect to his commander and mutiny; and was pronounced guilty by a jury of twelve. A council of forty voted his death. The witnesses had contradicted themselves as if in terror of Drake's displeasure; and some plainly pleaded that the jealous crew of the *Marygold* were doing an innocent gentleman to death. The one thing Drake would not do, was carry the trouble maker along on the voyage. Like dominant spirits world over, he did not permit a life more or less to obstruct his purpose. He granted Doughty a choice of fates—to be marooned in Patagonia, or suffer death on the spot. Protesting his innocence, Doughty spurned the least favor from his rival. He refused the choice.

Solemnly the two, accuser and accused, took Holy Communion together. Solemnly each called on God as witness to the truth. A day each spent in prayer, these pirate fellows, who mixed their religion with their robbery, perhaps using piety as sugar-coating for their ill-deeds. Then they dined together in the {149} commander's tent,—Fletcher, the horrified chaplain, looking on,—drank hilariously to each other's healths, to each other's voyage whatever the end might be, looked each in the eye of the other without quailing, talking nonchalantly, never flinching courage nor balking at the grim shadow of their own stubborn temper. Doughty then rose to his feet, drank his last bumper, thanked Drake graciously for former kindness, walked calmly out to the old scaffold, laid his head on the block, and suffered death. Horror fell on the crew. Even Drake was shaken from his wonted calm; for he sat apart, his velvet cloak thrown back, slapping his crossed knees, and railing at the defenders of the dead man.[4] To rouse the men, he had solemn service held for the crew, and for the first time revealed to them his project for the voyage on the Pacific. After painting the glories of a campaign against Spanish ports of the South Seas, he wound up an inspiriting address with the rousing assurance that after this voyage, "*the worst boy aboard would never nede to goe agayne to sea, but be able to lyve in England like a right good gentleman.*" Fletcher, the chaplain, who secretly advocated the dead man's cause, was tied to a mast pole in bilboes, with the inscription hung to his neck—"*Falsest knave that liveth.*"

On August 17 they departed from "the port {150} accursed," for the Straits of Magellan, that were to lead to Spanish wealth on the Pacific.[5]

The superstitious crews' fears of disaster for the death of Doughty seemed to become very real in the terrific tempests that assailed the three ships as they entered the straits. Gales lashed the cross tides to a height of thirty feet, threatening to swamp the little craft. Mountains emerged shadowy through the mists on the south. Roiling waters met the prows from end to end of the straits. Topsails were dipped, psalms of thanks chanted, and prayers held as the ships came out on the west side into the Pacific on the 6th of September. In honor of the first English vessel to enter this ocean, Drake renamed his ship "*Golden Hind.*" {151} The gales continued so furiously, Drake jocosely called the sea,

Mare Furiosum, instead of Pacific. The first week of October storms compelled the vessels to anchor. In the raging darkness that night, the explosive rip of a snapping hawser was heard behind the stern of the *Golden Hind*. Fearful cries rose from the waves for help. The dark form of a phantom ship lurched past in the running seas—the *Marygold* adrift, loose from her anchor, driving to the open storm; fearful judgment—as the listeners thought—for the crew's false testimony against Doughty; for, as one old record states, "they could by no means help {152} spooming along before the sea;" and the *Marygold* was never more seen.

The Golden Hind.

[Illustration: The Golden Hind.]

Meanwhile like disaster had befallen the *Golden Hind*, the cable snapping weak as thread against the drive of tide and wind. Only the *Elizabeth* kept her anchor grip, and her crew became so panic-stricken, they only waited till the storm abated, then turned back through the straits, swift heels to the stormy, ill-fated sea, and steered straight for England, where they moored in June. Towed by the *Golden Hind*, now driving southward before the tempest, was a jolly-boat with eight men. The mountain seas finally wrenched the tow-rope from the big ship, and the men were adrift in the open boat. Their fortunes are a story in itself. Only one of the eight survived to reach England after nine years' wandering in Brazil.[6]

Onward, sails furled, bare poles straining to the storm, drifted Drake in the *Golden Hind*. Luck, that so often favors daring, or the courage, that is its own talisman, kept him from the rocks. With battened hatches he drove before what he could not {153} stem, southward and south, clear down where Atlantic and Pacific met at Cape Horn, now for the first time seen by navigator. Here at last, on October 30, came a lull. Drake landed, and took possession of this earth's end for the Queen. Then he headed his prow northward for the forbidden waters of the Pacific bordering New Spain. Not a Spaniard was seen up to the Bay of San Filipe off Chile, where by the end of November Drake came on an Indian fisherman. Thinking the ship Spanish, the fellow offered to pilot her back eighteen miles to the harbor of Valparaiso.

Spanish vessels lay rocking to the tide as Drake glided into the port. So utterly impossible was it deemed for any foreign ship to enter the Pacific, that the Spanish commander of the fleet at anchor dipped colors in salute to the pirate heretic, thinking him a messenger from Spain, and beat him a rattling welcome on the drum as the *Golden Hind* knocked keels with the Spanish bark. Drake, doubtless, smiled as he returned the salute by a wave of his plumed hat. The Spaniards actually had wine jars out to drown the newcomers ashore, when a quick clamping of iron hooks locked the Spanish vessel in death grapple to the *Golden Hind*. An English sailor leaped over decks to the Spanish galleon with a yell of "*Downe, Spanish dogges!*" The crew of sixty English pirates had swarmed across the vessel like hornets before the poor hidalgo knew what had happened. Head over heels, down the hatchway, reeled the astonished dons. Drake clapped down {154} hatches, and had the Spaniards trapped while his men went ashore to sack the town. One Spaniard had succeeded in swimming across to warn the port.[7] When Drake landed, the entire population had fled to the hills. Rich plunder in wedges of pure gold, and gems, was carried off from the fort. Not a drop of blood was shed. Crews of the scuttled vessels were set ashore, the dismantled ships sent drifting to open sea. The whole fiasco was conducted as harmlessly as a melodrama, with a moral thrown in; for were not these zealous Protestants despoiling these zealous Catholics, whose zeal, in turn, had led them to despoil the Indian? There was a moral; but it wore a coat of many colors.

Francis Drake.

[Illustration: Francis Drake.]

The Indian was rewarded, and a Greek pilot forced on board to steer to Lima, the great treasury of Peruvian gold. Giving up all hope of the other English vessels joining him, Drake had paused at Coquimbo to put together a small sloop, when down swooped five hundred Spanish soldiers. In the wild scramble for the *Golden Hind*, one sailor was left behind. He was torn to pieces by the Spaniards before the eyes of Drake's crew. Northling again sailed Drake, piloted inshore by the Greek to Tarapaca, where Spanish treasure was sent out over the hills to await the call of ship; and sure enough, sound asleep in the sunlight, fatigued from his trip lay a Spanish carrier, {155} thirteen bars of silver piled beside him on the sand. When that carrier wakened, the ship had called! Farther on the English moored and went inland to see if more treasure might be coming over the hills. Along the sheep trails came a lad whistling as he drove eight Peruvian sheep laden with black leather sacks full of gold.

Drake's men were intoxicated with their success. It was impossible to attack Panama with only the *Golden Hind*; but what if the *Golden Hind* could catch the *Glory of the South Seas*—the splendid Spanish galleon that yearly carried Peruvian gold up to Panama? Drake gained first news of the treasure ship being afloat while he was rifling three barks at Aricara below Lima; but he knew coureurs were already speeding overland to warn the capital against the *Golden Hind*. Drake pressed sail to outstrip the land messenger, and glided into Callao, the port of Lima, before the thirty ships lying dismantled had the slightest inkling of his presence.

Viceroy Don Francisco de Toledo of Lima thought the overland coureur mad. A pirate heretic in the South Seas! Preposterous! Some Spanish rascal had turned pirate; so the governor gathered up two thousand soldiers to march with all speed for Callao, with hot wrath and swift punishment for the culprit. Drake had already sacked Callao, but he had missed the treasure ship. She had just left for Panama. The *Golden Hind* was lying outside the port becalmed {156} when Don Toledo came pouring his two thousand soldiers down to the wharves. The Spaniards dashed to embark on the rifled ships with a wild halloo! He was becalmed, the blackguard pirate,—whoever he was,—they would tow out! Divine Providence had surely given him into their hands; but just as they began rowing might and main, a fresh wind ruffled the water. The *Golden Hind* spread her wings to the wind and was off like a bird! Drake knew no ship afloat could outsail his swift little craft; and the Spaniards had embarked in such haste, they had come without provisions. Famine turned the pursuers back near the equator, the disgusted viceroy hastening to equip frigates that would catch the English pirate when famine must compel him to head southward.

Drake slackened sail to capture another gold cargo. The crew of this caravel were so grateful to be put ashore instead of having their throats cut, that they revealed to Drake the stimulating fact that the *Glory of the South Seas*, the treasure ship, was only two days ahead laden with golden wealth untold.

It was now a wild race for gold—for gold enough to enrich every man of the crew; for treasure that might buy up half a dozen European kingdoms and leave the buyer rich; for gold in huge slabs the shape of the legendary wedges long ago given the rulers of the Incas by the descendants of the gods; gold to be had for the taking by the striking of one sure blow at England's enemy! Drake called on the crew to acquit {157} themselves like men. The sailors answered with a shout. Every inch of sail was spread. Old muskets and cutlasses were scoured till they shone like the sun. Men scrambled up the mast poles to gaze seaward for sight of sail to the fore. Every nerve was braced. They were now across the equator. A few hundred miles more, and the *Glory of the South Seas* would lie safe inside the strong harbor of Panama. Drake ordered the thirty cannon ready for action, and in a loud voice offered the present of his own golden chain to the man who should first descry the sails of the Spanish treasure. For once his luck failed him. The wind suddenly fell. Before Drake needed to issue the order, his "brave boys" were over decks and out in the small boats rowing for dear life, towing the *Golden Hind*. Day or night from February twenty-fourth, they did not slack, scarcely pausing to eat or sleep. Not to lose the tremendous prize by seeing the *Glory of the South Seas* sail into Panama Bay at the last lap of the desperate race, had these bold pirates ploughed a furrow round the world, daring death or devil!

At three in the afternoon of March the 1st, John Drake, the commander's brother, shouted out from the mast top where he clung, "Sail ho!" and the blood of every Englishman aboard jumped to the words! At six in the evening, just off Cape Francisco, they were so close to the *Glory of the South Seas*, they could see that she was compelled to sail slowly, owing to the weight of her cargo. So unaware of danger was {158} the captain that he thought Drake some messenger sent by the viceroy, and instead of getting arms in readiness and pressing sail, he lowered canvas, came to anchor, and waited![8] Drake's announcement was a roaring cannonade that blew the mast poles off the Spanish ship, crippling her like a bird with wings broken. For the rest, the scene was what has been enacted wherever pirates have played their game—a furious fusillade from the cannon mouths belching from decks and port-holes, the unscathed ship riding down on the staggering victim like a beast on its prey, the clapping of the grappling hooks that bound the captive to the sides of her victor, the rush over decks, the flash of naked sword, the decks swimming in blood, and the quick surrender. The booty from this treasure ship was roughly estimated at twenty-six tons of pure silver, thirteen chests of gold plate, eighty pounds of pure gold, and precious jewels— emeralds and pearls—to the value in modern money of seven hundred and twenty thousand dollars.

Drake realized now that he dared not return to England by the Straits of Magellan. All the Spanish frigates of the Pacific were on the watch. The *Golden Hind* was so heavily freighted with treasure, it was actually necessary to lighten ballast by throwing spices and silks overboard. One can guess that the orchestra played a stirring refrain off Cape Francisco that night. The Northeast Passage from Asia to Europe was {159} still a myth of the geographers. Drake's friend, Frobisher, had thought he found it on the Atlantic side. After taking counsel with his ten chosen advisers, Drake decided to give the Spanish frigates the slip by returning through the mythical Northeast Passage. Stop was made at Guatalco, off the west coast of New Spain, for repairs. Here, the poor Portuguese pilot brought all the way from the islands off the west coast of Africa, was put ashore. [9] He was tortured by the Spaniards for piloting Drake to the South Seas. In the course of rifling port and ship at Guatalco, charts to the Philippines and Indian Ocean were found; so that even if the voyage to England by the Northeast Passage proved impossible, the *Golden Hind* could follow these charts home round the world by the Indian Ocean and Good Hope up Africa.

It was needless for Drake to sack more Spanish floats. He had all the plunder he could carry. From the charts he learned that the Spaniards always struck north for favorable winds. Heading north, month after month, the *Golden Hind* sailed for the shore that should have led northeast, and that puzzled the mariners by sheering west and yet west; fourteen hundred leagues she sailed along a leafy wilderness of tangled trees and ropy mosses, beauty and decay, the froth of the beach combers aripple on the very roots of the {160} trees; dolphins coursing round the hull like greyhounds; flying fish with mica for wings flitting over the decks; forests of seaweed warning out to deeper water. Then, a sudden cold fell, cold and fogs that chilled the mariners of tropic seas to the bone. The veering coast pushed them out farther westward, far north of what the Spanish charts showed. Instead of flying fish now, were whales, whales in schools of thousands that gambolled round the *Golden Hind*. As the north winds—"frozen nimphes," the record calls them—blew down the cold Arctic fogs, Drake's men thought they were certainly nearing the Arctic regions. Where were they? Plainly lost, lost somewhere along what are now known as Mendocino, and Blanco, and Flattery. In a word, perhaps up as far as Oregon, and Washington. One record says they went to latitude 43. Another record, purporting to be more correct, says 48. The Spaniards had been north as far as California, but beyond this, however far he may have gone, Drake was a discoverer in the true sense of the word. Mountains covered with snow they saw, and white cliffs, and low shelving shores, which is more descriptive of Oregon and Washington than California; but only the sudden transition from tropic heat to chilling northern fogs can explain the crew's exaggerated idea of cold along the Pacific coast. Land was sighted at 42, north of Mendocino, and an effort made to anchor farther north; but contrary winds and a rock bottom gave insecure mooring. {161} This was not surprising, as it was on this coast that Cook and Vancouver failed to find good harborage.

The coast still seemed to trend westward, dispelling hopes of a Northeast Passage, and if the world could have accepted Drake's conclusions on the matter, a deal of expenditure in human life and effort might have been saved.

Two centuries before the deaths of Bering and Cook, trying to find that Passage, Drake's chronicler wrote: "*The cause of this extreme cold we conceive to be the large spreading of the Asian and American continent, if they be not fully joined, yet seem they to come very neere, from whose high and snow-covered mountains, the north and north-west winds send abroad their frozen nimphes to the infecting of the whole air—hence comes it that in the middest of their summer, the snow hardly departeth from these hills at all; hence come those thicke mists and most stinking fogges, ... for these reasons we coniecture that either there is no passage at all through these Northerne coasts, which is most likely, or if there be, that it is unnavigable.... Adde there unto, that though we searched the coast diligently even unto the 48 degree, yet found we not the land to trend in any place towards the East, but rather running continually North-west, as if it went directly to meet with Asia.... of which we infallibly concluded rather than coniectured, that there was none.*"

Giving up all idea of a Northeast Passage, Drake turned south, and on June 17 anchored in a bay now {162} thoroughly identified as Drake's Bay, north of San Francisco.

The next morning, while the English were yet on the *Golden Hind*, came an Indian in a canoe, shouting out oration of welcome, blowing feather down on the air as a sign of dovelike peace, and finally after three times essaying courage, coming near enough the English to toss a rush basket full of tobacco into the ship. In vain Drake threw out presents to allure the Indian on board. The terrified fellow scampered ashore, refusing everything but a gorgeous hat, that floated out on the water. For years the legend of Drake's ship was handed down as a tradition among the Indians of this bay.[10]

By the 21st tents were erected, and a rude fortification of stone thrown round in protection where the precious cargo of gold could be stored while the ship was to be careened and scraped. At the foot of the hill, the poor Indians gathered and gazed spellbound at the sight of this great winged bird of the ocean, sending thirty cannon trundling ashore, and herself beginning to rise up from the tide on piles and scaffolding. As Drake sent the assembled tribe presents, the Indians laid down their bows and spears. So marvellously did the wonders of the white men grow—sticks that emitted puffs of fire (muskets), a ship so large it could have carried their tribe, clothing in velvet and gold braid gorgeous as the plumage of a {163} bird, cutlasses of steel—that by the 23d great assemblages of Indians were on their knees at the foot of the hill, offering sacrifices to the wonderful beings in the fort. Whatever the English pirate's faults, he deserves credit for treating the Indians with an honor that puts later navigators to shame. When he saw them gashing bodies in sacrifice, his superstition took fire with fear of Divine displeasure for the sacrilege; and the man who did not scruple to treat black slaves picked up among the Spaniards baser than he would have treated dogs, now fell "to prayers," as the old chronicle says, reading the Bible aloud, and setting his crew to singing psalms, and pointing to the sky, at which the Indians grunted approvals of "ho—ho!"

Three days later came coureurs from the "King of the Indians"—the chief—bidding the strangers prepare for the great sachem's visit. The coureurs advanced gyrating and singing; so that the English saw in this strange people nomads like the races of Scripture, whose ceremony was one of song and dance. The warriors preceding the chief carried what the English thought "a sceptre," but what we moderns would call a peace-pipe. The chains in their hands were probably strings of bears' claws, or something like wampum; the "crowns of feathers," plumed head-dresses; the gifts in the rush baskets borne by the women to the rear, maize and tobacco.

Drake drew his soldiers up in line, and with trumpets sounding and armor at gleam marched out to {164} welcome the Indian chief. Then the whole company of savages broke out in singing and dancing. Drake was signalled to sit down in the centre. Barely had he obeyed when to the shouting and dancing of the multitude, "a chain" was thrown over his neck, "a crown" placed on his head, and "the sceptre" put in his hand. According to Indian custom, Drake was welcomed by the ceremony of adoption in the tribe, "the sceptre" being a peace-pipe; "the crown," an Indian warrior's head-dress. Far otherwise the ceremony appeared to the romantic treasure hunters. "*In the name and to the use of Her Most Excellent Majesty*," records the chaplain, "*he (Drake) tooke the sceptre, crowne, and dignity of the sayd countrie into his hand*;" though, added the pious chaplain of pirates, when he witnessed the Indians bringing the sick to be healed by the master pirate's touch,—"*we groane in spirit to see the power of Sathan so farre prevails.*"

The Crowning of Drake in California.

[Illustration: The Crowning of Drake in California.]

To avert disaster for the sacrilege of the sacred touch of healing, Drake added to his prayers strong lotions and good ginger plasters. Sometime in the next five weeks, Drake travelled inland with the Indians, and because of patriotism to his native land and the resemblance of the white sand cliffs to that land, called the region "New Albion." "New Albion" would be an offset to "New Spain." Drake saw himself a second Cortés, and nailed to a tree a brass plate on which was graven the Queen's name, the year, the free surrender of the country to the {165} Queen, and Drake's own name; for, says the chaplain, quite ignorant of Spanish voyages, "*the Spaniards never had any dealing, or so much as set a foot in this country, the utmost of their discoveries reaching only many degrees Southward of this place.*"

Drake's misunderstanding of the Indian ceremony would be comical if it were not that later historians have solemnly argued whether an act of possession by a pirate should hold good in international law.

On the 23d of July the English pirate bade farewell to the Indians. As he looked back from the sea, they were running along the hilltops burning more of the fires which he thought were sacrifices.

Following the chart taken from the Spanish ship, Drake steered for the Philippines, thence southward through the East Indies to the Indian Ocean, and past Good Hope, back to Plymouth, where he came to anchor on September 26, 1580. Bells were set ringing. Post went spurring to London with word that Drake, the corsair, who had turned the Spanish world upside down, had come home. For a week the little world of England gave itself up to feasting. Ballads rang with the fame of Drake. His name was on every tongue. One of his first acts was to visit his old parents. Then he took the *Golden Hind* round the Channel to be dry-docked in Deptford.

For the once, the tactful Queen was in a quandary. Complaints were pouring in from Spain. The {166} Spanish ambassador was furious, and presented bills of sequestration against Drake, but as the amount sequestered, pending investigation, was only fifty-six thousand pounds, one may suspect that Elizabeth let Drake protect in his own way what he had taken in his own way.

For six months, while the world resounded with his fame, the court withheld approval. Jealous courtiers "deemed Drake the master thief of the unknown world," till Elizabeth cut the Gordian knot by one of her defiant strokes. On April 4 she went in state to dine on the *Golden Hind*, to the music of those stringed instruments that had harped away Drake's fear of death or devil as he ploughed an English keel round the world. After the dinner, she bade him fall to his knees and with a light touch of the sword gave him the title that was seal of the court's approval. The *Golden Hind* was kept as a public relic till it fell to pieces on the Thames, and the wood was made into a memorial chair for Oxford.

The Silver Map of the World. Both sides of a medal struck off at the time of Drake's return to England, commemorating his voyage around the world. The faint dotted line shows the course sailed by him in the Golden Hind.

[Illustration: The Silver Map of the World. Both sides of a medal struck off at the time of Drake's return to England, commemorating his voyage around the world. The faint dotted line shows the course sailed by him in the *Golden Hind*.]

After all the perils Drake saw in the subsequent war—Cadiz and the Armada—it seems strange that he should return to the scene of his past exploits to die. He was with Hawkins in the campaign of 1595 against Spain in the New World. Things had not gone well. He had not approved of Hawkins's plans of attack, and the venture was being bungled. Sick of the equatorial fever, or of chagrin from failure, Drake died off Porto Bello in the fifty-first year of his age. His body {167} was placed in a leaden coffin, and solemnly committed to that sea where he had won his first glory.[11]

[1] This is but a brief epitome of the Spaniard's swelling words. Only the Heavens above were omitted from Spain's claim.

[2] The exact position of the English towards the port is hard to give, at the site of Vera Cruz has been changed three times.

[3] This halfway station was known as Venta Cruz. Seven of the traders lost their lives in Drake's attack.

[4] The *Hakluyt Society Proceedings*, 1854, give all details of this terrible crime. Fletcher, the chaplain, thought Doughty innocent; but Drake considered the chaplain "the falsest knave that liveth."

[5] Don Francisco de Zarate, commander of a Spanish ship scuttled by Drake off Guatalco, gives this description to the Spanish government of the Englishman's equipage: "The general of the Englishmen is the same who five years ago took Nombre de Dios, about thirty-five years old, short, with a ruddy beard, one of the greatest mariners there are on the sea, alike for his skill and power of command. His ship is a galleon of four hundred tons, a very fast sailer, and there are aboard her, one hundred men, all skilled hands and of warlike age, and all so well trained that they might be old soldiers—they keep their harquebusses clean. He treats them with affection, they him with respect. He carries with him nine or ten gentlemen cadets of high families in England. These are his council. He calls them together, tho' he takes counsel of no one. He has no favorite. These are admitted to his table, as well as a Portuguese pilot whom he brought from England. (?) He is served with much plate with gilt borders engraved with his arms and has all possible kinds of delicacies and scents, which … the Queen gave him. (?) None of the gentlemen sit or cover in his presence without first being ordered once or even several times. The galleon carries thirty pieces of heavy ordnance, fireworks and ammunition. They dine and sup to the music of violins. He carries carpenters, caulkers, careeners. The ship is sheathed. The men are paid and not regular pirates. No one takes plunder and the slightest fault is punished." The don goes on to say that what troubled him most was that Drake captured Spanish charts of the Pacific, which would guide other intruders on the Pacific.

[6] The eight castaways in the shallop succeeded in passing back through the straits. At Plata they were attacked by the Indians; four, wounded, succeeded in escaping. The others were captured. Reaching islands off the coast of Patagonia, two of the wounded died. The remaining two suffered shipwreck on a barren island, where the only food was fruit; the only drink, the juice of the fruits. Making a raft of floating planks ten feet long, the two committed themselves to God and steered for the mainland. Here Pilcher died two hours after they had landed from drinking too much water. The survivor, Peter Carder, lived among the savages of Brazil for eight years before he escaped and got passage to England, where he related his adventures to Queen Elizabeth. The Queen gave him twenty-two angels and sent him to Admiral Howard for employment. *Purchas' Pilgrims*, Vol. IV.

[7] The plunder of this port was 60,000 pesos of gold, jewels, and goods (pesos about 8 shillings, $2); 1770 jars of wine, together with the silver of the chapel altar, which was given to Fletcher.

[8] The captain was a Biscayan, one Juan de Anton.

[9] Nuno Silva is the name of this pilot. It is from his story that many of the details of this part of the voyage are obtained.

[10] See Professor George Davidson's pamphlet on *Drake*.

[11] To give even a brief account of Drake's life would fill a small encyclopaedia. The story of his first ruin off Vera Cruz, of his campaign of vengeance, of his piratical voyage to the Pacific, of his doings with the California Indians, of his fight in the Armada—any one of these would fill an ordinary volume. Only that part of his life bearing on American exploration has been given here, and that sacrificed in detail to keep from cumbering the sweep of his adventure. No attempt has been made to pass judgment on Drake's character. Like Baranof of a later day, he was a curious mixture of the supremely selfish egoist, and of the religious enthusiast, alternately using his egoism as a support for his religion, and his religion as a support for his egoism; and each reader will probably pass judgment on Drake according as the reader's ideal of manhood is the altruist or the egoist, the Christ-type or "the great blond beast" of modern philosophic thought, the man supremely indifferent to all but self, glorying in triumph though it be knee-deep in blood. Nor must we moderns pass too hypocritical judgment on the hero of the Drake type. Drake had invested capital in his venture. He had the blessing of Church and State on what he was about to do, and what he did was *to take* what he had strength and dexterity to take independent of the Ten Commandments, which is not so far different from many commercial methods of to-day. We may appear as unmoral in our methods to future judges as Drake appears to us. Just as no attempt has been made to analyze Drake's character—to balance his lack of morals with his courage—so minor details, that would have led off from the main

current of events, have been omitted. For instance, Drake spilled very little Spanish blood and was Christian in his treatment of the Indians; but are these credit marks offset by his brutality toward the black servants whom the pirates picked up among the Spaniards, of whom one poor colored girl was marooned on a Pacific island to live or die or rot? To be sure, the Portuguese pilot taken from a scuttled caravel off the west coast of Africa on the way out, and forced to pilot Drake to the Pacific, was well treated on the voyage. At least, there is no mention to the contrary; but when Drake had finished with the fellow, though the English might have known very well what terrible vengeance Spain would take, the pilot was dumped off on the coast of New Spain, where, one old record states, he was tortured, almost torn to pieces, for having guided Drake.

The great, indeed, primary and only authorities for Drake's adventures are, of course, Hakluyt, Vol. III; for the fate of the lost crews, *Purchas' Pilgrims*, Vol. III and Vol. I, Book II, and Vol. IV; and the *Hakluyt Society Proceedings*, 1854, which are really a reprint of *The World Encompassed*, by Francis Fletcher, the chaplain, in 1628, with the addition of documents contemporary with Fletcher's by unknown writers. The title-page of *The World Encompassed* reads almost like an old ballad—"*for the stirring up of heroick spirits to benefit their countries, and eternize their names by like {168} attempts.*" Kohl and Davidson's *Reports of the Coast and Geodetic Survey*, 1884 and 1886, are also invaluable as establishing Drake's land-fall in California. Miller Christy's Silver Map of the World gives a splendid facsimile of the medal issued to commemorate Drake's return, of which the original is in the British Museum. Among biographers, Corbett's *Drake*, and Barrow's *Life of Sir Francis Drake*, give full details of his early and personal life, including, of course, his great services in the Armada.

Furious controversy has waged over Drake on two points: Did he murder Doughty? Did he go as far north on the west coast of America as 48 degrees? Hakluyt's account says 43 degrees; *The World Encompassed*, by Fletcher, the chaplain, says 48 degrees, though all accounts agree it was at 38 degrees he made harbor. I have not dealt with either dispute, stating the bare facts, leaving each reader to draw his own conclusions, though it seems to me a little foolish to contend that the claim of the 48th degree was an afterthought interpolated by the writer to stretch British possessions over a broader swath; for even two hundred years after the issue of the Silver Map of the World, when Cook was on this coast, so little was known of the west shores of America by Englishmen that men were still looking out for a Gamaland, or imaginary continent in the middle of the Pacific.

The words of the narrative bearing on America are: "We came to 42 degree of North latitude, where on the night following (June 3) we found such alterations of heat, into extreme and nipping cold, that our men in general did grievously complain thereof, some of them feeling their health much impaired thereby; neither was it that this chanced in the night alone, but the day following carried with it not only the markes, but the stings and force of the night ...; besides that the pinching and biting air was nothing altered, the very ropes of our ship were stiffe, and the rain which fell was an unnatural congealed and frozen substance so that we seemed to be rather in the frozen Zone than any where so neere unto the sun or these hotter climates ... it came to that extremity in sayling but two degrees farther to the northward in our course, that though seamen lack not good stomachs ... it was a question whether hands should feed their mouths, or rather keepe from the pinching cold that did benumme them ... our meate as soone as it was remooved from the fire, would presently in a manner be frozen up, and our ropes and tackling in a few days were growne to that stiffnesse ... yet would not our general be discouraged but as well by comfortable speeches, of the divine providence, and of God's loving care over his children, out of the Scriptures ... the land in that part of America, beares farther out into the West than we before imagined, we were neerer on it than we were aware; yet the neerer still we came unto it, the more extremity of cold did sease upon us. The fifth day of June, we were forced by contrary windes to runne in with the shoare, which we then first descried, and to cast anchor in a bad bay, the best roade we could for the present meete with, where we were not without some danger by reason of the many extreme gusts and flawes that beate upon us, which if they ceased, and were still at any time ... there followed most vile, thicke and stinking fogges against which the sea prevailed nothing {169} ... to go further North, the extremity of the cold would not permit us and the winds directly bent against us, having once gotten us under sayle againe, commanded us to the Southward whether we would or no.

"From the height of 48 degrees in which now we were to 38, we found the land by coasting alongst it, to be but low and plaine—every hill whereof we saw many but none were high, though it were in June, and the sunne in his nearest approach … being covered with snow.… In 38 deg. 30 min. we fell with a convenient and fit harborough and June 17 came to anchor therein, where we continued till the 23rd day of July following … neither could we at any time in whole fourteen days together find the aire so cleare as to be able to take the height of sunne or starre … after our departure from the heate we always found our bodies, not as sponges, but strong and hardened, more able to beare out cold, though we came out of the excesse of heate, then chamber champions could hae beene, who lye in their feather beds till they go to sea.

"… Trees without leaves, and the ground without greennes in these months of June and July … as for the cause of this extremity, they seem … chiefest we conceive to be the large spreading of the Asian and American continent, which (somewhat Northward of these parts) if they be not fully joyned, yet seeme they to come very neere one to the other. From whose high and snow-covered mountains, the North and Northwest winds (the constant visitants of those coasts) send abroad their frozen nimphes, to the infecting of the whole aire with this insufferable sharpnesse.… Hence comes the generall squalidnesse and barrennesse of the countrie, hence comes it that in the midst of their summer, the snow hardly departeth … from their hils at all, hence come those thicke mists and most stinking fogges, which increase so much the more, by how much higher the pole is raised … also from these reasons we coniecture that either there is no passage at all through these Northern coasts which is most likely or if there be, that yet it is unnavigable.… Add here unto, that though we searched the coast diligently, even unto the 48 degree, yet found we not the land to trend so much as one point in any place towards the East, but rather running on continually Northwest, as if it went directly to meet with Asia; and even in that height, when we had a franke winde to have carried us through, had there been a passage, yet we had a smoothe and calme sea, with ordinary flowing and renewing, which could not have beene had there been a frete; of which we rather infallibly concluded, then coniectured, that there was none.

"The next day, after coming to anchor in the aforesaid harbour, the people of the countrey showed themselves, sending off a man with great expedition to us in a canow, who being yet but a little from the shoare, and a great way from our ship, spake to us continually as he came rowing in. And at last at a reasonable distance, staying himself, he began more solemnly a long and tedious oration, after his manner, using in the deliverie thereof, many gestures and signes, mouing his hands, turning his head and body many wayes, and after his oration ended, with great show and reverence and submission returned backe to shoare again. He shortly came againe the second time in like manner, {170} and so the third time, when he brought with him (as a present from the rest) a bunch of feathers, much like the feathers of a blacke crowe, very neatly and artificially gathered upon a string, and drawne together into a round bundle, being verie cleane and finely cut, and bearing in length an equall proportion one with another a special cognizance (as we afterwards observed) which they … weare on their heads. With this also he brought a little basket made of rushes, and filled with an herbe which they called Tobah. Both which being tyed to a short rodde, he cast into our boate. Our generall intended to have recompenced him immediately with many good things he would have bestowed on him; but entering into the boate to deliver the same, he could not be drawne to receive them by any meanes, save one hat, which being cast into the water out of the ship, he took up (refusing utterly to meddle with any other thing) though it were upon a board put off unto him, and so presently made his returne. After which time our boate could row no way, but wondering at us as at gods, they would follow the same with admiration.…

"The third day following, viz., the 21, our ship having received a leake at sea, was brought to anchor neerer the shoare, that her goods being landed she might be repaired; but for that we were to prevent any danger that might chance against our safety, our Generall first of all landed his men, with all necessary provision, to build tents and make a fort for the defence of ourselves and our goods … which when the people of the country perceived us doing, as men set on fire to war in defence of their countrie, in great hast and companee, with such weapons as they had, they came down unto us, and yet with no hostile meaning or intent to hurt us: standing when they drew neerer, as men ravished in their mindes, with the sight of such things, as they never had scene or heard of before that time: their errand being rather with submission and feare to worship us as Gods, than to have warre with us as mortall men: which thing, as it did partly show itselfe at that instant, so did it more and more manifest itself afterwards, during the whole time of our abode amongst them. At this time, being veilled by signs to lay from them their bowes and arrowes, they did as they were directed and so did all the rest, as they came more and more by companies unto him, growing in a little while to a great number, both of men and women.

"… Our Generall, with all his company, used all meanes possible gently to intreate them, bestowing upon each of them liberally good and necessary things to cover their nakedness, withall signifying unto them we were no Gods but men, and had need of such things to cover our owne shame, teaching them to use them to the same ends, for which cause also we did eate and drinke in their presence, … they bestowed upon our Generall and diverse of our company, diverse things as feathers, cawles of networke, the quivers of their arrowes, made of faune skins, and the very skins of beasts that their women wore upon their bodies … they departed with joy to their houses, which houses are digged round within the earth, and have from the uppermost brimmes of the circle, clefts of wood set up, and joyned close together at the top, like our spires on the steeple of a church, which being covered with earth, … are very warme; the doore {171} in the most of them performs the office also of a chimney to let out the smoake; it's made in bignesse and fashion like to an ordinary scuttle in a ship, and standing slope-wise; the beds are the hard ground, onely with rushes strewed upon it and lying round about the house, have their fire in the middest, … with all expedition we set up our tents, and intrenched ourselves with walls of stone…. Against the end of two daies, there was gathered together a great assembly of men, women and children, bringing with them as they had before done, feathers and bagges of Tobah for present, or rather for sacrifices upon this persuasion that we were Gods.

"When they came to the top of the hill at the bottom whereof we had built our fort, they made a stand;" … "this bloodie sacrifice (against our wils) being thus performed, our generall, with his companie, in the presence of those strangers, fell to prayers; and by signes in lifting up our eyes and hands to heaven, signified unto them that that God whom we did serve and whom they ought to worship, was above: beseeching God, if it were his good pleasure, to open by some meanes their blinded eyes, that they might in due time be called to the knowledge of Him, the true and everliving God, and of Jesus Christ, whom he hath sent, the salvation of the Gentiles. In the time of which prayers, singing of Psalmes, and reading of certaine Chapters in the Bible, they sate very attentively, and observing the end of every pause, with one voice still cried 'oh' greatly rejoicing in our exercises."

"Our generall caused to be set up a monument of our being there, as also of her majesties and successors right and title to that kingdom, namely a plate of brasse, fast nailed to a great and firme poste; whereon is engraven her graces' name, and the day and year of our arrival there, and of the free giving up of the province and kingdom, both by the king and people, unto her majesties' hands: together with her highnesse picture and arms, in a piece of sixpence current English monie, shewing itselfe by a hole made of purpose through the plate; underneath was likewise engraven the name of our Generall….

"The Spaniards never had any dealings, or so much as set a foote in this country, the utmost of their discoveries reaching onely to many degrees Southward of this place."

The Spanish version of Drake's burial is, that the body was weighted with shot at the heels and heaved over into the sea, without coffin or ceremony.

{172}

CHAPTER VII
1728-1779
CAPTAIN COOK IN AMERICA

The English Navigator sent Two Hundred Years later to find the New Albion of Drake's Discoveries—He misses both the Straits of Fuca and the Mouth of the Columbia, but anchors at Nootka, the Rendezvous of Future Traders—No Northeast Passage found through Alaska—The True Cause of Cook's Murder in Hawaii told by Ledyard—Russia becomes Jealous of his Explorations

It seems impossible that after all his arduous labors and death, to prove his convictions, Bering's conclusions should have been rejected by the world of learning. Surely his coasting westward, southwestward, abreast the long arm of Alaska's peninsula for a thousand miles, should have proved that no open sea— no Northeast Passage—was here, between Asia and America. But no! the world of learning said fog had obscured Bering's observations. What he took for the mainland of America had been only a chain of islands. Northward of those islands was open sea between Asia and Europe, which might afford direct passage between East and West without circumnavigating the globe. In fact, said Dr. Campbell, {173} one of the most learned English writers of the day, "Nothing is plainer than that his (Bering's) discovery does not warrant any such supposition as that he touched the great continent making part of North America."

The moonshine of the learned men in France and Russia was even wilder. They had definitely proved, *even if there were no Gamaland*—as Bering's voyage had shown—then there must be a southern continent somewhere, to keep the balance between the northern and southern hemispheres; else the world would turn upside down. And there must also be an ocean between northern

Europe and northern Asia, else the world would be top-heavy and turn upside down. It was an age when the world accepted creeds for piety, and learned moonshine instead of scientific data; when, in a word, men refused to bow to fact!

All sorts of wild rumors were current. There was a vast continent in the south. There was a vast sea in the north. Somewhere was the New Albion, which Francis Drake had found north of New Spain. Just north of the Spanish possessions in America was a wide inlet leading straight through from the Pacific to the Atlantic, which an old Greek pilot—named Juan de Fuca—said he had traversed for the viceroy of New Spain.

Even stolid-going England was infected by the rage for imaginary oceans and continents. The Hudson's Bay Fur Company was threatened with a withdrawal {174} of its charter because it had failed to find a Northwest Passage from Atlantic to Pacific. Only four years after the death of Bering, an act of Parliament offered a reward of twenty thousand pounds to the officers and crew of any ships discovering a passage between Atlantic and Pacific north of 52 degrees. There were even ingenious fellows with the letters of the Royal Society behind their names, who affected to think that the great Athabasca Lake, which Hearne had found, when he tramped inland from the Arctic and Coppermine River, was a strait leading to the Pacific. Athabasca Lake might be the imaginary strait of the Greek pilot, Juan de Fuca. To be sure, two Hudson's Bay Company ships' crews—those under Knight and Barlow—had been totally lost fifty years before Hearne's tramp inland in 1771, trying to find that same mythical strait of Juan de Fuca westward of Hudson Bay.

But so furious did public opinion wax over a Northwest Passage at the very time poor Bering was dying in the North Pacific, that Captain Middleton was sent to Hudson Bay in 1741-1742 to find a way to the Pacific. And when Middleton failed to find water where the Creator had placed land, Dobbs, the patron of the expedition and champion of a Northwest Passage at once roused the public to send out two more ships—the *Dobbs* and *California*. Failure again! Theories never yet made Fact, never so much as added a hair's weight to Fact! Ellis, who was on board, affected to think that Chesterfield Inlet—a great arm of the sea, {175} westward of Hudson Bay—might lead to the Pacific. This supposition was promptly exploded by the Hudson's Bay Fur Company sending Captain Christopher and Moses Norton, the local governor of the company, up Chesterfield inlet for two hundred miles, where they found, not the Pacific, but a narrow river. Then the hue and cry of the learned theorists was—the Northwest Passage lay northward of Hudson Bay. Hearne was sent tramping inland to find —not sea, but land; and when he returned with the report of the great Athabasca Lake of Mackenzie River region, the lake was actually seized on as proof that there was a waterway to the Pacific. Then the brilliant plan was conceived to send ships by both the Atlantic and the Pacific to find this mythical passage from Europe to Asia. Pickersgill, who had been on the Pacific, was to go out north of Hudson Bay and work westward. To work eastward from the Pacific to the Atlantic was chosen a man who had already proved there was no great continental mass on the south, and that the world did not turn upside down, and who was destined to prove there was no great open ocean on the north, and still the world did not turn upside down. He was a man whose whole life had been based and built upon Fact, not Theory. He was a man who accepted Truth as God gave it to him, not as he had theorized it *ought* to be; a man who had climbed from a mud cottage to the position of the greatest navigator in the world—had climbed on top of facts mastered, not {176} of schoolgirl moonshine, or study-closet theories. That man was Captain James Cook.

Cook's life presents all the contrasts of true greatness world over. Like Peter the Great, of Russia, whose word had set in motion the exploration of the northwest coast of America, Cook's character consisted of elements that invariably lead to glory or ruin; often, both. The word "impossible" was not in his vocabulary. He simply did not recognize any limitations to what a man *might* do, could do, would do, if he tried; and that means, that under stress of risk or temptation, or opposition, a man's caution goes to the winds. With Cook, it was risk that caused ruin. With the Czar of Russia, it was temptation.

Born at Marton, a small parish of a north riding in the county of York, October 27, 1728, James Cook was the son of a day-laborer in an age when manual toil was paid at the rate of a few pennies a day. There were nine of a family. The home was a thatch-roofed mud cottage. Two years after Cook's birth, the father was appointed bailiff, which slightly improved family finances; but James was thirteen years of age before it was possible to send him to school. There, the progress of his learning was a gallop. He had a wizard-genius for figures. In three short years he had mastered all the Ayton school could teach him. At sixteen, his schooling was over. The father's highest ambition seems to have been for the son to become a successful shopkeeper in one of the small towns. The future {177} navigator was apprenticed to the village shop; but Cook's ambitions were not to be caged behind a counter.

Eastward rolled the North Sea. Down at Hull were heard seamen's yarns to make the blood of a boy jump. It was 1746. The world was ringing with tales of Bering on the Pacific, of a southern continent, which didn't exist, of the Hudson's Bay Fur Company's illimitable domain in the north, of La Vérendrye's wonderful discoveries of an almost boundless region westward of New France toward the uncharted Western Sea. In a year and a half, Cook had his fill of shopkeeping. Whether he ran away, or had served his master so well that the latter willingly remitted the three years' articles of apprenticeship, Cook now followed his destiny to the sea. According to the world's standards, the change seemed progress backward. He was articled to a ship-owner of Whitby as a common seaman on a coaler sailing between Newcastle and London. One can see such coalers any day—black as smut, grimed from prow to stern, with workmen almost black shovelling coal or hoisting tackling—pushing in and out among the statelier craft of any seaport. It is this stage in a great man's career which is the test. Is the man sure enough of himself to leave everything behind, and jump over the precipice into the unknown? If ever he wishes to return to what he has left, he will have just the height of this jump to climb back to the old place. The old place is a certainty. The unknown may engulf in failure. He {178} must chance that, and all for the sake of a faith in himself, which has not yet been justified; for the sake of a vague star leading into the misty unknown. He knows that he could have been successful in the old place. He does not know that he may not be a failure in the new place. Art, literature, science, commerce—in all —it is the men and women who have dared to risk being failures that have proved the mainspring of progress. Cook was sure enough of himself to exchange shopkeeper's linen for the coal-heaver's blue jeans, to risk following the star of his destiny to the sea.

Presently, the commonplace, grimy duties which he must fulfil are taking him to Dublin, to Liverpool, to Norway; and by the time he is twenty-two, he knows the Baltic trade well, and has heard all the pros and cons of the furious cackle which the schools have raised over that expedition of Bering's to the west coast of America. By the time he is twenty-four he is a first mate on the coal boats. Comes another vital change! When he left the shop, he felt all that he had to do to follow his destiny was to go to sea. Now the star has led him up to a blank wall. The only promotion he can obtain on these merchantmen is to a captainship; and the captaincy on a small merchantman will mean pretty much a monotonous flying back and forward like a shuttle between the ports of Europe and England.

Cook took a resolution that would have cost any {179} man but one with absolute singleness of purpose a poignant effort. At the age of twenty-seven, he decided to enter the Royal Navy. Now, in a democratic age, we don't talk about such things; but there are unwritten laws and invisible lines just the same. Standing on the captain's deck of an American warship not long ago, watching the deck hands below putting things shipshape, I asked an officer—"Is there any chance for those men to rise?"

"Yes, some," he answered tentatively, "but then, there is a difference between the men who have been trained for a position, and those who have worked up the line to it." If that difference exists in a democratic country and age, what was it for Cook in a country and at a time when lines of caste were hard and fast drawn? But he entered the navy on the *Eagle* under Sir Hugh Palliser, who, almost at once, transferred him from the forecastle to the quarterdeck. What was the explanation of such quick recognition? Therein lies the difference between the man who tries and succeeds, and the man who tries and fails. Cook had qualified himself for promotion. He was so fitted for the higher position, that the higher position could not do without him. Whether rocking on the Baltic, or waiting for the stokers to heave out coal at Liverpool, every moment not occupied by seaman's duties, Cook had filled by improving himself, by increasing his usefulness, by sharpening his brain, so that his brain could better direct his hands, by {180} studying mathematics and astronomy and geography and science and navigation. As some one has said—there are lots of people with hands and no brain; and there are lots of people with brains and no hands; but the kind who will command the highest reward for their services to the world are those who have the finest combination of brains *and* hands.

Captain James Cook.

[Illustration: Captain James Cook.]

Four years after Cook had joined the navy, he was master on the *Mercury* with the fleet before Quebec, making a chart of the St. Lawrence for Wolfe to take the troops up to the Heights of Abraham, piloting the boats to the attack on Montmorency, and conducting the embarkation of the troops, who were to win the famous battle, that changed the face of America.

Now the Royal Society wished to send some one to the South Seas, whose reliability was of such a recognized and steady-going sort, that his conclusions would be accepted by the public. Just twenty years from the time that he had left the shop, Cook was chosen for this important mission. What manner of man was he, who in that time had risen from life in a mud hut to the rank of a commander in the Royal Navy? In manner, he was plain and simple and direct, no flourish, no unnecessary palaver of showy words, not a word he did not mean. In form, he was six feet tall, in perfect proportion, with brown hair and eyes, alertly penetrating, with features sharp rather from habit or thought than from natural shape.

On this mission he left England in 1768, anchored at {181} the Society Islands of the South Seas in the spring of 1769, explored New Zealand in the fall of the same year, rounded Australia in 1770 and returned to England in 1771, the very year Hearne was trying to tramp it overland in search of a Northwest Passage. And he brought back no proof of that vast southern world which geographers had put on their maps. Promptly he was sent out on a second voyage to find or demolish that mythical continent of the southern hemisphere; and he demolished the myth of a southern continent altogether, returning from circumnavigating the globe just at the time when the furor of a Northwest Passage northward of Hudson Bay, northward even of Bering's course on the Pacific, was at its height.

The third voyage was to determine finally the bounds of western America, the possibilities of a passage between Europe and Asia by way of the Pacific. Two ships—the *Resolution*, four hundred and sixty tons, one hundred and twelve men, which Cook had used before, and the *Discovery*, three hundred tons, eighty men—were purchased at Hull, the old port of Cook's boyhood dreams. To secure the good will of the crews, two months' wages were paid in advance. Captain Clerke commanded the *Discovery*; and the two crews numbered men of whom the world was to hear more in connection with the northwest coast of America— a young midshipman, Vancouver, whose doings were yet to checkmate Spain; a young American, corporal {182} of marines, Ledyard, who was to have his brush with Russia; and other ambitious young seamen destined to become famous traders on the west coast of America.

The two ships left England in midsummer of 1776, crossed the equator in September when every man fresh to the episode was caught and ducked overrails in equatorial waters, rounded Good Hope, touched at the Society Islands of the first voyage, and by spring of 1778 had explored and anchored at the Sandwich Islands. Once on the Pacific, Cook mustered his crews and took them into his confidence; he was going to try for that reward of twenty thousand pounds to the crew that discovered a Northeast Passage; and even if he missed the reward, he was going to have a shy at the most northern latitude ever attempted by navigator—89 degrees; would they do it? The crew cheered. Whether they reached 89 degrees or not, they decided to preserve their grog for the intense cold to be encountered in the north; so that the daily allowance was now cut to half.

By March, the ships were off from the Sandwich Islands to the long swell of the Pacific, the slimy medusa lights covering the waters with a phosphorescent trail of fire all night, the rockweed and sea leek floating past by day telling their tale of some far land. Cook's secret commission had been very explicit: "You are to proceed on as direct a course as you can to the coast of New Albion, endeavoring to fall in with it in latitude 45 degrees north ... and are strictly enjoined {183} not to touch on any part of the Spanish dominions ... unless driven by accident ... and to be very careful not to give any umbrage to the subjects of his Catholic Majesty ... and if in further progress northward ... you find any subjects of a European prince ... you are not to give any cause of offence ... proceed northward to 65 degrees, carefully search for such inlets as appear pointing to Hudson Bay ... use your utmost endeavors to pass through." The commission shows that England was unaware Spain had pushed north of 45 degrees, and Russia north of 65 degrees; for Spain jealously kept her explorations secret, and Russia's were not accepted. The commission also offered a reward for any one going within 1 degree of the Pole. It may be added —the offer is still open.

For days after leaving the Sandwich Islands, not a bird was to be seen. That was a bad omen for land. Land must be far, indeed; and Cook began to fear there might be as much ocean in that northern hemisphere as the geographers of Russia and France—who actually tabulated Bering's discoveries as an island— had placed on the maps. But in the first week of March, a sea-gull came swimming over the crest of a wave. Where did she come from? Then an albatross was seen wheeling above the sea. Then, on March 6, two lonely land seals went plying past; and whales were noticed. Surely they were nearing the region that Drake, the English freebooter, had seen and named New Albion two hundred years before. {184} Suddenly, on the morning of March 7, the dim offing ahead showed thin, sharp, clear lines. The lines rose higher as the ship approached. They cut themselves against the sky in the form of mountains and hills with purple mist lying in the valleys. It was the New Albion at latitude 44 degrees 33 minutes, which Drake had discovered. The day was hazy and warm. Cook's crews wondered why Drake had complained of such cold. By night they found out. A roaring hurricane burst from the northern darkness with squalls of hail and snow and sleet, that turned the shore to one long reach of whitened cliffs straight up and down out of the sea. In commemoration, they called the first landfall, Cape Foulweather; and, in spite of the commission to sail north, drove under bare poles before the storm to 43 degrees, naming the two capes passed Perpetua and Gregory. Only by the third week of March had the storm abated enough for them to turn north again.[1]

Now, whether the old Greek pilot, Juan de Fuca, lied or dreamed, or only told a yarn of what some Indian had told him, it was along this coast that he had said the straits leading to the east side of America lay; and Cook's two ships hugged the coast as close as they dared for fear of roaring breakers and a landward wind. On March 23 rocks were seen lying off a high point capped with trees, behind which might be a {185} strait; but a gale ashore and a lashing tide thundering over the rocks sent the ships scudding for the offing through fog and rain; and never a glimpse of a passage eastward could the crews obtain. Cook called the delusive point Cape Flattery and added: "It is in this very latitude (48 degrees 15 minutes) that geographers have placed the pretended Straits of Juan de Fuca; but we saw nothing like it; nor is there the least possibility that any such thing ever existed." But Cook was too far out to descry the narrow opening—but thirteen miles wide—of Juan de Fuca, where the steamers of three continents ply to-day; though the strait by no means led to Europe, as geographers thought.

All night a hard gale drove them northward. When the weather cleared, permitting them to approach the coast again, high mountains, covered with snow and forests, jagged through the clouds like tent peaks. Tremendous breakers roared over sunken rocks. Point Breakers, Cook called them. Then the wind suddenly fell; and the ships were becalmed directly opposite the narrow entrance of a two-horned cove sheltered by the mountains. The small boats had all been mustered out to tow the two ships in, when a slight breeze sprang up. The flotilla drifted inland just as three canoes, carved in bizarre shapes of birds' heads and eagle claws, came paddling across the inlet. Three savages were in one, six in the other, ten in the third. They came slowly over the water, singing some song of welcome, beating time with their paddles, {186} scattering downy white feathers on the air, at intervals standing up to harangue a welcome to the newcomers. Soon thirty canoes were around the ships with some ten warriors in each. Still they came, shoals of them, like fish, with savages almost naked, the harbor smooth as glass, the grand *tyee*, or great chief of the tribes, standing erect shouting a welcome, with long elf-locks streaming down his back. Women and children now appeared in the canoes. That meant peace. The women were chattering like magpies; the men gurgling and spluttering their surprise at the white visitors. For safety's sake the guns of the two ships were pointed ready; but the natives did not know the fear of a gun. It was the end of March when Cook first anchored off what he thought was the mainland of America. It was not mainland, but an island, and the harbor was one to become famous as the rendezvous of Pacific traders—Nootka!

Three armed boats commanded by Mr. King, and one under Cook, at once proceeded from the ships to explore and sound the inlet. The entrance had been between two rocky points four miles apart past a chain of sunken rocks. Except in a northwest corner of the inlet, since known as Snug Cove, the water was too deep for anchorage; so the two ships were moored to trees, the masts unrigged, the iron forge set to work on the shore; and the men began cutting timber for the new masts. And still the tiny specks dancing over the waves carrying canoe loads of savages to the English ships, {187} continued to multiply till the harbor seemed alive with warriors—two thousand at least there must have been by the first week of April after Cook's arrival. Some of the savages wore brightly painted wooden masks as part of their gala attire. Others carried totems—pieces of wood carved in the likeness of bird or beast to typify manitou of family or clan. By way of showing their prowess, some even offered the white men human skulls from which the flesh had not yet been taken. By this Cook knew the people were cannibals. Some were observed to be wearing spoons of European make as ornaments round their necks. What we desire to believe we easily accept. The white men did not ascribe the spoons to traders from New Spain on the south, or the Russian settlements to the north; but thought this place must be within trading distance of Hudson Bay, whence the Indians must have obtained the spoons. And so they cherished the hope of a Northeast Passage from this slim sign. In a few days fifteen hundred beaver and sea-otter had been obtained in trade, sixty-nine sea-otter—each of which was worth at that time one hundred dollars in modern money—for a handful of old nails.

To these deep-sea wanderers of Cook's crews, the harbor was as a fairy-land. Snow still covered the mountain tops; but a tangled forest of dank growth with roots awash in the ripple of the sea, stretched down the hillsides. Red cedar, spruce, fir,—of enormous growth, broader in girth than a cart and {188} wagon in length,—cypress with twisted and gnarled knots red against the rank green; mosses swinging from branch to branch in snaky coils wherever the clouds settled and rested; islands studding the sea like emerald gems; grouse drumming their spring song through the dark underbrush; sea-mew and Mother Carey's chickens screaming and clacking overhead; the snowy summits red as wine in the sunset glow—all made up an April scene long cherished by these adventurers of the North.

Early one morning in April the men cutting timber inland were startled to notice the underbrush alive with warriors armed. The first fear was of an ambush. Cook ordered the men to an isolated rock ready for defence; but the grand *tyee* or chief explained by signs that his tribe was only keeping off another tribe that wanted to trade with the white men. The worst trouble was from the inordinate thieving propensities of the natives. Iron, nails, belaying pins, rudders, anchors, bits of sail, a spike that could be pulled from the rotten wood of the outer keel by the teeth of a thief paddling below—anything, everything was snatched by the light-fingered gentry. Nor can we condemn them for it. Their moral standard was the Wolf Code of Existence—which the white man has elaborated in his evolution—to take whatever they had the dexterity and strength to take and to keep. When caught in theft, they did not betray as much sense of guilt as a dog stealing a bone. Why should they? Their {189} code was to take. The chief of the Nootkas presented Cook with a sea-otter cloak. Cook reciprocated with a brass-hilted sword.

By the end of April the ships had been overhauled, and Cook was ready to sail. Porpoise were coursing the sea like greyhounds, and the stormy petrels in a clatter; but Cook was not to be delayed by storm. Barely had the two ships cleared the harbor, when such a squall broke loose, they could do nothing but scud for open sea, turn tails to the wind, and lie helpless as logs, heads south. If it had not been for this storm, Cook would certainly have discovered that Nootka was on an island, not the coast of the mainland; but by the time the weather permitted an approach to land again, Friday, May 1, the ships were abreast that cluster of islands below the snowy cone of Mt. Edgecumbe, Sitka, where Chirikoff's Russians had first put foot on American soil. Cook was now at the northernmost limit of Spanish voyaging.

By the 4th of May Cook had sighted and passed the Fairweather Range, swung round westward on the old course followed by Bering, and passed under the shadow of St. Elias towering through the clouds in a dome of snow. On the 6th the ships were at Kyak, where Bering had anchored, and amid myriad ducks and gulls were approaching a broad inlet northward. Now, just as Bering had missed exploring this part of the coast owing to fog, so Cook had failed to trace that long archipelago of islands from Sitka Sound {190} northward; but here, where the coast trends straight westward, was an opening that roused hopes of a Northeast Passage. The *Resolution* had sprung a leak; and in the second week of May, the inlet was entered in the hope of a shelter to repair the leak and a way northeast to the Atlantic. Barely had the ships passed up the sound, when they were enshrouded in a fog that wiped out every outline; otherwise, the high coast of glacial palisades—two hundred feet in places and four miles broad—might have been seen landlocked by mountains; but Mr. Gore launched out in a small boat steering north through haze and tide-rip. Twenty natives were seen clad in sea-otter skins, by which—the white men judged—no Russians could have come to this sound; for the Russians would not have permitted the Indians to keep such valuable sea-otter clothing. The glass beads possessed by the natives were supposed to attest proximity to traders of Hudson Bay. With an almost animal innocence of wrong, the Indians tried to steal the small boat of the *Discovery*, flourishing their spears till the white crew mustered. At another time, when the *Discovery* lay anchored, few lanterns happened to be on deck. No sailors were visible. It was early in the morning and everybody was asleep, the boat dark. The natives swarmed up the ship's sides like ants invading a sugar canister. Looking down the hatches without seeing any whites, they at once drew their knives and began to plunder. The whites dashed up the hatchway and drove the {191} plunderers over the rails at sword point. East and north the small boats skirted the mist-draped shores, returning at midnight with word the inlet was a closed shore. There was no Northeast Passage. They called the spider-shaped bay Prince William Sound; and at ten in the morning headed out for sea.

Here a fresh disappointment awaited them. The natives of Prince William Sound had resembled the Eskimos of Greenland so much that the explorers were prepared to find themselves at the westward end of the American continent ready to round north into the Atlantic. A long ledge of land projected into the sea. They called this Cape Elizabeth, passed it, noted the reef of sunken rocks lying directly athwart a terrific tidal bore, and behold! not the end of the continent— no, not by a thousand miles—but straight across westward, beneath a smoking volcano that tinged the fog ruby-red, a lofty, naked spur three miles out into the sea, with crest hidden among the clouds and rock-base awash in thundering breakers. This was called Cape Douglas. Between these two capes was a tidal flood of perhaps sixty miles' breadth. Where did it come from? Up went hopes again for the Northeast Passage, and the twenty thousand pounds! Spite of driftwood, and roily waters, and a flood that ran ten miles an hour, and a tidal bore that rose twenty feet, up the passage they tacked, east to west, west to east, plying up half the month of June in rain and sleet, with the heavy pall of black smoke {192} rolling from the volcano left far on the offing! At last the opening was seen to turn abruptly straight east. Out rattled the small boats. Up the muddy waters they ran for nine miles till salt water became fresh water, and the explorers found themselves on a river. In irony, this point was called Turn-Again. The whole bay is now known as Cook's Inlet. Mr. King was sent ashore on the south side of Turn-Again to take possession. Twenty natives in sea-otter skins stood by watching the ceremony of flag unfurled and the land of their fathers being declared the possession of England. These natives were plainly acquainted with the use of iron; but "I will be bold to say," relates Cook, "they do not know the Russians, or they would not be wearing these valuable sea-otter skins."

No Northeast Passage here! So out they ply again for open sea through misty weather; and when it clears, they are in the green treeless region west of Cook's Inlet. Past Kadiak, past Bering's Foggy Island, past the Shumagins where Bering's first sailor to die of scurvy had been buried, past volcanoes throwing up immense quantities of blood-red smoke, past pinnacled rocks, through mists so thick the roar of the breakers is their only guide, they glide, or drift, or move by inches feeling the way cautiously, fearful of wreck.

Toward the end of June a great hollow green swell swings them through the straits past Oonalaska, northward at last! Natives are seen in green trousers {193} and European shirts; natives who take off their hats and make a bow after the pompous fashion of the Russians.

Twice natives bring word to Cook by letter and sign that the Russians of Oonalaska wish to see him. But Captain Cook is not anxious to see the Russians just now. He wants to forestall their explorations northward and take possession of the Polar realm for England. In August they are in Bristol Bay, north of the Aleutians, directly opposite Asia. Here Dr. Anderson, the surgeon, dies of consumption. Not so much fog now. They can follow the mainland. Far ahead there projects straight out in the sea a long spit of land backed by high hills, the westernmost point of North America—Cape Prince of Wales! Bering is vindicated! Just fifty years from Bering's exploration of 1728, the English navigator finds what Bering found: that America and Asia are *not* united; that no Northeast Passage exists; that no great oceanic body lies north of New Spain; that Alaska—as the Russian maps had it after Bering's death—is not an island.

Wind, rain, roily, shoaly seas breaking clear over the ship across decks drove Cook out from land to deeper water. With an Englishman's thoroughness for doing things and to make deadly sure just how the two continents lay to each other, Cook now scuds across Bering Strait thirty-nine miles to the Chukchee land of Siberia in Asia. How he praises the accuracy of poor {194} Bering's work along this coast: Bering, whose name had been a target for ridicule and contempt from the time of his death; whose death was declared a blunder; whose voyage was considered a failure; whose charts had been rejected and distorted by the learned men of the world.

The Ice Islands.

[Illustration: The Ice Islands.]

From the Chukchee villages of Asia, Cook sailed back to the American coast, passing north of Bering Straits directly in mid-channel. It is an odd thing, while very little ice-drift is met in Bering Sea, you have no sooner passed north of the straits than a white world surrounds you. Fog, ice, ice, fog—endlessly, with palisades of ice twelve feet high, east and west, far as the eye can see! The crew amuse themselves alternately gathering driftwood for fuel, and hunting {195} walrus over the ice. It is in the North Pacific that the walrus attains its great size —nine feet in length, broader across its back than any animal known to the civilized world. These piebald yellow monsters lay wallowing in herds of hundreds on the ice-fields. At the edge lay always one on the watch; and no matter how dense the fog, these walrus herds on the ice, braying and roaring till the surf shook, acted as a fog-horn to Cook's ships, and kept them from being jammed in the ice-drift. Soon two-thirds of the furs got at Nootka had spoiled of rain-rot. The vessels were iced like ghost ships. Tack back and forward as they might, no passage opened through the ice. Suddenly Cook found himself in shoal water, on a lee shore, long and low and shelving, with the ice drifting on his ships. He called the place Icy Cape. It was their farthest point north; and the third week of August they were compelled to scud south to escape the ice. Backing away toward Asia, he reached the North Cape there. It was almost September. In accordance with the secret instructions, Cook turned south to winter at the Sandwich Islands, passing Serdze Kamen, where Bering had turned back in 1728, East Cape on the Straits of Bering just opposite the American Prince of Wales, and St. Lawrence islands where the ships anchored.

Norton Sound was explored on the way back; and October saw Cook down at Oonalaska, where Ledyard was sent overland across the island to conduct the {196} Russian traders to the English ships. Three Russians came to visit Cook. One averred that he had been with Bering on the expedition of 1741, and the rough adventurers seemed almost to worship the Dane's memory. Later came Ismyloff, chief factor of the Russian fur posts in Oonalaska, attended by a retinue of thirty native canoes, very suave as to manners, very polished and pompous when he was not too convivial, but very chary of any information to the English, whose charts he examined with keenest interest, giving them to understand that the Empress of Russia had first claim to all those parts of the country, rising, quaffing a glass and bowing profoundly as he mentioned the august name. "Friends and fellow-countrymen glorious," the English were to the smooth-tongued Russian, as they drank each other's health. Learning that Cook was to visit Avacha Bay, Ismyloff proffered a letter of introduction to Major Behm, Russian commander of Kamchatka. Cook thought the letter one of commendation. It turned out otherwise. Fur traders, world over, always resented the coming of the explorer. Ismyloff was neither better nor worse than his kind. [2]

Heavy squalls pursued the ships all the way from Oonalaska, left on October 26, to the Sandwich Islands, reached in the new year 1779. A thousand canoes of enthusiastic natives welcomed Cook back to the sunny islands of the Pacific. Before the explorer {197} could anchor, natives were swimming round the ship like shoals of fish. When Cook landed, the whole population prostrated itself at his feet as if he had been a god. It was a welcome change from the desolate cold of the inhospitable north.

Situated midway in the Pacific, the Sandwich Islands were like an oasis in a watery waste to Cook's mariners. The ships had dropped anchor in the centre of a horn-shaped bay called Karakakooa, in Hawaii, about two miles from horn to horn. On the sandy flats of the north horn was the native village of Kowrowa: amid the cocoanut grove of the other horn, the village of Kakooa, with a well and Morai, or sacred burying-ground, close by. Between the two villages alongshore ran a high ledge of black coral rocks. In all there were, perhaps, four hundred houses in the two villages, with a population of from two to three thousand warriors; but the bay was the rallying place for the entire group of islands; and the islands numbered in all several hundred thousand warriors.

Picture, then, the scene to these wanderers of the northern seas: the long coral reef, wave-washed by bluest of seas; the little village and burying-ground and priests' houses nestling under the cocoanut grove at one end of the semicircular bay, the village where Terreeoboo, king of the island, dwelt on the long sand beach at the other end; and swimming through the water like shoals of fish, climbing over the ships' rigging like monkeys, crowding the decks of the *Discovery* {198} so that the ship heeled over till young chief Pareea began tossing the intruders by the scuff of the neck back into the sea—hundreds, thousands, of half-naked, tawny-skinned savages welcoming the white men back to the islands discovered by them. Chief among the visitors to the ship was Koah, a little, old, emaciated, shifty-eyed priest with a wry neck and a scaly, leprous skin, who at once led the small boats ashore, driving the throngs back with a magic wand and drawing a mystic circle with his wizard stick round a piece of ground near the Morai, or burying-place, where the white men could erect their tents beside the cocoanut groves. The magic line was called a *taboo*. Past the tabooed line of the magic wand not a native would dare to go. Here Captain King, assisted by the young midshipman, Vancouver, landed with a guard of eight or ten mariners to overhaul the ships' masts, while the rest of the two crews obtained provisions by trade.

Cook was carried off to the very centre of the Morai—a circular enclosure of solid stone with images and priests' houses at one end, the skulls of slain captives at the other. Here priests and people did the white explorer homage as to a god, sacrificing to him their most sacred animal—a strangled pig.

All went well for the first few days. A white gunner, who died, was buried within the sacred enclosure of the Morai. The natives loaded the white men's boats with provisions. In ten days the wan, gaunt {199} sailors were so sleek and fat that even the generous entertainers had to laugh at the transformation. Old King Terreeoboo came clothed in a cloak of gaudy feathers with spears and daggers at his belt and a train of priestly retainers at his heels to pay a visit of state to Cook; and a guard of mariners was drawn up at arms under the cocoanut grove to receive the visitor with fitting honor. When the king learned that Cook was to leave the bay early in February, a royal proclamation gathered presents for the ships; and Cook responded by a public display of fireworks.

Now it is a sad fact that when a highly civilized people meet an uncivilized people, each race celebrates the occasion by appropriating all the evil qualities of the other. Vices, not virtues, are the first to fraternize. It was as unfair of Cook's crew to judge the islanders by the rabble swarming out to steal from the ships, as it would be for a newcomer to judge the people of New York by the pickpockets and under-world of the water front. And it must not be forgotten that the very quality that had made Cook successful—the quality to dare—was a danger to him here. The natives did not violate the sacred *taboo*, which the priest had drawn round the white men's quarters of the grove. It was the white men who violated it by going outside the limit; and the conduct of the white sailors for the sixteen days in port was neither better nor worse than the conduct of sailors to-day who go on a wild spree with the lowest elements of the harbor. {200} The savages were quick to find out that the white gods were after all only men. The true story of what happened could hardly be written by Captain King, who finished Cook's journal; though one can read between the lines King's fear of his commander's rashness. The facts of the case are given by the young American, John Ledyard, of Connecticut, who was corporal of marines and in the very thick of the fight.

At the end of two weeks the white seamen were, perhaps, satiated of their own vices, or suffering from the sore head that results from prolonged spreeing. At all events the thieving, which had been condoned at first, was now punished by soundly flogging the natives. The old king courteously hinted it was time for the white men to go. The mate, who was loading masts and rudder back on board the *Resolution*, asked the savages to give him a hand. The islanders had lost respect for the white men of such flagrant vices. They pretended to give a helping hand, but only jostled the mate about in the crowd. The Englishman lost his temper, struck out, and blustered. The shore rang with the shrill laughter of the throngs. In vain the chiefs of authority interposed. The commands to help the white men were answered by showers of stones directly inside the *taboo*. Ledyard was ordered out with a guard of sailors to protect the white men loading the *Resolution*. The guard was pelted black and blue. "There was nothing to do," relates Ledyard, "but move to new lands where our vices {201} were not known." At last all was in readiness to sail—one thing alone lacking—wood; and the white men dare not go inland for the needed wood.

So far the entire blame rested on the sailors. Now Cook committed his cardinal error. With that very dare and quickness to utilize every available means to an end—whether the end justified the means—Cook ordered his men ashore to seize the rail fence round the top of the stone burying-ground—the sacred Morai—as fuel for his ships. Out rushed the priests from the enclosure in dire distress. Was this their reward for protecting Cook with the wand of the sacred *taboo*? Two hatchets were offered the leading priest as pay. He spurned them as too loathsome to be touched. Leading the way, Cook ordered his men to break the fence down, and proffered three hatchets, thrusting them into the folds of the priest's garment. Pale and quivering with rage, the priest bade a slave remove the profaning iron. Down tumbled the fence! Down the images on poles! Down the skulls of the dead sacred to the savage as the sepulchre to the white man! It may be said to the credit of the crew, that the men were thoroughly frightened at what they were ordered to do; but they were not too frightened to carry away the images as relics. Cook alone was blind to risk. As if to add the last straw to the Hawaiians' endurance, when the ships unmoored and sailed out from the bay, where but two weeks before they had been so royally welcomed, they carried {202} eloping wives and children from the lower classes of the two villages.

It was one of the cases where retribution came so swift it was like a living Nemesis. If the weather had continued fair, doubtless wives and children would have been dumped off at some near harbor, the incident considered a joke, and the Englishmen gone merrily on their way; but a violent gale arose. Women and children were seized with a seasickness that was no joke. The decks resounded with such wails that Cook had to lie to in the storm, put off the pinnace, and send the visitors ashore. What sort of a tale they carried back, we may guess. Meanwhile the storm had snapped the foremast of the *Resolution*. As if rushing on his ruin, Cook steered back for the bay and anchored midway between the two villages. Again the tents were pitched beside the Morai under the cocoanut groves. Again the wand was drawn round the tenting place; but the white men had taught the savages that the *taboo* was no longer sacred. Where thousands had welcomed the ships before, not a soul now appeared. Not a canoe cut the waters. Not a voice broke the silence of the bay.

The sailors were sour; Cook, angry. When the men rowed to the villages for fresh provisions, they were pelted with stones. When at night-time the savages came to the ships with fresh food, they asked higher prices and would take only daggers and knives in pay. Only by firing its great guns could the {203} *Discovery* prevent forcible theft by the savages offering provisions; and in the scuffle of pursuit after one thief, Pareea—a chief most friendly to the whites—was knocked down by a white man's oar. "I am afraid," remarked Cook, "these people will compel me to use violent measures." As if to test the mettle of the tacit threat, Sunday, daybreak, February 14, revealed that the large rowboat of the *Discovery* had been stolen.

When Captain King, who had charge of the guard repairing the masts over under the cocoanut grove came on board Sunday morning, he found Cook loading his gun, with a line of soldiers drawn up to go ashore in order to allure the ruler of the islands on board, and hold him as hostage for the restitution of the lost boat. Clerke, of the *Discovery*, was too far gone in consumption to take any part. Cook led the way on the pinnace with Ledyard and six marines. Captain King followed in the launch with as many more. All the other small boats of the two ships were strung across the harbor from Kakooa, where the grove was, to Kowrowa, where the king dwelt, with orders to fire on any canoe trying to escape.

Before the fearless leader, the savages prostrated themselves in the streets. Cook strode like a conqueror straight to the door of the king's abode. It was about nine in the morning. Old Terreeoboo—peace lover and lazy—was just awake and only too willing to go aboard with Cook as the easiest way out {204} of the trouble about the stolen boat. But just here the high-handedness of Cook frustrated itself. That line of small boats stretched across the harbor began firing at an escaping canoe. A favorite chief was killed. Word of the killing came as the old king was at the water's edge to follow Cook; and a wife caught him by the arm to drag him back. Suddenly a throng of a thousand surrounded the white men. Some one stabs at Phillips of the marines. Phillips's musket comes down butt-end on the head of the assailant. A spear is thrust in Cook's very face. He fires blank shot. The harmlessness of the shot only emboldens the savages. Women are seen hurrying off to the hills; men don their war mats. There is a rush of the white men to get positions along the water edge free for striking room; of the savages to prevent the whites' escape. A stone hits Cook. "What man did that?" thunders Cook; and he shoots the culprit dead. Then the men in the boats lose their heads, and are pouring volleys of musketry into the crowds.

"It is hopeless," mutters Cook to Phillips; but amid a shower of stones above the whooping of the savages, he turns with his back to the crowd, and shouts for the two small boats to cease firing and pull in for the marines. His caution came too late.

His back is to his assailants. An arm reached out—a hand with a dagger; and the dagger rips quick as a flash under Cook's shoulder-blade. He fell without a groan, face in the water, and was hacked to pieces {205} before the eyes of his men. Four marines had already fallen. Phillips and Ledyard and the rest jumped into the sea and swam for their lives. The small boats were twenty yards out. Scarcely was Phillips in the nearest, when a wounded sailor, swimming for refuge, fainted and sank to the bottom. Though half stunned from a stone blow on his head and bleeding from a stab in the back, Phillips leaped to the rescue, dived to bottom, caught the exhausted sailor by the hair of the head and so snatched him into the boat. The dead and the arms of the fugitives had been deserted in the wild scramble for life.

The Death of Cook.

[Illustration: The Death of Cook.]

Meanwhile the masts of the *Resolution*, guarded by {206} only six marines, were exposed to the warriors of the other village at the cocoanut grove. Protected by the guns of the two ships under the direction of Clerke, who now became commander, masts and men were got aboard by noon. At four that afternoon, Captain King rowed toward shore for Cook's body. He was met by the little leprous priest Koah, swimming halfway out. Though tears of sorrow were in Koah's treacherous red-rimmed eyes as he begged that Clerke and King might come ashore to parley. King judged it prudent to hold tightly on the priest's spear handle while the two embraced.

Night after night for a week, the conch-shells blew their challenge of defiance to the white men. Fires rallying to war danced on the hillsides. Howls and shouts of derision echoed from the shore. The stealthy paddle of treacherous spies could be heard through the dark under the keel of the white men's ships. Cook's clothing, sword, hat, were waved in scorn under the sailors' faces. The women had hurried to the hills. The old king was hidden in a cave, where he could be reached only by a rope ladder; and emissary after emissary tried to lure the whites ashore. One pitch-dark night, paddles were heard under the keels. The sentinels fired; but by lantern light two terrified faces appeared above the rail of the *Resolution*. Two frightened, trembling savages crawled over the deck, prostrated themselves at Clerke's feet, and slowly unrolled a small wrapping of cloth that revealed a small {207} piece of human flesh—the remains of Cook. Dead silence fell on the horrified crew. Then Clerke's stern answer was that unless the bones of Cook were brought to the ships, both native villages would be destroyed. The two savages were former friends of Cook's and warned the whites not to be allured on land, nor to trust Koah, the leper priest, on the ships.

Again the conch-shells blew their challenge all night through the darkness. Again the war fires danced; but next morning the guns of the *Discovery* were trained on Koah, when he tried to come on board. That day sailors were landed for water and set fire to the village of the cocoanut groves to drive assailants back. How quickly human nature may revert to the beast type! When the white sailors returned from this skirmish, they carried back to the ships with them, the heads of two Hawaiians they had slain. By Saturday, the 20th, masts were in place and the boats ready to sail. Between ten and eleven o'clock in the morning, a long procession of people was seen filing slowly down the hills preceded by drummers and a white flag. Word was signalled that Cook's bones were on shore to be delivered. Clerke put out in a small boat to receive the dead commander's remains—from which all flesh had been burned. On Sunday, the 21st, the entire bay was tabooed. Not a native came out of the houses. Silence lay over the waters. The funeral service was read on board the *Resolution*, and the coffin committed to the deep.

{208} A curious reception awaited the ships at Avacha Bay, Kamchatka, whence they now sailed. Ismyloff's letter commending the explorers to the governor of Avacha Bay brought thirty Cossack soldiers floundering through the shore ice of Petropaulovsk under the protection of pointed cannon. Ismyloff, with fur trader's jealousy of intrusion, had warned the Russian commander that the English ships were pirates like Benyowsky, the Polish exile, who had lately sacked the garrisons of Kamchatka, stolen the ships, and sailed to America. However, when Cook's letters were carried overland to Bolcheresk, to Major Behm, the commander, all went well. The little log-thatched fort with its windows of talc opened wide doors to the far-travelled English. The Russian ladies of the fort donned their China silks. The samovars were set singing. English sailors gave presents of their grog to the Russians. Russian Cossacks presented their tobacco to the English, adding three such cheers as only Cossacks can give and a farewell song.

In 1779 Clerke made one more attempt to pass through the northern ice-fields from Pacific to Atlantic; but he accomplished nothing but to go over the ground explored the year before under Cook. On the 5th of July at ten P.M. in the lingering sunlight of northern latitudes, just as the boats were halfway through the Straits of Bering, the fog lifted, and for the first time in history—as far as known—the westernmost part of America, Cape Prince of Wales, and the {209} eastern-most part of Asia, East Cape, were simultaneously seen by white men.

Finding it impossible to advance eastward, Clerke decided there was no Northeast Passage by way of the Pacific to the Atlantic; and on the 21st of July, to the cheers of his sailors, announced that the ships would turn back for England.[3]

Poor Clerke died of consumption on the way, August 22, 1779, only thirty-eight years of age, and was buried at Petropaulovsk beside La Croyére de l'Isle, who perished on the Bering expedition. The boats did not reach England till October of 1780. They had not won the reward of twenty thousand pounds; but they had charted a strange coast for a distance of three thousand five hundred miles, and paved the way for the vast commerce that now plies between Occident and Orient.[4]

[1] The question may occur, why in the account of Cook's and Bering's voyage, the latitude is not oftener given. The answer is, the latitudes as given by Cook and Bering vary so much from the modern, it would only confuse the reader trying to follow a modern map.

[2] This is the Ismyloff who was marooned by Benyowsky.

[3] The authority for Cook's adventures is, of course, his own journal, *Voyage to the Pacific Ocean*, London, 1784, supplemented by the letters and journals of men who were with him, like Ledyard, Vancouver, Portlock, and Dixon, and others.

[4] In reiterating the impossibility of finding a passage from ocean to ocean, either northeast or northwest, no disparagement is cast on such feats as that of Nordenskjöld along the north of Asia, in the *Vega* in 1882.

By "passage" is meant a waterway practicable for ocean vessels, not for the ocean freak of a specially constructed Arctic vessel that dodges for a year or more among the ice-floes in an endeavor to pass from Atlantic to Pacific, or *vice versa*.

CHAPTER VIII
1785-1792
ROBERT GRAY, THE AMERICAN DISCOVERER OF THE COLUMBIA

Boston Merchants, inspired by Cook's Voyages, outfit two Vessels under Kendrick and Gray for Discovery and Trade on the Pacific—Adventures of the First Ship to carry the American Flag around the World —Gray attacked by Indians at Tillamook Bay—His Discovery of the Columbia River on the Second Voyage—Fort Defence and the First American Ship built on the Pacific

It is an odd thing that wherever French or British fur traders went to a new territory, they found the Indians referred to American traders, not as "Americans," but "Bostons" or "*Bostonnais*." The reason was plain. Boston merchants won a reputation as first to act. It was they who began a certain memorable "Boston Tea Party"; and before the rest of the world had recovered the shock of that event, these same merchants were planning to capture the trade of the Pacific Ocean, get possession of all the Pacific coast not already preëmpted by Spain, Russia, or England, and push American commerce across the Pacific to Asia.

{211} What with slow printing-presses and slow travel, the account of Cook's voyages on the Pacific did not become generally known in the United States till 1785 or 1786. Sitting round the library of Dr. Bulfinch's residence on Bowdoin Square in Boston one night in 1787, were half a dozen adventurous spirits for whom Cook's account of the fur trade on the Pacific had an irresistible fascination. There was the doctor himself. There was his son, Charles, of Harvard, just back from Europe and destined to become famous as an architect. There was Joseph Barrell, a prosperous merchant. There was John Derby, a shipmaster of Salem, a young man still, but who, nevertheless, had carried news of Lexington to England. Captain Crowell Hatch of Cambridge, Samuel Brown, a trader of Boston, and John Marden Pintard of the New York firm of Lewis Pintard Company were also of the little coterie.

Departure of the Columbia and the Lady Washington. Drawn by George Davidson, a member of the Expedition. Photographed by courtesy of the present owner, Mrs. Abigail Quincy Twombly.

If Captain Cook's crew had sold one-third of a water-rotted cargo of otter furs in China for ten thousand dollars, why, these Boston men asked themselves, could not ships fitted expressly for the fur trade capture a fortune in trade on that unoccupied strip of coast between Russian Alaska, on the north, and New Spain, on the south?

"There is a rich harvest to be reaped by those who are on the ground first out there," remarked Joseph Barrell.

Then the thing was to be on the ground first—that {212} was the unanimous decision of the shrewd-headed men gathered in Bulfinch's study.

Charles Bulfinch.

[Illustration: Charles Bulfinch.]

The sequence was that Charles Bulfinch and the other five at once formed a partnership with a capital of fifty thousand dollars, divided into fourteen shares, for trade on the Pacific. This was ten years before Lewis and Clark reached the Columbia, almost twenty years before Astor had thought of his Pacific Company. The Columbia, a full-rigged two-decker, two hundred and twelve tons and eighty-three feet long, mounting {213} ten guns, which had been built fourteen years before on Hobart's Landing, North River, was immediately purchased. But a smaller ship to cruise about inland waters and collect furs was also needed; and for this purpose the partners bought the *Lady Washington*, a little sloop of ninety tons. Captain John Kendrick of the merchant marine was chosen to command the *Columbia*, Robert Gray, a native of Rhode Island, who had served in the revolutionary navy, a friend of Kendrick's, to be master of the *Lady Washington*. Kendrick was of middle age, cautious almost to indecision; but Gray was younger with the daring characteristic of youth.

In order to insure a good reception for the ships, letters were obtained from the federal government to foreign powers. Massachusetts furnished passports;

and the Spanish minister to the United States gave letters to the viceroy of New Spain. Just how the information of Boston plans to intrude on the Pacific coast was received by New Spain may be judged by the confidential commands at once issued from Santa Barbara to the Spanish officer at San Francisco: *"Whenever there may arrive at the Port of San Francisco, a ship named the Columbia said to belong to General Wanghington (Washington) of the American States, under command of John Kendrick which sailed from Boston in September 1787 bound on a voyage of Discovery and of Examination of the Russian Establishments on the Northern Coast of this Peninsula, you {214} will cause said vessel to be secured together with her officers and crew."*

Orders were also given Kendrick and Gray to avoid offence to any foreign power, to treat the natives with kindness and Christianity, to obtain a cargo of furs on the American coast, to proceed with the same to China to be exchanged for a cargo of tea, and to return to Boston with the tea. The holds of the vessels were then stowed with every trinket that could appeal to the savage heart, beads, brass buttons, ear-rings, calico, tin mirrors, blankets, hunting-knives, copper kettles, iron chisels, snuff, tobacco. The crews were made up of the very best class of self-respecting sea-faring men. Woodruff, Kendrick's first mate, had been with Cook. Joseph Ingraham, the second mate, rose to become a captain. Robert Haswell, the third mate, was the son of a British naval officer. Richard Howe went as accountant; Dr. Roberts, as surgeon; Nutting, formerly a teacher, as astronomer; and Treat, as fur trader. Davis Coolidge was the first mate under Gray on the *Lady Washington*.

Some heroes blunder into glory. These didn't. They deliberately set out with the full glory of their venture in view. Whatever the profit and loss account might show when they came back, they were well aware that they were attempting the very biggest and most venturesome thing the newly federated states had essayed in the way of exploration and trade. To {215} commemorate the event, Joseph Barrell had medals struck in bronze and silver showing the two vessels on one side, the names of the outfitters on the other. All Saturday afternoon sailors and officers came trundling down to the wharf, carpet bags and seamen's chests in tow, to be rowed out where the Columbia and Lady Washington lay at anchor. Boston was a Sabbath-observing city in those days; but even Boston could not keep away from the two ships heaving to the tide, which for the first time in American history were to sail around an unknown world. All Saturday night and Sunday morning the sailors scoured the decks and put berths shipshape; and all Sunday afternoon the visitors thronged the decks. By night outfitters and relatives were still on board. The medals of commemoration were handed round. Health and good luck and God speed were drunk unto the heel taps. Songs resounded over the festive board. It was all "mirth and glee" writes one of the men on {216} board. But by daybreak the ships had slipped cables. The tide, that runs from round the underworld, raced bounding to meet them. A last dip of land behind; and on Monday, October 1, 1787, the ships' prows were cleaving the waters of their fate.

Medals commemorating Columbia and Lady Washington cruise.

[Illustration: Medals commemorating *Columbia* and *Lady Washington* cruise.]

The course lay from Boston to Cape Verde Islands, from Verde Islands to the Falklands north of Cape Horn, round Cape Horn, up the west coast of South America, touching at Masafuera and Juan Fernandez, and thence, without pause, to the west coast of North America. At Cape Verde, Gray hired a valet, a colored boy, Marcus Lopez, destined to play an important part later. Crossing the equator, the sailors became hilarious, playing the usual pranks of ducking the men fresh to equatorial waters. So long did the ships rest at the Verde Islands, taking in fresh provisions, that it was January before the Falkland Islands were reached. Here Kendrick's caution became almost fear. He was averse to rounding the stormy Horn in winter. Roberts, the surgeon, and Woodruff, who had been with Cook, had become disgusted with Kendrick's indecision at Cape Verde, and left, presumably taking passage back on some foreign cruiser. Haswell, then, went over as first mate to Gray. Mountain seas and smashing gales assailed the ships from the time they headed for the Horn in April of 1788. The *Columbia* was tossed clear up on her beam ends, and sea after sea crashed over the little {217} *Lady Washington*, drenching everything below decks like soap-suds in a rickety tub. Then came a hurricane of cold winds coating the ship in ice like glass, till the yard-arms looked like ghosts. Between scurvy and cold, there was not a sailor fit to man the decks. Somewhere down at 57 degrees south, westward of the Horn, the smashing seas and driving winds separated the two ships; but as they headed north, bright skies and warm winds welcomed them to the Pacific. At Masafuera, off Chile, the ships would have landed for fresh water; but a tremendous backwash of surf forewarned reefs; and the *Lady Washington* stretched her sails for the welcome warm winds, and tacked with all speed to the north. A few weeks later, Kendrick was compelled to put in for Juan Fernandez to repair the *Columbia* and rest his scurvy-stricken crew. They were given all aid by the governor of the island, who was afterward reprimanded by the viceroy of Chile and degraded from office for helping these invaders of the South Seas.

Meantime the little sloop, guided by the masterful and enthusiastic Gray, showed her heels to the sea. Soon a world of deep-sea, tropical wonders was about the American adventurers. The slime of medusa lights lined the long foam trail of the *Lady Washington* each night. Dolphins raced the ship, herd upon herd, their silver-white bodies aglisten in the sun. Schools of spermaceti-whales to the number of twenty at a time gambolled lazily around the prow. Stormy petrels, {218} flying-fish, sea-lions, began to be seen as the boat passed north of the seas bordering New Spain. Gentle winds and clear sunlight favored the ship all June. The long, hard voyage began to be a summer holiday on warm, silver seas. The *Lady Washington* headed inland, or where land should be, where Francis Drake two centuries before had reported that he had found New Albion. On August 2, somewhere near what is now Cape Mendocino, daylight revealed a rim of green forested hills above the silver sea. It was New Albion, north of New Spain, the strip of coast they had come round the world to find. Birds in myriads on myriads screamed the joy that the crew felt over their find; but a frothy ripple told of reefs; and the *Lady Washington* coasted parallel with the shore-line northward. On August 4, while the surf still broke with too great violence for a landing, a tiny speck was seen dancing over the waves like a bird. As the distance lessened, the speck grew and resolved itself to a dugout, or long canoe, carved with bizarre design stem and stern, painted gayly on the keel, carrying ten Indians, who blew birds' down of friendship in midair, threw open their arms without weapons, and made every sign of friendship. Captain Gray tossed them presents over the deck rail; but the whistle of a gale through the riggings warned to keep off the rock shore; and the sloop's prow cut waves for the offing. All night camp-fires and columns of smoke could be seen on shore, showing that the coast was inhabited. Under {219} clouds of sail, the sloop beat north for ten days, passing many savages, some of whom held up sea-otter to trade, others running along the shore brandishing their spears and shouting their war-cry. Two or three at a time were admitted on board to trade; but they evinced such treacherous distrust, holding knives ready to strike in their right hand, that Gray was cautious.

During the adverse wind they had passed one opening on the coast that resembled the entrance to a river. Was this the fabled river of the West, that Indians said ran to the setting sun? Away up in the Athabasca Country of Canadian wilds was another man, Alexander Mackenzie, setting to himself that same task of finding the great river of the West. Besides, in 1775, Heceta, the Spanish navigator from Monterey, had drifted close to this coast with a crew so stricken with scurvy not a man could hoist anchor or reef sails. Heceta thought he saw the entrance to a river; but was unable to come within twenty miles of the opening to verify his supposition. And now Gray's crew were on the watch for that supposed river; but more mundane things than glory had become pressing needs. Water was needed for drinking. The ship was out of firewood. The live stock must have hay; and in the crew of twelve, three-quarters were ill of the scurvy. These men must be taken ashore. Somewhere near what is now Cape Lookout, or Tillamook Bay, the rowboat was launched to sound, safe anchorage found, and the *Lady Washington* towed in harbor.

{220} The *Lady Washington* had anchored about half a mile from shore, but the curiously carved canoes came dancing over the waves in myriads. Gray noticed the natives were all armed with spears and knives, but they evinced great friendliness, bringing the crew baskets of berries and boiled crabs and salmon, in exchange for brass buttons. They had anchored at ten on the night of August 14, and by the afternoon of the 15th the Indians were about the sloop in great numbers, trading otter skins for knives, axes, and other arms—which, in itself, ought to have put the crew on guard. When the white men went ashore for wood and water, the Indians stood silently by, weapons in hand, but offered no hostility. On the third day in harbor an old chief came on board followed by a great number of warriors, all armed. Gray kept careful guard, and the old Indian departed in possession of the stimulating fact that only a dozen hands manned the *Lady Washington*. Waiting for the tide the next afternoon, Haswell and Coolidge, the two mates, were digging clams on shore. Lopez, the black man, and seven of the crew were gathering grass for the stock. Only three men remained on the sloop with Captain Gray. Only two muskets and three or four cutlasses had been brought ashore. Haswell and Coolidge had their belt pistols and swords. The two mates approached the native village. The Indians began tossing spears, as Haswell thought, to amuse their visitors. That failing to inspire these white men, {221} rash as children, with fear, the Indians formed a ring, clubbed down their weapons in pantomime, and executed all the significant passes of the famous war-dance. "It chilled my veins," says Haswell; and the two mates had gone back to their clam digging, when there was a loud, angry shout. Glancing just where the rowboat lay rocking abreast the hay cutters, Haswell saw an Indian snatch at the cutlass of Lopez, the black, who had carelessly stuck it in the sand. With a wild halloo, the thief dashed for the woods, the black in pursuit, mad as a hornet.

Haswell went straight to the chief and offered a reward for the return of the sword, or the black man. The old chief taciturnly signalled for Haswell to do his own rescuing.

Theft and flight had both been part of a design to scatter the white men. "They see we are ill armed," remarked Haswell to the other. Bidding the boat row abreast with six of the hay cutters, the two mates and a third man ran along the beach in the direction Lopez had disappeared. A sudden turn into a grove of trees showed Lopez squirming mid a group of Indians, holding the thief by the neck and shouting for "help! help!" No sooner had the three whites come on the scene, than the Indians plunged their knives in the boy's back. He stumbled, rose, staggered forward, then fell pierced by a flight of barbed arrows. Haswell had only time to see the hostiles fall on his body like a pack of wolves on prey, when more Indians {222} emerged from the rear, and the whites were between two war parties under a shower of spears. A wild dash was made to head the fugitives off from shore. Haswell and Coolidge turned, pistols in hand, while the rowboat drew in. Another flight of arrows, when the mates let go a charge of pistol shot that dropped the foremost three Indians. Shouting for the rowers to fire, Haswell, Coolidge, and the sailor plunged into the water. To make matters worse, the sailor fainted from loss of blood, and the pursuers threw themselves into the water with a whoop. Hauling the wounded man in the boat, the whites rowed for dear life. The Indians then launched their canoes to pursue, but by this time Gray had the cannon of the *Lady Washington* trained ashore, and three shots drove the hostiles scampering. For two days tide and wind and a thundering surf imprisoned Gray in Murderers' Harbor, where he had hoped to find the River of the West, but met only danger. All night the savages kept up their howling; but on the third day the wind veered. All sails set, the sloop scudded for the offing, glad to keep some distance between herself and such a dangerous coast.

The advantage of a small boat now became apparent. In the same quarter, Cook was compelled to keep out from the coast, and so reported there were no Straits of Fuca. By August 21 the sloop was again close enough to the rocky shore to sight the snowy, opal {223} ranges of the Olympus Mountains. By August 26 they had passed the wave-lashed rocks of Cape Flattery, and the mate records; "I am of opinion that the Straits of Fuca exist; for in the very latitude they are said to lie, the coast takes a bend, probably the entrance."

Building the first American Ship on the Pacific Coast. Photographed by courtesy of Mrs. Abigail Quincy Twombly, a descendant of Gray.

[Illustration: Building the first American Ship on the Pacific

By September, after frequent stops to trade with the Indians, they were well abreast of Nootka, where Cook had been ten years before. A terrible ground-swell of surf and back-wash raged over projecting reefs. The Indians, here, knew English words enough to tell Gray that Nootka lay farther east, and that a Captain Meares was there with two vessels. A strange sail appeared inside the harbor. Gray thought it was the belated *Columbia* under Kendrick; but a rowboat came out bearing Captain Meares himself, who breakfasted with the Americans on September 17, and had his long-boats tow the *Lady Washington* inside Nootka, where Gray was surprised to see two English snows under Portuguese colors, with a cannon-mounted garrison on shore, and a schooner of thirty tons, the *Northwest-America*, all ready to be launched. This was the first ship built on the northwest coast. Gray himself later built the second. Amid salvos of cannon from the *Lady Washington*, the new fur vessel was launched from her skids; and in her honor September 19 was observed as a holiday, Meares and Douglas, the two English captains, entertaining Gray and his officers. Meares had come from China in {224} January, and during the summer had been up the Straits of Fuca, where another English captain, Barclay, had preceded him. Then Meares had gone south past Flattery, seeking in vain for the River of the West. Gales and breakers had driven him off the coast, and the very headland which hid the mouth of the Columbia, he had named Cape Disappointment, because he was so sure—in his own words—"that the river on the Spanish charts did not exist." He had also been down the coast to that Tillamook, or Cape Meares, where Gray's valet had been murdered. This was in July, a month before the assault on Gray; and if Haswell's report of Meares's cruelty be accepted—taking furs by force of arms—that may have explained the hostility to the Americans. Meares was short of provisions to go to China, and Gray supplied them. In return Meares set his workmen to help clean the keel of the *Lady Washington* from barnacles; but the Englishman was a true fur trader to the core. In after-dinner talks, on the day of the launch, he tried to frighten the Americans away from the coast. Not fifty skins in a year were to be had, he said. Only the palisades and cannon protected him from the Indians, of whom there were more than two thousand hostiles at Nootka, he reported. They could have his fort for firewood after he left. He had purchased the right to build it from the Indians. (Whether he acknowledged that he paid the Indians only two old pistols for this privilege, is not recorded.) At all events, it {225} would not be worth while for the Americans to remain on the coast. The Americans listened and smiled. Meares offered to carry any mail to China, and on the 2d was towed out of port by Gray and the other English captain, Douglas; but what was Gray's astonishment to receive the packet of mail back from Douglas. Meares had only pretended to carry it out in order that none of his crew might be bribed to take it, and then had sent it back by his partner, Douglas—true fur trader in checkmating the moves of rivals. Later on, when Meares's men were in desperate straits in this same port, they wondered that the Americans stood apart from the quarrel, if not actually siding with Spain.

On September 23 appeared a strange sail on the offing—the *Columbia*, under Kendrick, sails down and draggled, spars storm-torn, two men dead of scurvy, and the crew all ill.

October 1 celebrated a grand anniversary of the departure from Boston the previous year. At precisely midday the *Columbia* boomed out thirteen guns. The sloop set the echoes rocketing with another thirteen. Douglas's ship roared out a salute of seven cannon shots, the fort on land six more, and the day was given up to hilarity, all hands dining on board the *Columbia* with such wild fowl as the best game woods in the world afforded, and copious supply of Spanish wines. Toasts were drunk to the first United States ship on the Pacific coast of America. On October 26 {226} Douglas's ship and the fur trader, *Northwest-America*, were towed out, bound for the Sandwich Islands, and the Americans were left alone on the northwest coast, the fort having been demolished, and the logs turned over to Kendrick for firewood.

Feather Cloak worn by a son of an Hawaiian Chief, at the celebration in honor of Gray's return. Photographed by courtesy of Mrs. Joy, the present owner.

[Illustration: Feather Cloak worn by a son of an Hawaiian Chief, at the celebration in honor of Gray's return. Photographed by courtesy of Mrs. Joy, the present owner.]

The winter of 1788-1789 passed uneventfully except that the English were no sooner out of the harbor, than the Indians, who had kept askance of the Americans, came in flocks to trade. Inasmuch as Cook's name is a household word, world over, for what he did on the Pacific coast, and Gray's name barely known outside the city of Boston and the state of {227} Oregon, it is well to follow Gray's movements on the *Lady Washington*. March found him trading south of Nootka at Clayoquot, named Hancock, after the governor of

Massachusetts. April saw him fifty miles up the Straits of Fuca, which Cook had said did not exist. Then he headed north again, touching at Nootka, where he found Douglas, the Englishman, had come back from the Sandwich Islands with the two ships. Passing out of Nootka at four in the afternoon of May 1, he met a stately ship, all sails set, twenty guns pointed, under Spanish colors, gliding into the harbor. It was the flag-ship of Don Joseph Martinez, sent out to Bering Sea on a voyage of discovery, with a consort, and now entering Nootka to take possession in the name of Spain. Martinez examined Gray's passports, learned that the Americans had no thought of laying claim to Nootka and, finding out about Douglas's ship inside the harbor, seemed to conclude that it would be wise to make friends of the Americans; and he presented Gray with wines, brandy, hams, and spices.

"She will make a good prize," was his sententious remark to Gray about the English ship.

Rounding northward, Gray met the companion ship of the Spanish commander. It will be remembered Cook missed proving that the west coast was a chain of islands. Since Cook's time, Barclay, an Englishman, and Meares had been in the Straits of Fuca. Dixon had discovered Queen Charlotte Island; but {228} the cruising of the little sloop, *Lady Washington*, covered a greater area than Meares's, Barclay's and Dixon's ships together. First it rounded the north end of Vancouver, proving this was island, not continent. These northern waters Gray called Derby Sound, after the outfitter. He then passed up between Queen Charlotte Island and the continent for two hundred miles, calling this island Washington. It was northward of Portland Canal, somewhere near what is now Wrangel, that the brave little sloop was caught in a terrific gale that raged over her for two hours, damaging masts and timbers so that Gray was compelled to turn back from what he called Distress Cove, for repairs at Nootka. At one point off Prince of Wales Island, the Indians willingly traded two hundred otter skins, worth eight thousand dollars, for an old iron chisel.

In the second week of June the sloop was back at Nootka, where Gray was not a little surprised to find the Spanish had erected a fort on Hog Island, seized Douglas's vessel, and only released her on condition that the little fur trader *Northwest-America* should become Spanish property on entering Nootka.

Gray and Kendrick now exchanged ships, Gray, who had proved himself the swifter navigator, going on the *Columbia*, taking Haswell with him as mate. In return for one hundred otter skins, Gray was to carry the captured crew of the *Northwest-America* to China for the Spaniards. On July 30, 1789, he left Vancouver Island. Stop was made at Hawaii for {229} provisions, and Atto, the son of a chief, boarded the *Columbia* to visit America. On December 6 the *Columbia* delivered her cargo of furs to Shaw & Randall of Canton, receiving in exchange tea for Samuel Parkman, of Boston. It was February, 1790, before the Columbia was ready to sail for Boston, and dropping down the river she passed the *Lady Washington*, under Kendrick, in a cove where the gale hid her from Gray.

John Derby, from the portrait by Gilbert Stuart, by courtesy of the owner, Dr. George B. Shattuck.

[Illustration: John Derby, from the portrait by Gilbert Stuart, by courtesy of the owner, Dr. George B. Shattuck.]

On August 11, 1790, after rounding Good Hope and touching at St. Helena, Gray entered Boston. It was the first time an American ship had gone round the world, almost fifty thousand miles, her log-book showed, and salvos of artillery thundered a welcome. General Lincoln, the port collector, was first on board to shake Gray's hand. The whole city of Boston was on the wharf to cheer him home, and the explorer walked up the streets side by side with Atto, the Hawaiian boy, gorgeous in helmet and cloak of yellow plumage. Governor Hancock gave a public reception to Gray. The *Columbia* went to the shipyards to be overhauled, and the shareholders met.

Owing to the glutting of the market at Canton, the sea-otter had not sold well. Practically the venture of these glory seekers had not ended profitably. The voyage had been at a loss. Derby and Pintard sold out to Barrell and Brown. But the lure of glory, or the wilds, or the venture of the unknown, was on the others. They decided to send the *Columbia* back at {230} once on a second voyage. Perhaps, this time, she would find that great River of the West, which was to be to the Pacific coast what the Hudson was to the East.

Map of Gray's two voyages, resulting in the discovery of the Columbia.

[Illustration: Map of Gray's two voyages, resulting in the

Coolidge and Ingraham now left the *Columbia* for ventures of their own to the Pacific. Haswell, whose diary, with Gray's log-book, gives all details of the voyage, went as first mate. George Davidson, an artist, Samuel Yendell, a carpenter, Haskins, an accountant of Barrell's Company, Joshua Caswell of Maiden, Abraham Waters, and John Boit were the new men to enlist for the venturesome voyage. The *Columbia* left Boston for a second voyage September 28, 1790, and reached Clayoquot on the west coast of Vancouver Island on June 5, 1791. True to his nature, Gray lost not a day, but was off for the sea-otter harvest of the north, up Portland Canal near what is now Alaska. The dangers of the first voyage proved a holiday compared to this trip. Formerly, Gray had treated the Indians with kindness. Now, he found kindness was mistaken only for fear. Joshua Caswell, Barnes, and Folger had been sent up Portland Canal to reconnoitre. Whether ambushed or openly assaulted, they never returned. Only Caswell's body was found, and buried on the beach. Later, when the grave was revisited, the body had been stolen, in all likelihood for cannibal rites, as no more degraded savages exist than those of this archipelago. Over on Queen Charlotte Island, Kendrick, who had returned from China on the *Lady Washington*, {232} was having his own time. One day, when all had gone below decks to rest, a taunting laugh was heard from the hatchway. Kendrick rushed above to find Indians scrambling over the decks of the *Lady Washington* like a nest of disgruntled hornets. A warrior flourished the key of the ammunition chest, which stood by the hatchway, in Kendrick's face with the words: "Key is mine! So is the ship!"

If Kendrick had hesitated for the fraction of a second, all would have been lost, as on Astor's ship a few years later; but before the savages had time for any concerted signal, he had seized the speaker by the scruff of the neck, and tossed him into the sea. In a second every savage had scuttled over decks; but the scalp of Kendrick's son Solomon was found on the beach. Henceforth neither Kendrick nor Gray allowed more than ten savages on board at a time, and Kendrick at once headed south to take the harvest of furs to China. At Nootka things had gone from bad to worse between the English and the Spaniards. Though Kendrick bought great tracts of land from the Indian chiefs at Nootka for the price of a copper kettle, he judged it prudent to keep away from a Spanish commander, whose mission it was to capture the ships of rival traders; so the American sloop moored in Clayoquot, south of Nootka, where Gray found Kendrick ready to sail for China by September.

At Clayoquot was built the first American fort on the Pacific coast. Here Gray erected winter quarters. {233} The *Columbia* was unrigged and beached. The dense forest rang with the sound of the choppers. The enormous spruce, cedar, and fir trees were hewn into logs for several cabins and a barracks, the bark slabs being used as a palisade. Inside the main house were quarters for ten men. Loopholes punctured all sides of the house. Two cannon were mounted outside the window embrasures, one inside the gate or door. The post was named Fort Defence. Sentinels kept guard night and day. Military discipline was maintained, and divine service held each Sunday. On October 3 timbers were laid for a new ship, to be called the *Adventure*, to collect furs for the *Columbia*. All the winter of 1791-1792, Gray visited the Indians, sent medicines to their sick, allowed his men to go shooting with them, and even nursed one ill chief inside the barracks; but he was most careful not to allow women or more than a few warriors inside the fort.

What was his horror, then, on February 18, when Atto, the Hawaiian boy, came to him with news that the Indians, gathered to the number of two thousand, and armed with at least two hundred muskets got in trade, had planned the entire extermination of the whites. They had offered to make the Hawaiian boy a great chief among them if he would steal more ammunition for the Indians, wet all the priming of the white men's arms, and join the conspiracy to let the savages get possession of fort and ship. In the history of American pathfinding, no explorer was ever in greater {234} danger. Less than a score of whites against two thousand armed warriors! Scarcely any ammunition had been brought in from the *Columbia*. All the swivels of the dismantled ship were lying on the bank. Gray instantly took advantage of high tide to get the ship on her sea legs, and out from the bank. Swivels were trundled with all speed back to the decks. For that night a guard watched the fort; but the next night, when the assault was expected, all hands were on board, provisions had been stowed in the hold, and small arms were loaded. The men were still to mid-waist in water, scraping barnacles from the keel, when a whoop sounded from the shore; but the change in the ship's position evidently upset the plans of the savages, for they withdrew. On the morning of the 20th the woods were seen to be alive with ambushed men; and Haswell had the cannon loaded with canister fired into the woods. At eleven that very morning, the chief, at the head of the plot, came to sell otter skins, and ask if some of the crew would not visit the village. Gray jerked the skins from his arms, and the rascal was over decks in terror of his life. That was the end of the plot. On the 23d the *Adventure* was launched, the second vessel built on the Pacific, the first American vessel built there at all; and by April 2 Haswell was ready to go north on her. Gray on the *Columbia* was going south to have another try at that great River of the West, which Spanish charts represented.

{235} Without a doubt, if the river existed at all, it was down behind that Cape Disappointment where Meares had failed to go in, and Heceta been driven back. Just what Gray did between April 2 and May 7 is a matter of guessing. Anyway, Captain George Vancouver sent out from England to settle the dispute about Nootka, at six o'clock on the morning of April 29, just off the wave-lashed rocks of Cape Flattery, and within sight of Olympus's snowy sky-line, noticed a ship on the offing carrying American colors. He sent Mr. Puget and Mr. Menzies to inquire.

They brought back word that Gray "had been off the mouth of a river in 46 degrees 10 minutes where the outset and reflux was so strong as to prevent entering for nine days," and that Gray had been fifty miles up the Straits of Fuca.

Both facts were distasteful to Vancouver. He had wished to be the first to explore the Straits of Fuca, and on only April 27, had passed an opening which he pronounced inaccessible and not a river, certainly not a river worthy of his attention. Yet the exact words of Captain Bruno Heceta, the Spaniard, in 1775 were: "These currents … cause me to believe that the place is the mouth of some great river.… I did not enter and anchor there because … if we let go the anchor, we had not enough men to get it up. (Thirty-five were down with scurvy.) … At the distance of three or four leagues, I lay too. I experienced heavy currents, which made it impossible to enter the {236} bay, as I was far to leeward.… These currents, however, convince me that a great quantity of water rushed from this bay on the ebb of the tide."

So the Spaniard failed to enter, and now the great English navigator went on his way, convinced there was no River of the West; but Robert Gray headed back south determined to find what lay behind the tremendous crash of breakers and sand bar. On the 7th of May, the rowboat towed the *Columbia* into what is now known as Gray's Harbor, where he opened trade with the Indians, and was presently so boldly overrun by them, that he was compelled to fire into their canoes, killing seven. Putting out from this harbor on the 10th, he steered south, keeping close ashore, and was rewarded at four o'clock on the morning of the 11th by hearing a tide-rip like thunder and seeing an ocean of waters crashing sheer over sand bar and reef with a cataract of foam in midair from the drive of colliding waves. Milky waters tinged the sea as of inland streams. Gray had found the river, but could he enter? A gentle wind, straight as a die, was driving direct ashore. Gray waited till the tide seemed to lift or deepen the waters of the reef, then at eight in the morning, all sails set like a bird on wing, drove straight for the narrow entrance between reefs and sand. Once across the bar, he saw the mouth of a magnificent river of fresh water. He had found the River of the West.

Gray describes the memorable event in these simple {237} words: "May 11th ... at four A.M. saw the entrance of our desired port bearing east-southeast, distance six leagues ... at eight A.M. being a little to windward of the entrance of the harbor, bore away, and ran in east-southeast between the breakers.... When we were over the bar, we found this to be a large river of fresh water, up which we steered. Many canoes came alongside. At one P.M. came to (anchor). ..."

A View of the Columbia River.

[Illustration: A View of the Columbia River.]

By the 14th, Gray had ascended the river twenty or thirty miles from the sea, but was compelled to turn, as he had taken a shallow channel. Dropping down with the tide, he anchored on the 19th and went ashore, where he planted coins under a tree, took {238} possession in the name of the United States, and named the river "Columbia." On the 20th, he crossed the bar and was out again on the Pacific. The most of men would have rested, satisfied with half he had done. Not so Gray. He headed the *Columbia* north again for the summer's trade in what is now known as southern Alaska. Only damages to the *Columbia* drove her down to Nootka in July, where Don Quadra, the new Spanish commander, and Captain Vancouver were in conference over those English ships seized by Martinez. To Quadra, Gray sold the little *Adventure*, pioneer of American shipbuilding on the Pacific, for seventy-five otter skins. From Spanish sources it is learned Gray's cargo had over three thousand otter skins, and fifteen thousand other peltries; so the second voyage may have made up for the loss of the first.

At the Mouth of the Columbia River.

[Illustration: At the Mouth of the Columbia River.]

On October 3 the *Columbia* left America for China; and on July 29, 1793, came to the home harbor of Boston. Sometime between 1806 and 1809, Gray died in South Carolina, a poor man. It is doubtful if his widow's petition to Congress ever materialized in a reward for any of his descendants. Kendrick, eclipsed by his brilliant assistant, was accidentally killed in Hawaii by the wad of a gun fired by a British vessel to salute the *Lady Washington*. From the date 1793 or 1795 the little sloop drops out of sea-faring annals.

What is Gray's place among pathfinders and naval {239} heroes? Where does his life's record leave him? It was not spectacular work. It was not work backed by a government, like Bering's or Cook's. It was the work of an individual adventurer, like Radisson east of the Rockies. Gray was a man who did much and said little. He was not accompanied by a host of scientists to herald his fame to the world. Judged solely by results, what did he accomplish? The same for the United States that Cook did for England. He led the way for the American flag around the world. Measuring purely by distance, his ship's log would compare well with Cook's or Vancouver's. The same part of the Pacific coast which they {240} explored, he explored, except that he did not go to northern Alaska; and he compensated for that by discovering the great river, which they both said had no existence. And yet, who that knows of Cook and Vancouver, knows as much of Gray? Authentic histories are still written that speak of Gray's discovery doubtfully. Gray did much, but said little; and the world is prone to take a man at his own valuation. Yet if the world places Cook and Vancouver in the niches of naval heroes, Gray must be placed between them.

There is a curious human side to the story of these glory seekers, too. Bulfinch was so delighted over the discovery of the Columbia, that he had his daughter christened "Columbia," to which the young lady objected in later years, so that the name was dropped. In commemoration of Don Quadra's kindness in repairing the ship *Columbia*, Gray named one of his children Quadra. The curios brought back by Ingraham on the first voyage were donated to Harvard. Descendants of Gray still have the pictures drawn by Davidson and Haswell on the second voyage. The sea chest carried round the world by Gray now rests in the keeping of an historical society in Portland; and the feather cloak worn up the street by the boy Atto, when he marched in the procession with Gray, is treasured in Boston.[1]

[1] Much concerning Gray's voyages can be found in the accounts of contemporary navigators like Meares and Vancouver; but the essential facts of the voyages are obtainable from the records of Gray's log-book, and of diaries kept by his officers. {241} Gray's log-book itself seems to have passed into the hands of the Bulfinch family. From a copy of the original, Thomas Bulfinch reprinted the exact entry of the discovery on May 11, 1792, in his *Oregon and Eldorado, a Romance of the Rivers*, Boston, 1866. The log-book is now on file in the Department of State, Washington; but that part from which Bulfinch made his extract is missing; nor is it known where this section was lost as it was in 1816 that Mr. Charles Bulfinch made a copy of this section from the original. Greenhow's *Oregon and California*, Boston, 1844, issued under the auspices of Congress, gives the log-book in full from May 7th to May 21st. Hubert Howe Bancroft in his *Northwest Coast*, Volume I, 1890, reproduces the diary in full of Haswell for both voyages. It is from Haswell that the fullest account of the Indian plots are obtained; but at the time of the discovery of the Columbia, Haswell was on the little sloop *Adventure*, and what he reports is from hearsay. His words in the entry of June 14 are; "They (the *Columbia*) had very disagreeable weather but ... good success... They discovered a harbor in latitude 46 degrees 53 minutes north.... This is Gray's Harbor. Here they were attacked by the natives, and the savages had a considerable slaughter made among them. They next entered Columbia River, and went up it about thirty miles, and doubted not it was navigable upwards of a hundred miles.... The ship (*Columbia*) during the cruise had collected upwards of seven hundred sea-otter skins and fifteen thousand skins of other species." The pictures made by Davidson, the artist, on the second voyage, owned by collectors in Boston, tell their own story. From all these sources, and from the descendants of Gray, the Rev. Edward G. Porter collected data for his lecture before the Massachusetts Historical Society, afterward published in the *New England Magazine* of June, 1892. The *Massachusetts Historical Proceedings* for 1892 have, by all odds, the most complete collection of data bearing on Gray. The archives include the medal and three of Davidson's drawings, also papers relating to the *Columbia* presented by Barrell. The Salem Institute has also some data on the ships. The *Massachusetts Proceedings* for 1869-1870 also give, from the Archives of California, the letter of Governor Don Pedro Fages of Santa Barbara to Don Josef Arguello of San Francisco, warning the latter against the American navigators. Greenhow obtained from the Hydrographical Office at Madrid the report of Captain Bruno Heceta's voyage in 1775, when he sighted the mouth of a river supposed to be the Columbia.

CHAPTER IX
1778-1790
JOHN LEDYARD, THE FORERUNNER OF LEWIS AND CLARK

A New England Ne'er-do-well, turned from the Door of Rich Relatives, joins Cook's Expedition to America —Adventure among the Russians of Oonalaska—Useless Endeavor to interest New England Merchants in Fur Trade—A Soldier of Fortune in Paris, he meets Jefferson and Paul Jones and outlines Exploration of Western America—Succeeds in crossing Siberia alone on the Way to America, but is thwarted by Russian Fur Traders

When his relatives banged the door in his face, turning him destitute in the streets of London, if John Ledyard could have foreseen that the act would indirectly lead to the Lewis and Clark exploration of the great region between the Mississippi and the Pacific, he would doubtless have regarded the unkindness as Dick Whittington did the cat, that led on to fortune. He had been a dreamer from the time he was born in Groton, opposite New London, Connecticut—the kind of a dreamer whose moonshine lights the path of other men to success; but his wildest dreams never dared the bigness of an empire many times greater than the original states of the Union.

{243} Instead he had landed at Plymouth, ragged, not a farthing in the bottom of his pockets, not a farthing's possession on earth but his hopes. Those hopes were to reach rich relatives in London, who might give him a lift to the first rung of the world's climbers. He was twenty-five years old. He had burned his ships behind him. That is, he had disappointed all his relatives in America so thoroughly that he could never again turn for help to the home hands.

They had designed him for a profession, these New England friends. If Nature had designed him for the same thing, it would have been all right; but she hadn't. The son of a widowed mother, the love of the sea, of pathless places, of what is just out of sight over the dip of the horizon, was in his blood from his father's side. Friends thought he should be well satisfied when he was sent to live with his grandfather at Hartford and apprenticed to the law; but John Ledyard hated the pettifogging of the law, hated roofed-over, walled-in life, wanted the kind of life where men do things, not just dicker, and philosophize, and compromise over the fag-ends of things other men have done. At twenty-one years of age, without any of the prospects that lure the prudent soul, he threw over all idea of law.[1]

Friends were aghast. Manifestly, the boy had {244} brains. He devoured information, absorbed facts like an encyclopaedia, and observed everything. The Greek Testament and Ovid were his companions; yet he rebelled at the immured existence of the scholar. At that time (1772), Dartmouth was the rendezvous of {245} missionaries to the Indians. The college itself held lectures to the singing of the winds through the forests around it. The blowing of a conch-shell called to lessons; and a sort of wildwood piety pervaded the atmosphere. Urged by his mother, Ledyard made one more honest attempt to fit his life to a stereotyped form, and came to study at Dartmouth for the missionary's career.

It was not a success. When he thought to get a foretaste of the missionary vocation by making a dugout and floating down the whole length of Connecticut River, one hundred and forty miles, the scholarly professors were shocked. And when he disappeared for four months to make a farther test by living among the Mohawks, the faculty was furious. His friends gave him up as hopeless, a ne'er-do-well; and Ledyard gave over the farce of trying to live according to other men's patterns.

Ledyard in his dugout, from a contemporaneous print.

[Illustration: Ledyard in his dugout, from a contemporaneous print.]

What now determined him was what directs the most of lives—need for bread and butter. He became a common sailor on the ship of a friend in New London, and at twenty-five landed in Plymouth, light of heart as he was light of purse. The world was an oyster to be opened by his own free lance; and up he tramped from Plymouth to London in company with an Irishman penniless as himself, gay as a lark, to the world's great capital with the world's great prizes for those with the wits to win them. A carriage with driver {246} and footman in livery wearing the armorial design of his own Ledyard ancestors rolled past in the street. He ran to the coachman, asked the address, and presented himself at the door of the ancestral Ledyards, hope beating high. The relationship was to be the key to open all doors. And the door of the ancestral Ledyards was shut in his face. The father was out. The son put no stock in the story of the ragged stranger. He did not even know that Ledyards existed in America. What was to hinder any common tramp trumping up such a story? Where were the tattered fellow's proofs? Ledyard came away with just enough wholesome human rage to keep him from sinking to despair, or to what is more unmanning, self-pity. He had failed before, through trying to frame his life to other men's plans. He had failed now, through trying to win success through other men's efforts—a barnacle clinging to the hull of some craft freighted with fortune. Perhaps, too, he fairly and squarely faced the fact that if he was to be one whit different from the beggar for whom he had been mistaken, he must build his own life solely and wholly on his own efforts.

On he wandered, the roar of the great city's activities rolling past him in a tide. His rage had time to cool. Afternoon, twilight, dark; and still the tide rolled past him; *past him* because like a stranded hull rotting for lack of use, he had put himself *outside* the tide of human effort. He must build up his own career. That was the fact he had wrested out of his {247} rage; but unless his abilities were to rot in some stagnant pool, he must launch out on the great tide of human work. Before he had taken that resolution, the roar of the city had been terrifying—a tide that might swamp. Now, the thunder of the world's traffic was a shout of triumph. He would launch out, let the tide carry him where it might.

All London was resounding with the project of Cook's third voyage round the world—the voyage that was to settle forever how far America projected into the Pacific. Recruits were being mustered for the voyage. It came to Ledyard in an inspiration—the new field for his efforts, the call of the sea that paved a golden path around the world, the freedom for shoulder-swing to do all that a man was worth. Quick as flash, he was off—going *with* the tide now, not a derelict, not a stranded hull—off to shave, and wash, and respectable-ize, in order to apply as a recruit with Cook.

In the dark, somewhere near the sailors' mean lodgings, a hand touched him. He turned; it was the rich man's son, come profuse of apologies: his father had returned; father and son begged to proffer both financial aid and hospitality—Ledyard cut him short with a terse but forcible invitation to go his own way. That the unknown colonial at once received a berth with Cook as corporal of marines, when half the young men of England with influence to back their applications were eager to join the voyage, speaks well for the sincerity of the new enthusiasm.

{248} Cook left England in midsummer of 1776. He sighted the Pacific coast, northward of what is now San Francisco, in the spring of 1778. Ledyard was the first American to see the land that lay beyond the Rockies. It was not a narrow strip as men had thought, but a broad belt a thousand miles long by a thousand broad, an unclaimed world; for storms drove Cook offshore here; and the English discoverer did not land till abreast of British America.

At Nootka thousands of Indians flocked round the two vessels to trade. For some trinkets of glass beads and iron, Ledyard obtained one thousand five hundred skins for Cook. Among the Indians, too, he saw brass trinkets, that must have come all the way from New Spain on the south, or from the Hudson's Bay Fur Company on the east. What were the merchants of New York and

Philadelphia doing, that their ships were not here reaping a harvest of wealth in furs? If this were the outermost bound of Louisiana, Louisiana might some day be a part of the colonies now struggling for their liberties; and Ledyard's imagination took one of those leaps that win a man the reputation of a fool among his contemporaries, a hero to future generations. "If it was necessary that a European should discover the existence of the continent," he afterward wrote, "in the name of Amor Patriae let a native explore its resources and boundaries... It is my wish to be the man."

Cook's ships passed north to Oonalaska. Only {249} twenty-five years before, the Indians of Oonalaska had massacred every white settlement on the island. Cook wished to send a message to the Russian fur traders. Not many men could be risked from the ship. Fired with the ambition to know more of the coast which he had determined to explore, Ledyard volunteered to go for the Russians with two Indian guides. The pace was set at an ambling run over rocks that had cut Ledyard's boots to tatters before nightfall. He was quite unarmed; and just at dark the way seemed to end at a sandy shore, where the waves were already chopping over on the rising tide, and spiral columns of smoke betrayed the underground mud huts of those very Indian villages that had massacred the Russians a quarter of a century before. The guides had dived somewhere underground and, while Ledyard stood nonplussed, came running back carrying a light skin boat which they launched. It was made of oiled walrus hide stretched like a drum completely round whalebones, except for two manholes in the top for the rowers. Perpheela, the guide, signalled Ledyard to embark; and before the white man could solve the problem of how three men were to sit in two manholes, he was seized head and heels, and bundled clear through a manhole, lying full length imprisoned like Jonah in the whale. Then the swish of dipping paddles, of the cold waves above and beneath, shut out by parchment thin as tissue paper, told Ledyard that he was being carried out to sea, spite of dark and storm, {250} in a craft light as an air-blown bladder, that bounced forward, through, under, over the waves, undrownable as a fish.

There was nothing to do but lie still. The slightest motion might have ruptured the thin skin keel. On he was borne through the dark, the first American in history to travel by a submarine. At the end of what seemed ages—it could not have been more than two hours—after a deal of bouncing to the rising storm with no sound but the whistling of wind and rush of mountain seas, the keel suddenly grated pebbles. Starlight came through the vacated manholes; but before Ledyard could jump out, the boat was hoisted on the shoulders of four men, and carried on a run overland. The creak of a door slammed open. A bump as the boat dumped down to soft floor; and Ledyard was dazzled by a glare of light to find himself in the mess room of the Russian barracks on Captain Harbor, in the presence of two bearded Russian hunters gasping speechless with surprise to see a man emerging from the manhole like a newly hatched chicken from an egg.

Fur rugs covered the floor, the walls, the benches, the berth beds lining the sides of the barnlike Russian barracks. The windows were of oiled bladder skin; the lamps, whale-oil in stone basins with skin for wick. Arms were stacked in the corner. The two Russians had been sitting down to a supper of boiled salmon, when Ledyard made his unannounced {251} entrance. By signs he explained that Captain Cook's ships were at a near harbor and that the English commander desired to confer with Ismyloff, chief factor of the Russians. Rising, kissing their hands ceremoniously as they mentioned the august name and taking off their fur caps, the Russians made solemn answer that all these parts, with a circumambient wave, belonged to the Empress of Russia; that they were her subjects—with more kissing of the hands. Russia did not want foreigners spying on her hunting-grounds. Nevertheless, Ledyard was given a present of fresh Chinese silk underwear, treated to the hottest Russian brandy in the barracks, and put comfortably to bed on a couch of otter skins. From his bed, he saw the Indians crowd in for evening services before a little Russian crucifix, the two traders leading prayers. These were the tribes, whom the Russians had hunted with dogs fifty years before; and who in turn had slain all Russians on the Island. A better understanding now prevailed.

In the morning Ledyard looked over the fur establishment; galliots, cannon-mounted in the harbor for refuge in case of attack; the huge lemon-yellow, red-roofed store-room that might serve as barracks or fort for a hundred men; the brigades of eight, of nine, of eleven hundred Indian hunters sailing the surfs under the leadership of Ismyloff, the chief factor. Oonalaska was the very centre of the sea-otter hunt. Here, eighteen thousand otter a year were taken. At once, {252} Ledyard realized how he could pay the cost of exploring that unclaimed world between New Spain and Alaska: by turning fur trader as Radisson, and La Salle, and the other explorers had done.

Ismyloff himself, who had been out with his brigade when Ledyard came, went to visit the Englishman; but Ismyloff had little to say, little of Benyowsky, the Polish pirate, who had marooned him; less of Alaska; and the reason for taciturnity was plain. The Russian fur traders were forming a monopoly. They told no secrets to the world. They wanted no intruders on their hunting-ground. Could Ledyard have known that the surly, bearded Russian was to blast his new-born ambitions; could Ismyloff have guessed that the eager, young, beardless corporal of marines was indirectly to be the means of wresting the Pacific coast from Russia—each might have smiled at the tricks of destiny.

Ledyard had two more years to serve in the British navy when he returned from Cook's voyage. By another trick of destiny he was sent out on a battle ship to fight against his native country in the Revolutionary War. It was a time when men wore patriotic coats of many colors. His ship lay at anchor off Long Island. He had not seen his mother for seven years, but knew that the war had reduced her to opening a lodging house for British officers. Asking for a week's furlough, Ledyard went ashore, proceeded to his mother's {253} house, knocked at the door, and was taken as a lodger by her without being recognized, which was, perhaps, as well; for the house was full of British spies. Ledyard waited till night. Then he went to her private apartments and found her reading with the broad-rimmed, horn-framed spectacles of those days. He took her hands. "Look at me," he said. One glance was enough. Then he shut the door; and the door remains shut to the world on what happened there.

That was the end of British soldiering for Ledyard. He never returned to the marines. He betook himself to Hartford, where he wrote an account of Cook's voyage. Then he set himself to move heaven and earth for a ship to explore that unknown coast from New Spain to Alaska. This was ten years before Robert Gray of Boston had discovered the Columbia; twenty years before the United States thought of buying Louisiana, twenty-five years before Lewis and Clark reached the Pacific. Many influences worked against him. Times were troublous. The country had not recovered sufficiently from the throes of the Revolution to think of expanding territory. Individually and collectively, the nation was desperately poor. As for private sailing masters, they smiled at Ledyard's enthusiasm. An unclaimed world? What did they care? Where was the money in a venture to the Pacific? When Ledyard told how Russia was reaping a yearly harvest of millions in furs, even his old friend, Captain Deshon, whose boat had {254} carried him to Plymouth, grew chary of such roseate prospects. It was characteristic of Ledyard that the harder the difficulties proved, the harder grew his determination to overcome. He was up against the impossible, and instead of desisting, gritted his teeth, determined to smash a breach through the wall of the impossible, or smash himself trying. For six months he besieged leading men in New York and Philadelphia, outlining his plans, meeting arguments, giving proofs for all he said of Pacific wealth, holding conference after conference. Robert Morris entered enthusiastically into the scheme; but what with shipmasters' reluctance to embark on such a dangerous voyage and the general scarcity of funds, the patience of both Ledyard and Morris became exhausted. Ledyard's savings had meanwhile dwindled down to $4.27.

In Europe, Cook's voyage was beginning to create a stir. The Russian government had projected an expedition to the Pacific under Joseph Billings, Cook's assistant astronomer. These Russian plans aimed at no less than dominance on the Pacific. Forts were to be built in California and Hawaii. In England and India, private adventurers, Portlock, Dixon, Meares, Barclay, were fitting out ships for Pacific trade. Some one advised Ledyard to attempt his venture in the country that had helped America in the Revolution, France; and to France he sailed with money loaned by Mr. Sands of New York, in 1784.

{255} In Paris Ledyard met two of the most remarkable men in American history, Paul Jones, the naval hero, and Jefferson. To them both he told the marvels of Pacific wealth, and both were far-sighted enough to share his dreams. It was now that Jefferson began to formulate those plans that Lewis and Clark afterward carried out. The season was too late for a voyage this year, but Paul Jones loaned Ledyard money and arranged to take out a ship of four hundred tons the following year. The two actually went over every detail together. Jones was to carry the furs to China, Ledyard with assistants, surgeon, and twenty soldiers to remain at the fur post and explore.

But Paul Jones was counting on the support of the American government; and when he found that the government considered Ledyard's promises visionary, he threw the venture over in a pique.

Was Ledyard beaten? Jefferson and he talked over the project day after day. Ledyard was willing to tramp it across the two Siberias on foot, and to chance over the Pacific Ocean in a Russian fur-trading vessel, if Jefferson could obtain permission from the Russian Empress. Meanwhile, true soldier of fortune, without money, or influence, he lived on terms of intimacy with the fashion of

Paris.

"I have but five French crowns," he wrote a friend. "The Fitzhughes (fellow-roomers) haven't money for tobacco. Such a set of moneyless rascals never {256} appeared since the days of Falstaff." Again—"Sir James Hall, on his way from Paris to Cherbourg, stopped his coach at our door. I was in bed, but having flung on my robe de chambre, met him at the door.... In walking across the chamber, he laughingly put his hand on a six livre piece and a louis d'or on my table, and with a blush asked me how I was in the money way. Blushes beget blushes. 'If fifteen guineas,' said he, 'will be of any service to you, here they are. You have my address in London.'"

While waiting the passports from the Empress of Russia, he was invited by Sir James Hall to try his luck in England. The very daring of the wild attempt to cross Siberia and America alone appealed to the English. Half a dozen men, friends of Cook, took the venture up, and Ledyard found himself in the odd position of being offered a boat by the country whose navy he had deserted. Perhaps because of that desertion all news of the project was kept very quiet. A small ship had slipped down the Thames for equipments, when the government got wind of it. Whether the great Hudson's Bay Company of England opposed the expedition as intrusion on its fur preserve, or the English government objected to an American conducting the exploration for the expansion of American territory, the ship was ordered back, and Ledyard was in no position to confront the English authorities. Again he was checkmated, and fell back on Jefferson's plan to cross the two Siberias on foot, and chance it over {257} the Pacific. His friends in London gathered enough money to pay his way to St. Petersburg.

January of 1787 saw him in Sweden seeking passage across the Baltic. Usually the trip to St. Petersburg was made by dog sleighs across the ice. This year the season had been so open, neither boats nor dog trains could be hired to make the trip. Ledyard was now thirty-six years old, and the sum of his efforts totalled to a zero. The first twenty-five years of his life he had wasted trying to fit his life to other men's patterns. The last five years he had wasted waiting for other men to act, men in New York, in Philadelphia, in Paris, in London, to give him a ship. He had done with waiting, with dependence on others. When boats and dog trains failed him now, he muffled himself in wolfskins to his neck, flung a knapsack on his back, and set out in midwinter to tramp overland six hundred miles north to Tornea at the head of the Baltic, six hundred miles south from

Tornea, through Finland to St. Petersburg. Snow fell continually. Storms raged in from the sea. The little villages of northern Sweden and Finland were buried in snow to the chimney-tops. Wherever he happened to be at nightfall, he knocked at the door of a fisherman's hut. Wherever he was taken in, he slept, whether on the bare floor before the hearth, or among the dogs of the outhouses, or in the hay-lofts of the cattle sheds. No more waiting for Ledyard! Storm or shine, early and late, he {258} tramped two hundred miles a week for seven weeks from the time he left Stockholm. When he marched into St. Petersburg on the 19th of March, men hardly knew whether to regard him as a madman or a wonder. Using the names of Jefferson and Lafayette, he jogged up the Russian authorities by another application for the passport. The passport was long in coming. How was Ledyard to know that Ismyloff, the Russian fur trader, whom he had met in Oonalaska, had written letters stirring up the Russian government to jealous resentment against all comers to the Pacific? Ledyard was mad with impatience. Days slipped into weeks, weeks into months, and no passport came. He was out of clothes, out of money, out of food. A draft on his English friends kept him from destitution. Just a year before, Billings, the astronomer of Cook's vessel, had gone across Siberia on the way to America for the Russian government. If Ledyard could only catch up to Billings's expedition, that might be a chance to cross the Pacific. As if to exasperate his impatience still more, he met a Scotch physician, a Dr. William Brown, now setting out for Siberia on imperial business, who offered to carry him along free for three thousand of the seven thousand miles to the Pacific. Perhaps the proceeds of that English draft helped him with the slow Russian authorities, but at last, on June 1, he had his passport, and was off with Dr. Brown. His entire earthly possessions at this time consisted of a few guineas, a suit of {259} clothes, and large debts. What was the crack-brained enthusiast aiming at anyway? An empire half the present size of the United States.

From St. Petersburg to Moscow in six days, drawn by three horses at breakneck pace, from Moscow to Kazan through the endless forests, on to the Volga, Brown and Ledyard hastened. By the autumn they were across the Barbary Desert, three thousand miles from St. Petersburg. Here Brown remained, and Ledyard went on with the Cossack mail carriers. All along the endless trail of two continents, the trail of East and West, he passed the caravans of the Russian fur traders, and learned the astonishing news that more than two thousand Russians were on the west coast of America. Down the Lena next, to Yakutsk, the great rendezvous of the fur traders, only one thousand miles more to the Pacific; and on the great plain of the fur traders near Yakutsk he at last overtook the Billings explorers on their way to America. Only one guinea was left in his pocket, and the Cossack commandant reported that the season was too far advanced for him to cross the Pacific. What did it matter? He would cross the Pacific with Billings in spring. He was nearer the realization of his hopes than ever before in his life; and surely his success in tramping twice the length of Sweden, and in crossing two continents when almost destitute augured well for his success in crossing from the Pacific to the Missouri.

Not for a moment was his almost childlike confidence {260} disturbed by a suspicion of bad faith, of intentional delay in issuing the passports, of excuses to hold him back at Yakutsk till the jealous fur traders could send secret complaints to St. Petersburg. Much less was he suspicious when Billings, his old friend of Cook's voyage, himself arrived, and invited him on a sled journey of exploration up the Lena while waiting.[2]

On sledges he went up the Lena River with a party of explorers. On the night of February 24 two or three of the officers and Ledyard were sitting in the mess room of Irkutsk playing cards. They might laugh *at* Ledyard. They also laughed *with* him. Wherever he went, went gayety. Gales of boisterous laughter were on the wind. Hopes as tenuous as the wind were in the air. One of the great Bering's sons was there, no doubt telling tales of discovery that set each man's veins jumping. Suddenly a tremendous jingling of bells announced some midnight arrival post-haste at the barracks' door. Before the card players had risen from their places, two Cossacks had burst into the room stamping snow from their feet. Marching straight over to Ledyard, they seized him roughly by the arms and arrested him for a French spy, displaying the Empress's written orders, brought all the way from St. Petersburg. To say that Ledyard was dumfounded is putting it mildly. Every man in the room knew that he was not a French spy. Every man {261} in the room knew that the arrest was a farce, instigated by the jealous fur traders whom Ismyloff's lying letters had aroused. For just a second Ledyard lost his head and called on Billings as a man of honor to confute the charge. However Ledyard might lose his head, Billings was not willing to lose his. He advised Ledyard not to provoke conflict with the Russian authorities, but to go back to St. Petersburg and disprove the charge. Was it a case of one explorer being jealous of another, or had Billings played Ledyard into the fur traders' trap? That will never be known. Certain it is, Billings made mess enough of his own expedition to go down to posterity as a failure. Some of the officers ran to get Ledyard a present of clothes and money. As he jumped into the waiting sledge and looked back over his shoulder at the group of faces smiling in the lighted doorway, he burst into a laugh, but it was the laugh of an embittered man, whose life had crumbled to ruin at one blow. The Cossacks whipped up the horses, and he was off on the long trail back, five thousand miles, every mile a sign post of blasted hopes. Without a word of explanation or the semblance of a trial on the false charge, he was banished out of St. Petersburg on pain of death if he returned.

Ragged, destitute, the best years of his life gone, he reached London, heartbroken. "I give up," he told the English friends, who had backed him with money, and what was better than money—faith. "I give up," {262} he wrote Jefferson, who afterward had Lewis and Clark carry out Ledyard's plans.

The men of the African Geographical Society in London tried to cheer him. When could he set out to explore the source of the Nile for them?

"To-morrow," answered Ledyard, with the heedlessness of one who has lost grip on life. The salary advanced paid off the moss-grown debts of his disappointed past, but he never reached the scene of his new venture. He died on the way at Cairo, in November, 1788, for all hope had already died in his heart. The world that has entered into the heritage of his aims has forgotten Ledyard; for the public acclaims only the heroes of success, and he was a hero of defeat. All that Lewis and Clark succeeded in doing for the West, backed by the prestige of government, Ledyard, the penniless soldier of fortune, had foreseen and planned with Jefferson in the attic apartments of Paris.[3]

[1] The world owes all knowledge of Ledyard's intimate life to Jared Sparks, who compiled his life of Ledyard from journals and correspondence collected by Dr. Ledyard and Henry Seymour of Hartford.

[2] In Sauer's account of the Billings Expedition, some excuse is given for the conduct of Billings on the ground that Ledyard had been insolent to the Russians.

[3] Ledyard's *Journal of Cook's Last Voyage*, Hartford, 1783, and Sparks's *Life of Ledyard*, Cambridge, 1829.

CHAPTER X
1779-1794
GEORGE VANCOUVER, LAST OF PACIFIC COAST EXPLORERS

Activities of Americans, Spanish, and Russians on the West Coast of America arouse England—Vancouver is sent out ostensibly to settle the Quarrel between Fur Traders and Spanish Governors at Nootka—Incidentally, he is to complete the Exploration of America's West Coast and take Possession for England of Unclaimed Territory—The Myth of a Northeast Passage dispelled forever

With Gray's entrance of the Columbia, the great drama of discovery on the northwest coast of America was drawing to a close.

After the death of Bering on the Commander Islands, and of Cook at Hawaii, while on voyages to prove there was no Northeast Passage, no open waterway between Pacific and Atlantic, it seems impossible that the myth of an open sea from Asia to Europe could still delude men; but it was in hunting for China that Columbus found America; and it was in hunting for a something that had no existence except in the foolish theories of the schoolmen that the whole northwest coast of America was exploited.

{264} Bering had been called "coward" for not sailing through a solid continent. Cook was accused of fur trading, "pottering in peltries," to the neglect of discovery, because his crews sold their sea-otter at profit. To be sure, the combined results of Bering's and Cook's voyages proved there was no waterway through Alaska to the Atlantic; but in addition to blackening the reputations of the two great navigators in order to throw discredit on their conclusions, the schoolmen bellicosely demanded—Might there not be a passage south of Alaska, between Russia's claim on the north and Spain's on the south? Both Bering and Cook had been driven out from this section of the coast by gales. This left a thousand miles of American coast unexplored. Cook had said there were no Straits of Fuca, of which the old Greek pilot in the service of New Spain had told legends of fictitious voyages two centuries before; yet Barclay, an East India English trader, had been up those very straits. So had Meares, another trader. So had Kendrick and Gray, the two Americans. This was the very section which Bering and Cook had left untouched; and who could tell where these straits might lead? They were like a second Mediterranean. Meares argued they might connect with Hudson Bay.

Then Spain had forced matters to a climax by seizing Meares's vessels and fort at Nootka as contraband. That had only one meaning: Spain was trying to lay hands on everything from New Spain to Russian {265} territory on the north. If Spain claimed all north to the Straits of Fuca, and Russia claimed all south to the Straits of Fuca, where was England's claim of New Albion discovered by Sir Francis Drake, and of all that coast which Cook had sighted round Nootka?

Captain George Vancouver, formerly midshipman with Cook, was summoned post-haste by the British Admiralty. Ostensibly, his mission was to receive back at Nootka all the lands which the Spaniards had taken from Meares, the trader. Really, he was to explore the coast from New Spain on the south, to Russian America on the north, and to hold that coast for England. That Spain had already explored the islands of this coast was a mere detail. There remained the continental shore still to be explored. Besides, Spain had not followed up her explorations by possession. She had kept her navigations secret. In many cases her navigators had not even landed.

Captain George Vancouver.

[Illustration: Captain George Vancouver.]

Vancouver was still in his prime, under forty. Serving in the navy from boyhood, he had all a practical seaman's contempt for theories. This contempt was given point by the world's attitude toward Cook. Vancouver had been on the spot with Cook. He knew there was no Northeast Passage. Cook had proved that. Yet the world refused credence.

For the practical navigator there remained only one course, and that course became the one aim, the consuming ambition of Vancouver's life—to destroy the {266} last vestige of the myth of a Northeast Passage; to explore the northwest coast of America so thoroughly there would not remain a single unknown inlet that could be used as a possible prop for the schoolmen's theories, to penetrate every inlet from California to Alaska—mainland and island; to demonstrate that not one possible opening led to the Atlantic. This was to be the object of Vancouver's life, and he carried it out with a thoroughness that left nothing for subsequent explorers to do; but he died before the record of his voyages had been given to the world.

The two ships, *Discovery* and *Chatham*, with a supply ship, the *Daedalus*, to follow later, were fitted out for long and thorough work. Vancouver's vessel, the *Discovery*, carried twenty guns with a crew of a hundred men. The tender, *Chatham*, under Broughton, had ten guns and forty-five men. With Vancouver went Menzies, and Puget, and Baker, and Johnstone—names that were to become place marks on the Pacific. The *Discovery* and *Chatham* left England in the spring of 1791. A year later found them cutting the waves from Hawaii for America, the New Albion of Drake's discovery, forgotten by England until Spain's activity stimulated memory of the pirate voyage.

A swashing swell met the ships as they neared America. Phosphorescent lights blue as sulphur flame slimed the sea in a trail of rippling fire; and a land bird, washed out by the waves, told of New Albion's shore. {267} For the first two weeks of April, the *Discovery* and *Chatham* had driven under cloud of sail and sunny skies; but on the 16th, just when the white fret of reefs ahead forewarned land, heavy weather settled over the ships. To the fore, bare, majestic, compact as a wall, the coast of New Albion towered out of the surf near Mendocino. Cheers went up from the lookout for the landfall of Francis Drake's discovery. Then torrents of rain washed out surf and shore. The hurricane gales, that had driven all other navigators out to sea from this coast, now lashed Vancouver. Such smashing seas swept over decks, that masts, sails, railings, were wrenched away.

Was it ill-luck or destiny, that caught Vancouver in this gale? If he had not been driven offshore here, he might have been just two weeks before Gray on the *Columbia*, and made good England's claim of all territory between New Spain and Alaska. When the weather cleared on April 27, the ocean was turgid, plainly tinged river-color by inland waters; but ground swell of storm and tide rolled across the shelving sandbars. Not a notch nor an opening breached through the flaw of the horizon from the ocean to the source of the shallow green. Vancouver was too far offshore to see that there really was a break in the surf wash. He thought—and thought rightly—this was the place where the trader, Meares, had hoped to find the great River of the West, only to be disappointed and to name the point Cape Disappointment. Vancouver was {268} not to be fooled by any such fanciful theories. "Not considering this opening worthy of more attention," he writes, "I continued to the northwest." He had missed the greatest honor that yet remained for any discoverer on the Pacific. Within two weeks Gray, the American, heading back to these baffling tides with a dogged persistence that won its own glory, was to succeed in passing the breakers and discovering the Columbia. As the calm permitted approach to the shore again, forests appeared through the haze—that soft, velvet, caressing haze of the dreamy, lazily swelling Pacific—forests of fir and spruce and pine and cypress, in all the riot of dank spring growth, a dense tangle of windfall and underbrush and great vines below, festooned with the light green stringy mosses of cloud line overhead and almost impervious to sunlight. Myriad wild fowl covered the sea. The coast became beetling precipice, that rolled inland forest-clad to mountains jagging ragged peaks through the clouds. This was the Olympus Range, first noticed by Meares, and to-day seen for miles out at sea like a ridge of opalescent domes suspended in mid-heaven.

Vancouver was gliding into the Straits of Fuca when the slender colors of a far ship floated above the blue horizon outward bound. Another wave-roll, and the flag was seen to be above full-blown sails and a square-hulled, trim little trader of America. At six in the morning of April 29, the American saluted with a {269} cannon-shot. Vancouver answered with a charge from his decks, rightly guessing this was Robert Gray on the *Columbia.*

The Columbia in a Squall.

[Illustration: The *Columbia* in a Squall.]

Puget and Menzies were sent to inquire about Gray's cruise. They brought back word that Gray had been fifty miles up the Straits of Fuca; and—most astounding to Vancouver's ambitions—that the American had been off the mouth of a river south of the straits at 46 degrees 10 minutes, where the tide prevented entrance for nine days. "The river Mr. Gray mentioned," says Vancouver, "should be south of Cape Disappointment. This we passed on the forenoon of the 27th; and if any inlet or river be found, it must be a {270} very intricate one, inaccessible ... owing to reefs and broken water.... I was thoroughly convinced, as were most persons on board, that we could not possibly have passed any cape ... from Mendocino to Classet (Flattery)."

Keen to prove that no Northeast Passage existed by way of the Straits of Fuca, Vancouver headed inland, close to the south shore, where craggy heights offered some guidance through the labyrinth of islands and fog. Eight miles inside the straits he anchored for the night. The next morning the sun rose over one of the fairest scenes of the Pacific coast—an arm of the sea placid as a lake, gemmed by countless craggy islands. On the land side were the forested valleys rolling in to the purple folds of the mountains; and beyond, eastward, dazzling as a huge shield of fire in the sunrise, a white mass whiter than the whitest clouds, swimming aerially in mid-heaven. Lieutenant Baker was the first to catch a glimpse of the vision for which every western traveller now watches, the famous peak seen by land or sea for hundreds of miles, the playground of the jagged green lightnings on the hot summer nights; and the peak was named after him.— Mount Baker.

For the first time in history white men's boats plied the waters of the great inland sea now variously known as Admiralty Inlet, Puget Sound, Hood Canal. There must be no myth of a Northeast Passage left lurking in any of the many inlets of this spider-shaped sea. {271} Vancouver, Menzies, Puget, and Johnstone set out in the small boats to penetrate every trace of water passage. Instead of leading northeast, the tangled maze of forest-hidden channels meandered southward. Savages swarmed over the water, paddling round and round the white men, for all the world like birds of prey circling for a chance to swoop at the first unguarded moment. Tying trinkets to pieces of wood, Puget let the gifts float back as peace-offerings to woo good will. The effect was what softness always is to an Indian spoiling for a fight, an incentive to boldness. When Puget landed for noon meal, a score of redskins lined up ashore and began stringing their bows for action. Puget drew a line along the sand with his cutlass and signalled the warriors to keep back. They scrambled out of his reach with a great clatter. It only needed some fellow bolder than the rest to push across the line, and massacre would begin. Puget did not wait. By way of putting the fear of the Lord and respect for the white man in the heart of the Indian, he trained the swivel of the small boat landward, and fired in midair. The result was instant. Weapons were dropped. On Monday, midday, June 4, Vancouver and Broughton landed at Point Possession. Officers drew up in line. The English flag was unfurled, a royal salute fired, and possession taken of all the coast of New Albion from latitude 39 to the Straits of Fuca, which Vancouver named Gulf of Georgia. Just a month before, Gray, the American, had preceded this act of {272} possession by a similar ceremony for the United States on the banks of the Columbia.

The sum total of Vancouver's work so far had been the exploration of Puget Sound, which is to the West what the Gulf of St. Lawrence is to the East. For Puget Sound and its allied waters he had done exactly what Carrier accomplished for the Atlantic side of America. His next step was to learn if the Straits of Fuca leading northward penetrated America and came out on the Atlantic side. That is what the old Greek pilot in the service of New Spain, Juan de Fuca, had said some few years after Drake and Cavendish had been out on the coast of California.

Though Vancouver explored the Pacific coast more thoroughly than all the other navigators who had preceded him,—so thoroughly, indeed, that nothing was left to be done by the explorers who came after him, and modern surveys have been unable to improve upon his charts,—it seemed his ill-luck to miss by just a hair's breadth the prizes he coveted. He had missed the discovery of the Columbia. He was now to miss the second largest river of the Northwest, the Fraser. He had hoped to be the first to round the Straits of Fuca, disproving the assumption that they led to the Atlantic; and he came on the spot only to learn that the two English traders, Meares and Barclay, the two Americans, Kendrick and Gray, and two Spaniards, Don Galiano and Don Valdes, had already proved {273} practically that this part of the coast was a large island, and the Straits of Fuca an arm of the Pacific Ocean.

Fifty Indians, in the long dugouts, of grotesquely carved prows and gaudy paint common among Pacific tribes, escorted Vancouver's boats northward the second week in June through the labyrinthine passageways of cypress-grown islets to Burrard Inlet. To Peter Puget was assigned the work of coasting the mainland side and tracing every inlet to its head waters. Johnstone went ahead in a small boat to reconnoitre the way out of the Pacific. On both sides the shores now rose in beetling precipice and steep mountains, down which foamed cataracts setting the echo of myriad bells tinkling through the wilds. The sea was tinged with milky sediment; but fog hung thick as a blanket; and Vancouver passed on north without seeing Fraser River. A little farther on, toward the end of June, he was astonished to meet a Spanish brig and schooner exploring the straits. Don Galiano and Don Valdes told him of the Fraser, which he had missed, and how the Straits of Fuca led out to the North Pacific. They had also been off Puget Sound, but had not gone inland, and brought Vancouver word that Don Quadra, the Spanish emissary, sent to restore to England the fort from which Meares, the trader, had been ousted, had arrived at Nootka on the other side of the island, and was waiting. The explorers all proceeded up the straits together; but the little Spanish crafts were unable {274} to keep abreast of the big English vessels, so with a friendly cheer from both sides, the English went on alone.

Strange Indian villages lined the beetling heights of the straits. The houses, square built and of log slabs, row on row, like the streets of the white man, were situated high on isolated rocks, inaccessible to approach except by narrow planking forming a causeway from rock walls across the sea to the branches of a tree. In other places rope ladders formed the only path to the aerial dwellings, or the zigzag trail up the steep face of a rock down which defenders could hurl stones. Howe's Sound, Jervis Canal, Bute Inlet, were passed; {275} and in July Johnstone came back with news he had found a narrow channel out to the Pacific.

The Discovery on the Rocks.

[Illustration: The Discovery on the Rocks.]

The straits narrowed to less than half a mile with such a terrific tide wash that on Sunday, July 29, the ships failed to answer to the helm and waves seventeen feet high dashed over decks. Progress was made by hauling the boats alongshore with ropes braced round trees. By the first of August a dense fog swept in from the sea. The *Discovery* crashed on a sunken rock, heeling over till her sails were within three inches of water. Ballast was thrown overboard, and the next tide-rush lifted her. By August 19 Vancouver had proved—if any doubt remained—that no Northeast Passage was to be found by way of the Straits of Fuca.[1] Then, veering out to sea at midnight through squalls {276} of rain, he steered to Nootka for the conference with Spain.

Vancouver came to Nootka on the 28th of August. Nootka was the grand rallying place of fur traders on the Pacific. It was a triangular sound extending into the shores of Vancouver Island. On an island at the mouth of the sound the Spaniards had built their fort. This part of the bay was known as Friendly Cove. To the north was Snug Cove, where Cook had anchored; to the south the roadstead of the fur traders. Mountains rose from the water-line; and on a terrace of hills above the Spanish fort was the native village of Maquinna, the Indian chief.

{277} Here, then, came Vancouver, met at the harbor mouth by a Spanish officer with pilot to conduct the *Discovery* to the Spanish fort of Nootka. The *Chatham*, the *Daedalus*, Vancouver's store ship, two or three English fur-trading ships, Spanish frigates bristling with cannon, were already at anchor; and the bright Spanish pennant, red and yellow, waved to the wind above the cannon-mounted, palisaded log fort of Nootka.

Indian Settlement at Nootka.

[Illustration: Indian Settlement at Nootka.]

Donning regimentals, Lieutenant Puget marched solemnly up to the fort to inform Don Juan de la Bodega y Quadra, representative of Spain, that Captain George Vancouver, representative of England, had arrived at Nootka to await the pleasure of New Spain's commander. It was New Spain's pleasure to receive England's salute; and Vancouver's guns roared out a volley of thirteen shots to the amaze of two thousand or more savages watching from the shores. Formally accompanied by his officers, Vancouver then paid his respects to New Spain. Don Quadra returned the compliment by breakfasting next morning on board the

Discovery, while his frigates in turn saluted England by a volley of thirteen guns. In all this solemn parade of formality, Maquinna, lord of the wild domain, began to wonder what part he was to play, and ventured to board the *Discovery*, clad in a garb of nature, to join the breakfast of the leaders; when he was summarily cuffed overboard by the guard, who failed to recognize the Indian's quality. Don Quadra then gave a grand dinner to the English, to which the irate Maquinna {278} was invited. Five courses the dinner had, with royal salutes setting the echoes rolling in the hills. Seventeen guns were fired to the success of Vancouver's explorations. Toasts were drunk, foaming toasts to glory, and the navigators of the Pacific, and Maquinna, grand chief of the Nootkas, who responded by rising in his place, glass in hand, to express regret that Spain should withdraw from the North Pacific. It was then the brilliant thought flashed on Don Quadra to win the friendship of the Indians for all the white traders on the Pacific coast through a ceremonious visit by Vancouver and himself to Maquinna's home village, twenty miles up the sound.

Cutter and yawl left Friendly Cove at eight in the morning of September 4, coming to Maquinna's home village at two in the afternoon. Don Quadra supplied the dinner, served in style by his own Spanish lackeys; and the gallant Spaniard led Maquinna's only daughter to the seat at the head of the spread, where the young squaw did the honors with all the hauteur of the Indian race. Maquinna then entertained his visitors with a sham battle of painted warriors, followed by a mask dance. Not to be outdone, the whites struck up fife and drum, and gave a wild display of Spanish fandangoes and Scotch reels. In honor of the day's outing, it was decided to name the large island which Vancouver had almost circumnavigated, Quadra and Vancouver.

When Maquinna returned this visit, there were fireworks, and more toasts, and more salutes. All this {279} was very pleasant; but it was not business. Then Vancouver requested Don Quadra to ratify the international agreement between England and Spain; but there proved to be a wide difference of opinion as to what that agreement meant. Vancouver held that it entailed the surrender of Spain's sovereignty from San Francisco northward. Don Quadra maintained that it only surrendered Spanish rights north of Juan de Fuca, leaving the northwest coast free to all nations for trade. With Vancouver it was all or nothing. Don Quadra then suggested that letters be sent to Spain and England for more specific instructions. For this purpose Lieutenant Broughton was to be despatched overland across Mexico to Europe. It was at this stage that Robert Gray came down from the north on the damaged *Columbia*, to receive assistance from Quadra. Within three weeks Gray had sailed for Boston, Don Quadra for New Spain, and Vancouver to the south, to examine that Columbia River of Gray's before proceeding to winter on the Sandwich Islands.

The three English ships hauled out of Nootka in the middle of October, steering for that new river of Gray's, of which Vancouver had expressed such doubt. The foaming reefs of Cape Disappointment were sighted and the north entrance seen just as Gray had described it. The *Chatham* rode safely inside the heavy cross swell, though her small boat smashed to chips among the breakers; but on Sunday, October {280} 21, such mountainous seas were running that Vancouver dared not risk his big ship, the *Discovery*, across the bar. Broughton was intrusted to examine the *Columbia* before setting out to England for fresh orders.

The *Chatham* had anchored just inside Cape Disappointment on the north, then passed south to Cape Adams, using Gray's chart as guide. Seven miles up the north coast, a deep bay was named after Gray. Nine or ten Indian dugouts with one hundred and fifty warriors now escorted Broughton's rowboat upstream. The lofty peak ahead covered with snow was named Mt. Hood. For seven days Broughton followed the river till his provision ran out, and the old Indian chief with him explained by the signs of pointing in the direction of the sunrise and letting water trickle through his fingers that water-falls ahead would stop passage. Somehow, Broughton seemed to think because Gray, a private trader, had not been clad in the gold-braid regimentals of authority, his act of discovery was void; for Broughton landed, and with the old chief assisting at the ceremony by drinking healths, took possession of all the region for England, "having" as the record of the trip explains, "every reason to believe that the subjects of no other civilized nation or state had ever entered this river before; in this opinion he was confirmed by Mr. Gray's sketch, in which it does not appear that Mr. Gray either saw or was ever within five leagues of the entrance."

{281} Any comment on this proceeding is superfluous. It was evidently in the hope that the achievement of Gray—an unassuming fur trader, backed by nothing but his own dauntless courage—would be forgotten, which it certainly was for fifty years by nearly all Americans. Three days later, on November 3, Broughton was back down-stream at the *Chatham*, noting the deserted Indian village of Chinook as he passed to the harbor mouth. On November 6, in heavy rain, the ship stood out for sea, passing the *Jenny* of Bristol, imprisoned inside the cape by surf. Broughton landed to reconnoitre the passage out. The wind calmed next day, and a breach was descried through the surf. The little trading ship led the way, Broughton following, hard put to keep the *Chatham* headed for the sea, breakers rolling over her from stem to stern, snapping the tow-rope of the launch and washing a sailor overboard; and we cannot but have a higher respect for Gray's feat, knowing the difficulties that Broughton weathered.

Meanwhile Vancouver on the *Discovery* had coasted on down from the mouth of the Columbia to Drake's Bay, just outside the Golden Gate of San Francisco, where the bold English pirate had anchored in 1579. By nightfall of November 14 he was inside the spacious harbor of San Francisco. Two men on horseback rode out from the Spanish settlement, a mile back from the water front, firing muskets as a salute to Vancouver. The next morning, a Spanish friar and {282} ensign came aboard the *Discovery* for breakfast, pointing out to Vancouver the best anchorage for both wood and water. While the sailors went shooting quail on the hills, or amused themselves watching the Indians floating over the harbor on rafts made of dry rushes and grass, the good Spanish padre conducted Vancouver ashore to the presidio, or house of the commandant, back from the landing on a little knoll surrounded by hills. The fort was a square area of adobe walls fourteen feet high and five deep, the outer beams filled in between with a plaster of solid mortar, houses and walls whitewashed from lime made of sea-shells. A small brass cannon gathered rust above one dilapidated carriage, and another old gun was mounted by being lashed to a rotten log. A single gate led into the fort, which was inhabited by the commandant, the guard of thirty-five soldiers, and their families. The windows of the houses were very small and without glass, the commandant's house being a rude structure thirty by fourteen feet, whitewashed inside and out, the floor sand and rushes, the furnishings of the roughest handicraft. The mission proper was three miles from the fort, with a guard of five soldiers and a corporal. Such was the beginning of the largest city on the Pacific coast to-day.

Broughton was now sent overland to England for instructions about the transfer of Nootka. Puget became commander of the *Chatham*. The store ship *Daedalus* was sent to the South Seas, and touching only {283} at Monterey, Vancouver sailed to winter in the Sandwich Islands. Here two duties awaited the explorer, which he carried out in a way that left a streak both of glory and of shame across his escutcheon. The Sandwich Islands had become the halfway house of the Pacific for the fur traders. How fur traders—riff-raff adventurers from earth's ends beyond the reach of law—may have acted among these simple people may be guessed from the conduct of Cook's crews; and Cook was a strict disciplinarian. Those who sow to the wind, need not be surprised if they reap the whirlwind. White men, welcomed by these Indians as gods, repaid the native hospitality by impressing natives as crews to a northern climate where the transition from semitropics meant almost certain death. For a fur trader to slip into Hawaii, entice women aboard, then scud off to America where the victims might rot unburied for all the traders cared—was considered a joke. How the joke caused Captain Cook's death the world knows; and the joke was becoming a little frequent, a little bold, a little too grim for the white traders' sense of security. The Sandwich Islanders had actually formed the plot of capturing every vessel that came into their harbors and holding the crews for extortionate ransom. How many white men were victims of this plot—to die by the assassin's knife or waiting for the ransom that never came—is not a part of this record. It was becoming a common thing to find white men living in a state of quasi-slavery among the {284} islanders, each white held as hostage for the security of the others not escaping. Within three years three ships had been attacked, one Spanish, one American, one English—the store ship *Daedalus* on the way out to Nootka with supplies for Vancouver. Two officers, Hergest and Gooch of the *Daedalus*, had been seized, stripped naked, forced at the point of spears up a hill to the native village, and cut to pieces. Vancouver determined to put a stop to such attacks. Arriving at the islands, he trained his cannon ashore, demanded that the murderers of the *Daedalus's* officers be surrendered, tried the culprits with all the solemnity and speed of English court-martial, sentenced them to death, had them tied up to the mast poles and executed. That is the blot against Vancouver; for the islanders had put up a trick. The real murderers had been leading chiefs. Not wishing to surrender these, the islanders had given Vancouver poor slaves quite guiltless of the crime.

In contrast to this wrong-headed demonstration of justice was Vancouver's other act. At Nootka he had found among the traders two young Hawaiian girls not more than fifteen and nineteen years of age, whom some blackguard trader had forcibly carried off. The most of great voyagers would not have soiled their gloves interfering with such a case. Cook had winked at such crimes. Drake, two hundred years before, had laughed. The Russians outdid either Drake or Cook. They dumped the victims overboard where the {285} sea told no tales. Vancouver might have been strict enough disciplinarian to execute the wrong men by way of a lesson; but he was consistent in his strictness. Round these two friendless savages he wrapped all the chivalry and the might of the English flag.

He received them on board the *Discovery*, treated them as he might have treated his own sisters, prevented the possibility of insult from the common sailors by having them at his own table on the ship, taught them the customs of Europeans toward women and the reasons for those customs, so that the young girls presently had the respect and friendship of every sailor on board the *Discovery*. In New Spain he had obtained clothing and delicacies for them that white women have; and in the Sandwich Islands took precautions against their death at the hands of Hawaiians for having been on the ship with strange men, by securing from the Sandwich Island chief the promise of his protection for them and the gifts of a home inside the royal enclosure.

April of 1793 saw Vancouver back again on the west coast of America. In results this year's exploring was largely negative; but the object of Vancouver's life was a negative one—to prove there was no passage between Pacific and Atlantic. He had missed the Columbia the previous year by standing off the coast north of Mendocino. So this year, he again plied up the same shore to Nootka. No fresh instructions had {286} come from England or Spain to Nootka; and Vancouver took up the trail of the sea where he had stopped the year before, carrying forward survey of island and mainland from Vancouver Island northward to the modern Sitka or Norfolk Sound. Gray, the American, had been attacked by Indians here the year before; and Vancouver did not escape the hostility of these notoriously treacherous tribes. Up Behm Canal the ships were visited by warriors wearing death-masks, who refused everything in exchange for their sea-otter except firearms. The canal here narrowed to a dark canyon overhung by beetling cliffs. Four large war canoes manned by several hundred savages daubed with war paint succeeded in surrounding the small launch, and while half the warriors held the boat to prevent it escaping, the rest had rifled it of everything they could take, from belaying-pins and sail rope to firearms, before Vancouver lost patience and gave orders to fire. At the shot the Indians were over decks and into the sea like water-rats, while forces ambushed on land began rolling rocks and stones down the precipices. One gains some idea of Vancouver's thoroughness by his work up Portland Canal, which was to become famous a hundred years later as the scene of boundary disputes. Here, so determined was he to prove none of the passages led to the Atlantic that his small boat actually cruised seven hundred miles without going more than sixty miles from ocean front. By October of 1793 Vancouver had demolished the myth of {287} a possible passage between New Spain and Russian America; for he had examined every inlet from San Francisco to what is now Sitka. While the results were negative to himself, far different were they to Russia. It was Vancouver's voyage northward that stirred the Russians up to move southward. In a word, if Vancouver had not gone up as far as Norfolk Sound or Sitka, the Russian fur traders would have drowsed on with Kadiak as headquarters, and Canada to-day might have included the entire gold-fields of Alaska.

Again Vancouver wintered in the Sandwich Islands. In the year 1794 he changed the direction of his exploring. Instead of beginning at New Spain and working north, he began at Russian America and worked south. Kadiak and Cook's Inlet were regarded as the eastern bounds of Russian settlement at this time, though the hunting brigades of the Russians scoured far and wide; so Vancouver began his survey eastward at Cook's Inlet. Terrific floods of ice banged the ships' bows as they plied up Cook's Inlet; and the pistol-shot reports of the vast icebergs breaking from the walls of the solid glacier coast forewarned danger; but Vancouver was not to be deterred. Again the dogged ill-luck of always coming in second for the prize he coveted marked each stage of his trip. Russian forts were seen on Cook's Inlet, Russian settlements on Prince William Sound, Russian flotillas of nine hundred {288} Aleutian hunters steering by instinct like the gulls spreading over the sea as far east as Bering Bay, or where the coast of Alaska dips southward. Everywhere he heard the language of Russia, everywhere saw that Russia regarded his explorations with jealousy as intrusion; everywhere observed that Russian and savage had come to an understanding and now lived as friends, if not brothers. Twice Baranof, the little Czar of the North, sent word for Vancouver to await a conference; but Vancouver was not keen to meet the little Russian potentate. One row at a time was enough; and the quarrel with Spain was still unsettled. The waters of to-day plied by the craft of gold seekers, Bering Bay, Lynn Canal, named after his birthplace, were now so thoroughly surveyed by Vancouver that his charts may still be used.

Reindeer Herd in Siberia.

[Illustration: Reindeer Herd in Siberia.]

Only once did the maze of waterways seem to promise a northeast passage. It was up Lynn Canal, where so many gold seekers have rushed to have their hopes dashed, like Vancouver. Two officers had gone up the channel in a small boat to see if any opening led to the Atlantic. Boisterous weather and tremendous tide had lashed the sea to foam. The long daylight was so delusive that the men did not realize it was nearly midnight. At ten o'clock they had rowed ashore, to rest from their fight with wave and wind, when armed Indians suddenly rushed down to the water's edge in battle array, spears couched. The exhausted rowers bent to the oars all night. At one place in their {289} retreat to open sea, the fog lifted to reveal the passage between precipices only a few feet wide with warriors' canoes on every side. A crash of musketry drove the assailants off. Two or three men kept guard with pointed muskets, while the oarsmen pulled through a rolling cross swell back to the protection of the big ships outside.

On August 19, as the ships drove south to Norfolk or Sitka Sound, the men suddenly recognized headlands where they had cruised the summer before. For a second they scarcely realized. Then they knew that their explorations from Alaska southward had come to the meeting place of their voyage from New Spain northward. Just a little more than fifty years from Bering's discoveries, the exploration of the northwest coast of America had been completed. Some one emitted an incoherent shout that the work was finished! The cheer was caught up by every man on board. Some one else recalled that it had been April when they set out on the fool-quest of the Northeast Passage; and a true April's fool the quest had proved! Then flags were run up; the wine casks brought out, the marines drawn up in line, and three such volleys of joy fired as those sailors alone could feel. For four years they had followed the foolish quest of the learned world's error. That night Vancouver gave a gala dinner to his crews. They deserved it. Their four years' cruise marked the close of the most heroic epoch on the Pacific coast. Vancouver had accomplished his life-work—there {290} was no northeast passage through the west coast of America.[2]

[1] The legend of Juan de Fuca became current about 1592, as issued in *Samuel Purchas' Pilgrims* in 1625, Vol. III: "A note made by Michael Lok, the elder, touching the strait of sea commonly called *Fretum Anian* in the South Sea through the North-West Passage of Meta Incognita." Lok met in Venice, in April, 1596, an old man called Juan de Fuca, a Greek mariner and pilot, of the crew of the galleon *Santa Anna* taken by Cavendish near southern California in 1587. The pilot narrated after his return to Mexico, he was sent by the viceroy with three vessels to discover the Strait of Anian. This expedition failing, he was again sent in 1592, with a small caravel in which "he followed the course west and northwest to latitude 47 north, there finding a broad inlet between 47 and 48, he entered, sailing therein more than twenty days … and found very much broader sea than was at the said entrance … a great island with a high pinnacle.... Being come into the North Sea … he returned to Acapulco." According to the story the old pilot tried to find his way to England in the hope of the Queen recouping him for goods taken by Cavendish, and furnishing him with a

ship to essay the Northeast Passage again. The old man died before Raleigh and other Englishmen could forward money for him to come to England. Whether the story is purely a sailor's yarn, or the pilot really entered the straits named after him, and losing his bearings when he came out in the Pacific imagined he was on the Atlantic, is a dispute among savants.

[2] The data of Vancouver's voyage come chiefly, of course, from the volume by himself, issued after his death, *Voyage of Discovery to the Pacific Ocean*, London, 1798. Supplementary data may be found in the records of predecessors and contemporaries like Meares's *Voyages*, London, 1790, Portlock's *Voyage*, London, 1789; Dixon's *Voyage*, London, 1789, and others, from whom nearly all modern writers, like Greenhow, Hubert Howe Bancroft, draw their information. The reports of Dr. Davidson in his Coast and Survey work, and his *Alaska Boundary*, identify many of Vancouver's landfalls, and illustrate the tremendous difficulties overcome in local topography. It is hardly necessary to refer to Begg and Mayne, and other purely local sketches of British Columbian coast lines; as Begg's *History* simply draws from the old voyages. Of modern works, Dr. Davidson's Survey works, and the official reports of the Canadian Geological Survey (Dawson), are the only ones that add any facts to what Vancouver has recorded.

{291}

PART III

EXPLORATION GIVES PLACE TO FUR TRADE—THE EXPLOITATION OF THE PACIFIC COAST UNDER THE RUSSIAN AMERICAN FUR COMPANY, AND THE RENOWNED LEADER BARANOF

{293}

CHAPTER XI
1579-1867
THE RUSSIAN AMERICAN FUR COMPANY

The Pursuit of the Sable leads Cossacks across Siberia, of the Sea-Otter, across the Pacific as far South as California—Caravans of Four Thousand Horses on the Long Trail Seven Thousand Miles across Europe and Asia—Banditti of the Sea—The Union of All Traders in One Monopoly—Siege and Slaughter of Sitka—How Monroe Doctrine grew out of Russian Fur Trade—Aims of Russia to dominate North Pacific

"*Sea Voyagers of the Northern Ocean*" they styled themselves, the Cossack banditti—robber knights, pirates, plunderers—who pursued the little sable across Europe and Asia eastward, just as the French *coureurs des bois* followed the beaver across America westward. And these two great tides of adventurers—the French voyager, threading the labyrinthine waterways of American wilds westward; the Russian voyager exchanging his reindeer sled and desert caravans for crazy rafts of green timbers to cruise across the Pacific eastward—were directed both to the same region, animated by the same impulse, the capture of the Pacific coast of America.

{294}

Raised Reindeer Sledges.

[Illustration: Raised Reindeer Sledges.]

The tide of adventure set eastward across Siberia at the very time (1579) Francis Drake, the English freebooter, was sacking the ports of New Spain on his way to California. Yermac, robber knight and leader of a thousand Cossack banditti, had long levied tribute of loot on the caravans bound from Russia to Persia. Then came the avenging army of the Czar. Yermac fled to Siberia, wrested the country from the Tartars, and obtained forgiveness from the Czar by laying a new realm at his feet. But these Cossack plunderers did not stop with Siberia. Northward were the ivory tusks of the frozen tundras. Eastward were precious furs of the snow-padded forests and mountains toward Kamchatka. For both ivory and furs the smugglers of the Chinese borderlands would pay a price. On pretence of collecting one-tenth tribute for the Czar, forward pressed the Cossacks; now on horseback,—wild {295} brutes got in trade from Tartars,—now behind reindeer teams through snowy forests where the spreading hoofs carried over drifts; now on rude-planked rafts hewn from green firs on the banks of Siberian rivers; on and on pushed the plunderers till the Arctic rolled before them on the north, and the Pacific on the east.[1] Nor did the seas of these strange shores bar the Cossacks. Long before Peter the Great had sent Vitus Bering to America in 1741, Russian voyagers had launched out east and north with a daredevil recklessness that would have done honor to prehistoric man. That part of their adventures is a record that exceeds the wildest darings of fiction. Their boats were called *kotches*. They were some sixty feet long, flat bottomed, planked with green timber. Not a nail was used. Where were nails to come from six thousand miles across the frozen tundras? Indeed, iron was so scarce that at a later day when ships with nails ventured on {296} these seas natives were detected diving below to pull the nails from the timbers with their teeth. Instead of nails, the Cossack used reindeer thongs to bind the planking together. Instead of tar, moss and clay and the tallow of sea animals calked the seams. Needless to say, there was neither canvas nor rope. Reindeer thongs supplied the cordage, reindeer hides the sails. On such rickety craft, "with the help of God and a little powder," the Russian voyagers hoisted sail and put to sea. On just such vessels did Deshneff and Staduchin attempt to round Asia from the Arctic into Bering Sea (1647-1650).

To be sure, the first bang of the ice-floes against the prow of these rickety boats knocked them into kindling-wood. Two-thirds of the Cossack voyagers were lost every year; and often all news that came of the crew was a mast pole washed in by the tide with a dead man lashed to the crosstrees. Small store of fresh water could be carried. Pine needles were the only antidote for scurvy; and many a time the boat came tumbling back to the home port, not a man well enough to stand before the mast.

Always it is what lies just beyond that lures. It is the unknown that beckons like the arms of the old sea sirens. Groping through the mists that hang like a shroud over these northern seas, hoar frosts clinging to masts and decks till the boat might have been some ghost ship in a fog world, the Cossack plunderers {297} sometimes caught glimpses far ahead—twenty, thirty, forty miles eastward—of a black line along the sea. Was it land or fog, ice or deep water? And when the wind blew from the east, strange land birds alighted on the yard-arms. Dead whales with the harpoons of strange hunters washed past the ship; and driftwood of a kind that did not grow in Asia tossed up on the tide wrack. It was the word brought back by these free-lances of the sea that induced Peter the Great to send Vitus Bering on a voyage of discovery to the west coast of America; and when the castaways of Bering's wreck returned with a new fur that was neither beaver nor otter, but larger than either and of a finer sheen than sable, selling the pelts to Chinese merchants for what would be from one hundred and fifty to two hundred dollars each in modern money, the effect was the same as the discovery of a gold mine. The new fur was the sea-otter, as peculiar to the Pacific as the seal and destined to lead the Cossacks on a century's wild hunt from Alaska to California. Cossacks, Siberian merchants, exiled criminals, banded together in as wild a stampede to the west coast of

America as ever a gold mine caused among civilized men of a later day.

The little *kotches* that used to cruise out from Siberian rivers no longer served. Siberian merchants advanced the capital for the building of large sloops. Cargo of trinkets for trade with American Indians was supplied in the same way. What would be fifty thousand dollars in modern money, it took to build and {298} equip one of these sloops; but a cargo of sea-otter was to be had for the taking—barring storms that yearly engulfed two-thirds of the hunters, and hostile Indians that twice wiped Russian settlements from the coast of America —and if these pelts sold for one hundred and fifty dollars each, the returns were ample to compensate risk and outlay. Provisions, cordage, iron, ammunition, firearms, all had to be brought from St. Petersburg, seven thousand miles to the Pacific coast. From St. Petersburg to Moscow, Kasan, the Tartar desert and Siberia, pack horses were used. It was a common thing for caravans of four or even five thousand pack horses employed by the Russian fur traders of America to file into Irkutsk of a night. At the head waters of the Lena, rafts and flatboats, similar to the old Mackinaw boats of American fur traders on the Missouri, were built and the cargo floated down to Yakutsk, the great rendezvous of Siberian fur traders. Here exiles acting as packers and Cossacks as overseers usually went on a wild ten days' spree. From Yakutsk pack horses, dog trains, and reindeer teams were employed for the remaining thousand miles to the Pacific; and this was the hardest part of the journey. Mountains higher than the Rockies had to be traversed. Mountain torrents tempestuous with the spring thaw had to be forded —ice cold and to the armpits of the drivers; and in winter time, the packs of timber wolves following on the heels of the cavalcade could only be driven off by the hounds kept to course down grouse and hare {299} for the evening meal. If an exile forced to act as transport packer fell behind, that was the last of him. The Russian fur traders of America never paused in their plans for a life more or less. Ordinarily it took three years for goods sent from St. Petersburg to reach the Pacific; and this was only a beginning of the hardships. The Pacific had to be crossed, and a coast lined with reefs like a ploughed field traversed for two thousand miles among Indians notorious for their treachery.

The vessels were usually crammed with traps and firearms and trinkets to the water-line. The crews of forty, or seventy, or one hundred were relegated to vermin-infested hammocks above decks, with short rations of rye bread and salt fish, and such scant supply of fresh water that scurvy invariably ravaged the ship whenever foul weather lengthened the passage. Having equipped the vessel, the Siberian merchants passed over the management to the Cossacks, whose pretence of conquering new realms and collecting tribute for the Czar was only another excuse for the same plunder in gathering sea-otter as their predecessors had practised in hunting the sable. Landsmen among Siberian exiles were enlisted as crew of their own free will at first, but afterward, when the horrors of wreck and scurvy and massacre became known, both exiles and Indians were impressed by force as fur hunters for the Cossacks. If the voyage were successful, half the {300} proceeds went to the outfitter, the remaining half to Cossacks and crew.

The boats usually sailed in the fall, and wintered on Bering Island. Here stores of salted meat, sea-lion and sea-cow, were laid up, and the following spring the ship steered for the Aleutians, or the main coast of Alaska, or the archipelago round the modern Sitka. Sloops were anchored offshore fully armed for refuge in case of attack. Huts were then constructed of driftwood on land. Toward the east and south, where the Indians were treacherous and made doubly so by the rum and firearms of rival traders, palisades were thrown up round the fort, a sort of balcony erected inside with brass cannon mounted where a sentry paraded day and night, ringing a bell every hour in proof that he was not asleep. Westward toward the Aleutians, where driftwood was scarce, the Russians built their forts in one of two places: either a sandy spit where the sea protected them on three sides, as at Captain Harbor, Oonalaska, and St. Paul, Kadiak, or on a high, rocky eminence only approachable by a zigzag path at the top of which stood cannon and sentry, as at Cook's Inlet. Chapel and barracks for the hunters might be outside the palisade; but the main house was inside, a single story with thatch roof, a door at one end, a rough table at the other. Sleeping berths with fur bedding were on the side walls, and every other available piece of wall space bristled with daggers and firearms ready {301} for use. If the house was a double-decker, as Baranof Castle at Sitka, powder was stored in the cellar. Counting-rooms, mess room, and fur stores occupied the first floor. Sleeping quarters were upstairs, and, above all, a powerful light hung in the cupola, to guide ships into port at night.

But these arrangements concerned only the Cossack officers of the early era, or the governors like Baranof, of a later day. The rank and file of the crews were off on the hunting-grounds with the Indians; and the hunting-grounds of the sea-otter were the storm-beaten kelp beds of the rockiest coast in the world. Going out in parties of five or six, the *promyshleniki*, as the hunters were called, promised implicit obedience to their foreman. Store of venison would be taken in a preliminary hunt. Indian women and children would be left at the Russian fort as hostages of good conduct, and at the head of as many as four, five hundred, a thousand Aleut Indian hunters who had been bludgeoned, impressed, bribed by the promise of firearms to hunt for the Cossacks, six Russians would set out to coast a tempestuous sea for a thousand miles in frail boats made of parchment stretched on whalebone. Sometimes a counter-tide would sweep a whole flotilla out to sea, when never a man of the hunting crew would be heard of more. Sometimes, when the hunters were daring a gale, riding in on the back of a storm to catch the sea-otter driven ashore to the kelp beds for a rest, the back-wash of a billow, or a sudden {302} hurricane of wind raising mountain seas, would crash down on the brigade. When the spray cleared, the few panic-stricken survivors were washing ashore too exhausted to be conscious that half their comrades had gone under. Absurd as it seems that these plunderers of the deep always held prayers before going off on a hunt—is it any wonder they prayed? It was in such brigades that the Russian hunters cruised the west coast of America from Bering Sea to the Gulf of California, and the whole northwest coast of America is punctuated with saints' names from the Russian calendar; for, like Drake's freebooters, they had need to pray.

Fur companies world over have run the same course. No sooner has game become scarce on the hunting-grounds, than rivals begin the merry game of slitting one another's throats, or instigating savages to do the butchering for them. That was the record of the Hudson's Bay Company and Nor'westers in Canada, and the Rocky Mountain men and American Company on the Missouri. Four years after Bering's crew had brought back word of the sea-otter in 1742, there were seventy-seven different private Russian concerns hunting sea-otter off the islands of Alaska. Fifty years later, after Cook, the English navigator, had spread authentic news of the wealth in furs to be had on the west coast of America, there were sixty different fur companies on the Pacific coast carrying {303} almost as many different flags. John Jacob Astor's ships had come round the Horn from New York and, sailing right into the Russian hunting-grounds, were endeavoring to make arrangements to furnish supplies to the Russians in exchange for cargoes of the fur-seals, whose rookeries had been discovered about the time sea-otter began to be scarce. Kendrick, Gray, Ingraham, Coolidge, a dozen Boston men were threading the shadowy, forested waterways between New Spain and Alaska.[2] Ships from Spain, from France, from London, from

[Illustration: John Jacob Astor.]

This was Gregory Ivanovich Shelikoff, a fur trader {304} of Siberia, accompanied to America and seconded by his wife, Natalie, who succeeded in carrying out many of his plans after his death. Shelikoff owned shares in two of the principal Russian companies. When he came to America accompanied by his wife, Baranof, another trader, and two hundred men in 1784, the Russian headquarters were still at Oonalaska in the Aleutians. Only desultory expeditions had gone eastward. Foreign ships had already come among the Russian hunting-grounds of the north. These Shelikoff at once checkmated by moving Russian headquarters east to Three Saints, Kadiak. Savages warned him from the island, threatening death to the Aleut Indian hunters he had brought. Shelikoff's answer was a load of presents to the hostile messenger. That failing, he took advantage of an eclipse of the sun as a sign to the superstitious Indians that the coming of the Russians was noted and blessed of Heaven. The unconvinced Kadiak savages responded by ambushing the first Russians to leave camp, and showering arrows on the Russian boats. Shelikoff gathered up his men, sallied forth, whipped the Indians off their feet, took four hundred prisoners, treated them well, and so won the friendship of the islanders. From the new quarters hunters were despatched eastward under Baranof and others as far as what is now Sitka. These yearly came back with cargoes of sea-otter worth two hundred thousand dollars. Shelikoff at once saw that if the Russian traders were to hold their own against {305} the foreign adventurers of all nations flocking to the Pacific, headquarters must be moved still farther eastward, and the prestige of the Russian government invoked to exclude foreigners. There were, in fact, no limits to the far-sighted ambitions of the man. Ships were to be despatched to California setting up signs of Russian possession. Forts in Hawaii could be used as a mid-Pacific arsenal and halfway house for the Russian fleet that was to dominate the North Pacific. A second Siberia on the west coast of America, with limits eastward as vague as the Hudson's Bay Company's claims westward, was to be added to the domains of the Czar. Whether the idea of declaring the North Pacific a *closed sea* as Spain had declared the South Pacific a *closed sea* till Francis Drake opened it, originated in the brain of Shelikoff, or his successors, is immaterial. It was the aggrandizement of the Russian American Fur Company as planned by Shelikoff from 1784 to 1796, that led to the Russian government trying to exclude foreign traders from the North Pacific twenty-five years later, and which in turn led to the declaration of the famous Monroe Doctrine by the United States in 1823—

that the New World was no longer to be the happy hunting-ground of Old World nations bent on conquest and colonization.

Like many who dream greatly, Shelikoff did not live to see his plans carried out. He died in Irkutsk in 1795; but in St. Petersburg, when pressing upon {306} the government the necessity of uniting all the independent traders in one all-powerful company to be given exclusive monopoly on the west coast of America, he had met and allied himself with a young courtier, Nikolai Rezanoff. [3] When Shelikoff died, Rezanoff it was who obtained from the Czar in 1799 a charter for the Russian American Fur Company, giving it exclusive monopoly for hunting, trading, and exploring north of 55 degrees in the Pacific. Other companies were compelled either to withdraw or join. Royalty took shares in the venture. Shareholders of St. Petersburg were to direct affairs, and Baranof, the governor, resident in America, to have power of life and death, despotic as a czar. By 1800 the capital of Russian America had been moved down to the modern Sitka, called Archangel Michael in the trust of the Lord's anointed protecting these plunderers of the sea. Shelikoff's dreams were coming true. Russia was checkmating the advances of England and the United States and New Spain. Schemes were in the air with Baranof for the impressment of Siberian exiles as peasant farmers among the icebergs of Prince William Sound, for the remission of one-tenth tribute in furs from the Aleuts on condition of free service as hunters with the company, and for the employment of Astor's ships as purveyors of provisions to Sitka, when there fell a bolt {307} from the blue that well-nigh wiped Russian possession from the face of America.

It was a sleepy summer afternoon toward the end of June in 1802. Baranof had left a guard of twenty or thirty Russians at Sitka and, confident that all was well, had gone north to Kadiak. Aleut Indians, impressed as hunters, were about the fort, for the fiery Kolosh or Sitkans of this region would not bow the neck to Russian tyranny. Safe in the mountain fastnesses behind the fort, they refused to act as slaves. How they regarded this invasion of their hunting-ground by alien Indians—Indians acting as slaves—may be guessed.[4] Whether rival traders, deserters from an American ship, living with the Sitkan Indians, instigated the conspiracy cannot be known. I have before me letters written by a fur trader of a rival company at that time, declaring if a certain trader did not cease his methods, that "pills would be bought at Montreal with as good poison as pills from London;" and the sentiment of the writer gives a true idea of the code that prevailed among American fur traders.

The fort at that time occupied a narrow strip between a dense forest and the rocky water front a few miles north of the present site. Whether the renegade American sailors living in the forests with the Kolosh betrayed all the inner plans of the fort, or the squaws daily passing in and out with berries kept their {308} countrymen informed of Russian movements, the blow was struck when the whites were off guard. It was a holiday. Half the Russians were outside the palisades unarmed, fishing. The remaining fifteen men seem to have been upstairs about midday in the rooms of the commander, Medvednikoff. Suddenly the sleepy sentry parading the balcony noticed Michael, chief of the Kolosh, standing on the shore shouting at sixty canoes to land quickly. Simultaneously the patter of moccasined feet came from the dense forest to the rear—a thousand Kolosh warriors, every Indian armed and wearing the death-mask of battle. Before the astounded sentry could sound an alarm, such a hideous uproar of shouts arose as might have come from bedlam let loose. The Indian always imitates the cries of the wild beast when he fights—imitates or sets free the wild beast in his own nature. For a moment the Russians were too dumfounded to collect their senses. Then women and children dashed for refuge upstairs in the main building, huddling over the trapdoor in a frenzy of fright. Russians outside the palisades ran for the woods, some to fall lanced through the back as they raced, others to reach shelter of the dense forest, where they lay for eight days under hiding of bark and moss before rescue came. Medvednikoff, the commander, and a dozen others, seem to have hurled themselves downstairs at the first alarm, but already the outer doors had been rammed. The panels of the inner door were slashed out. A flare of {309} musketry met the Russians full in the face. The defenders dropped to a man, fearless in death as in life, though one wounded fellow seems to have dragged himself to the balcony where he succeeded in firing off the cannon before he was thrown over the palisades, to be received on the hostiles' upturned spears. Meanwhile wads of burning birch bark and moss had been tossed into the fort on the powder magazines. A high wind fanned the flames. A terrific explosion shook the fort. The trap-door where the women huddled upstairs gave way. Half the refugees fell through, where they were either butchered or perished in the flames. The others plunged from the burning building through the windows. A few escaped to the woods. The rest— Aleut women, wives of the Russians—were taken captive by the Kolosh. Ships, houses, fortress, all were in flames. By nightfall nothing remained of Sitka but the brass and iron of the melted cannon. The hostiles had saved loot of some two thousand sea-otter skins.

All that night, and for eight days and nights, the refugees of the forest lay hidden under bark and moss. Under cover of darkness, one, a herdsman, ventured down to the charred ruins of Sitka. The mangled, headless bodies of the Russians lay in the ashes. At noon of the eighth day the mountains suddenly rocked to the echo of two cannon-shots from the bay. A ship had come. Three times one Russian ventured to the shore, and three times was chased back to the woods; {310} but he had seen enough. The ship was an English trader under Captain Barber, who finally heard the shouts of the pursued man, put off a small boat and rescued him. Three others were saved from the woods in the same way, but had been only a few days on the ship, when Michael, the Kolosh chief, emboldened by success, rowed out with a young warrior and asked the English captain to give up the Russians. Barber affected not to understand, lured both Indians on board, seized them, put them in irons, and tied them across a cannon mouth, when he demanded the restoration of all captives and loot; but the Sitkan chief probably had his own account of who suggested the massacre. Also it was to the English captain's interests to remain on good terms with the Indians. Anyway, the twenty captives were not restored till two other ships had entered port, and sent some Kolosh canoes to bottom with grape-shot. The savages were then set free, and hastening up to Kadiak, Barber levelled his cannon at the Russian fort and demanded thirty-seven thousand five hundred dollars' salvage for the rescue of the captives and loot. Baranof haggled the Englishman tired, and compromised for one-fifth the demand.

Two years passed, and the fur company was powerless to strike an avenging blow. Wherever the Russians led Aleuts into the Kolosh hunting-grounds, there had been ambush and massacre; but Baranof {311} bided his time. The Aleut Indian hunters, who had become panic-stricken, gradually regained sufficient courage again to follow the Russians eastward. By the spring of 1804 Baranof's men had gathered up eight hundred Aleut Indians, one hundred and twenty Russian hunters, four small schooners, and two sloops. The Indians in their light boats of sea-lion skin on whalebone, the Russians in their sail-boats, Baranof set out in April from St. Paul, Kadiak, with his thousand followers to wreak vengeance on the tribes of Sitka. Sea-otter were hunted on the way, so that it was well on in September before the brigades entered Sitka waters. Meanwhile aid from an unexpected quarter had come to the fur company. Lieutenant Krusenstern had prevailed on the Russian government to send supplies to the Russian American Company by two vessels around the world instead of caravans across Siberia. With Krusenstern went Rezanoff, who had helped the fur traders to obtain their charter, and was now commissioned to open an embassy to Japan. The second vessel under Captain Lisiansky proceeded at once to Baranof's aid at Sitka.

Baranof was hunting when Lisiansky's man-of-war entered the gloomy wilds of Sitka Sound. The fur company's two sloops lay at anchor with lanterns swinging bow and stern to guide the hunters home. The eight hundred hostiles had fortified themselves behind the site of the modern Sitka. Palisades the depth of two spruce logs ran across the front of the {312} rough barricade, loopholed for musketry, and protected by a sort of cheval-de-frise of brushwood and spines. At the rear of the enemy's fort ran sally ports leading to the ambush of the woods, and inside were huts enough to house a small town. By the 28th of September Baranof's Aleut Indian hunters had come in and camped alongshore under protection of cannon sent close inland on a small boat. It was a weird scene that the Russian officers witnessed, the enemy's fort, unlighted and silent as death, the Aleut hunters alongshore dancing themselves into a frenzy of bravado, the spruce torches of the coast against the impenetrable forest like fireflies in a thicket; an occasional fugitive canoe from the enemy attempting to steal through the darkness out of the harbor, only to be blown to bits by a cannon-shot. The ships began to line up and land field-pieces for action, when a Sitkan came out with overtures of peace. Baranof gave him the present of a gay coat, told him the fort must be surrendered, and chiefs sent to the Russians as hostages of good conduct. Thirty warriors came the next day, but the whites insisted on chiefs as hostages, and the braves retired. On October the first a white flag was run up on the ship of war. No signal answered from the barricade. The Russian ships let blaze all the cannon simultaneously, only to find that the double logs of the barricade could not be penetrated. No return fire came from the Sitkans. Two small boats were then landed to destroy the enemy's {313} stores. Still not a sign from the barricade. Raging with impatience, Baranof went ashore supported by one hundred and fifty men, and with a wild halloo led the way to rush the fort. The hostile Sitkans husbanded their strength with a coolness equal to the famous thin red line of British fame. Not a signal, not a sound, not the faintest betrayal of their strength or weakness till in the dusk Baranof was within gunshot of the logs, when his men were met with a solid wall of fire. The Aleuts stopped, turned, stampeded. Out sallied the Sitkans pursuing Russians and Aleuts to the water's edge, where the body of one dead Russian was brandished on spear ends. In the sortie fourteen of the Russian forces were killed, twenty-six wounded, among whom was Baranof, shot through the shoulder. The guns of the war ship were all that saved the retreat from a panic.

Lisiansky then undertook the campaign, letting drive such a brisk fire the next day that the Sitkans came suing for peace by the afternoon. Three days the cunning savages stayed the Russian attack on pretence of arranging hostages. Hailing the fort on the morning of the 6th and securing no answer, Lisiansky again played his cannon on the barricade. That night a curious sound, that was neither chant nor war-cry, came from the thick woods. At daylight carrion crows were seen circling above the barricade. Three hundred Russians landed. Approaching cautiously for fear of ambuscade, they clambered over the {314} palisades and looked. The fort was deserted. Naught of the Sitkans remained but thirty dead warriors and all their children, murdered during the night to prevent their cries betraying the retreat.

New Archangel, as it was called, was built on the site of the present Sitka. Sixteen short and forty-two long cannon mounted the walls. As many as seven hundred officers and men were sometimes on garrison duty. Twelve officers frequently dined at the governor's table; and here, in spite of bishops and priests and deacons who later came on the ground, the revellers of the Russian fur hunters held high carnival. Thirty-six forts and twelve vessels the Russian American fur hunters owned twenty years after the loss of Sitka. New Archangel became more important to the Pacific than San Francisco. Nor was it a mistake to move the capital so far south. Within a few years Russian traders and their Indians were north as far as the Yukon, south hunting sea-otter as far as Santa Barbara. To enumerate but a few of the American vessels that yearly hunted sea-otter for the Russians southward of Oregon and California, taking in pay skins of the seal islands, would fill a coasting list. Rezanoff, who had failed to open the embassy to Japan and so came across to America, spent two months in Monterey and San Francisco trying to arrange with the Spaniards to supply the Russians with provisions. He was received coldly by the Spanish governor till {315} a love affair sprang up with the daughter of the don, so ardent that the Russian must depart post-haste across Siberia for the Czar's sanction to the marriage. Worn out by the midwinter journey, he died on his way across Siberia.

Sitka from the Sea.

[Illustration: Sitka from the Sea.]

Later, in 1812, when the Russian coasters were refused watering privileges at

San Francisco, the Russian American Company bought land near Bodega, and settled their famous Ross, or California colony, with cannon, barracks, arsenal, church, workshops, and sometimes a population of eight hundred Kadiak Indians. Here provisions were gathered for Sitka, and hunters despatched for sea-otter of the south. The massacres on the Yukon and the clashes with the Hudson's Bay traders are a story by themselves. The other doings of these "Sea Voyagers" became matters of international history when they tried to exclude American and British traders from the Pacific. The fur hunters in the main were only carrying out the far-reaching plans of Shelikoff, who originated the charter for the company; but even Shelikoff could hardly foresee that the country which the Russian government was willing to sell to the United States in 1867 for seven million dollars, would produce more than twice that during a single year in gold. To-day all that remains to Russia of these sea voyagers' plundering are two small islands, Copper and Bering in Bering Sea.

---

[1] Coxe and Müller are the two great authorities on the early Russian fur trade. Data on later days can be found in abundance in Krusenstern's *Voyage*, London, 1813; Kohl's *History*, London, 1862; Langsdorff's *Travels*, London, 1813; Stejneger's *Contributions to Smithsonian*, 1884, and *Report on Commander Islands*; Elliott's *Our Arctic Province*; Dall's *Alaska*; Veniaminof's *Letters on Aleutians*; Cleveland's *Voyages*, 1842, Nordenskjöld's *Voyage of the Vega*; Macfie's *Vancouver Island*; Ivan Petroff's *Report on Alaska*, 1880; Lisiansky's *Voyage Round the World*; Sauer's *Geographical Account of Expedition to Northern Parts*; Kotzebue's *Voyages of Discovery*, 1819, and *New Voyage*, 1831; Chappe d'Auteroche's *Siberia* and Kracheninnikof's *Kamchatka*, 1764; Simpson's *Voyage Round World*, 1847; Burney's *Voyages*; Gmelin's *Siberia*, Paris, 1767; Greenhow's *Oregon*; Pallas's *Northern Settlements*; Broughton's *Voyage*, 1804; Berg's *Aleutian Islands*; Bancroft's *Alaska*; *Massa. Hist. Coll.*, 1793-1795; *U. S. Congressional Reports* from 1867; Martin's *Hudson's Bay Territories*, London, 1849.

[2] Over one hundred American ships had been on the Pacific coast of America before 1812.

[3] Rezanoff married the fur trader's daughter. The bride did not live long, nor does the union seem to have been a love affair; as Rezanoff's infatuation with the daughter of a Spanish don later seemed to indicate a heart-free lover.

[4] See Chapter XII.

CHAPTER XII
1747-1818
BARANOF, THE LITTLE CZAR OF THE PACIFIC

Baranof lays the Foundations of Russian Empire on the Pacific Coast of America—Shipwrecked on his
Way to Alaska, he yet holds his Men in Hand and turns the Ill-hap to Advantage—How he bluffs the
Rival Fur Companies in Line—First Russian Ship built in America—Adventures leading the Sea-otter
Hunters—Ambushed by the Indians—The Founding of Sitka—Baranof, cast off in his Old Age, dies
of Broken Heart

No wilder lord of the wild northland ever existed than that old madcap Viking
of the Pacific, Alexander Baranof, governor of the Russian fur traders. For thirty
years he ruled over the west coast of America from Alaska to southern
California despotic as a czar. And he played the game single-handed, no retinue
but convicts from Siberia, no subjects but hostile Indians.

Whether leading the hunting brigades of a thousand men over the sea in skin
canoes light as cork, or rallying his followers ambushed by hostiles repelling
invasion of their hunting-ground, or drowning hardships with seas of fiery
Russian brandy in midnight carousals, Baranof was supreme autocrat. Drunk or
{317} sober, he was master of whatever came, mutineers or foreign traders
planning to oust Russians from the coast of America. Baranof stood for all that
was best and all that was worst in that heroic period of Pacific coast history
when adventurers from all corners of the earth roamed the otter-hunting grounds
in quest of fortune. Each man was a law unto himself. There was fear of neither
man nor devil. The whole era might have been a page from the hero epic of
prehistoric days when earth was young, and men ranged the seas unhampered by
conscience or custom, magnificent beasts of prey, glorying in freedom and
bloodshed and the warring elements.

Alexander Baranof.

[Illustration: Alexander Baranof.]

Yet in person Baranof was far from a hero. He was wizened, sallow, small, a
margin of red hair round a head bald as a bowl, grotesque under a black wig tied
on with a handkerchief. And he had gone up in life much the way a monkey
climbs, by shifts and scrambles and prehensile hoists with frequent falls. It was

an ill turn of fortune that sent him to America in the first place. He had been managing a glass factory at Irkutsk, Siberia, where the endless caravans of fur traders passed. Born at Kargopol, East Russia, in 1747, he had drifted to Moscow, set up in a shop for himself at twenty-four, failed in business, and emigrated to Siberia at thirty-five. Tales of profit in the fur trade were current at Irkutsk. Tired of stagnating in what was an absolutely safe but unutterably monotonous life, Baranof left the factory and invested all his {318} savings in the fur trade to the Indians of northern Siberia and Kamchatka. For some years all went well. Baranof invested deeper, borrowing for his ventures. Then the Chukchee Indians swooped down on his caravans, stampeded the pack horses, scuttled the goods, and Baranof was a bankrupt. The rival fur companies on the west coast of America were now engaged in the merry game of cutting each other's throats—literally and without restraint. A strong hand was needed—a hand that could weld the warring elements into one, and push Russian trade far down from Alaska to New Spain, driving off the field those foreigners whose relentless methods—liquor, bludgeon, musket—were demoralizing the Indian sea-otter hunters.

Destitute and bankrupt, Baranof was offered one-sixth of the profits to become governor of the chief Russian company. On August 10, 1790, about the same time that John Jacob Astor also embarked in the fur trade that was to bring him in contact with the Russians, Baranof sailed to America.

Fifty-two men the ragamuffin crew numbered, exiles, convicts, branded criminals, raggedly clad and ill-fed, sleeping wherever they could on the littered and vermin-infested decks; for what did the lives of a convict crew matter? Below decks was crammed to the waterline with goods for trade. All thought for furs, small care for men; and a few days out from port, the water-casks were found to be leaking so badly that allowance {319} of drinking water was reduced; and before the equinoctial gales, scurvy had already disabled the crew. Baranof did not turn back, nor allow the strong hand of authority to relax over his men as poor Bering had. He ordered all press of sail, and with the winds whistling through the rigging and the little ship straining to the smashing seas, did his best to outspeed disease, sighting the long line of surf-washed Aleutian Islands in September, coasting from headland to headland, keeping well offshore for fear of reefs till the end of the month, when compelled to turn in to the mid-bay of Oonalaska for water. There was no ignoring the danger of the landing. A shore like the walls of a giant rampart with reefs in the teeth of a saw, lashed to a fury by beach combers, offered poor escape from death by scurvy. Nevertheless, Baranof effected anchorage at Koshigin Bay, sent the small boats ashore for water, watched his chance of a seaward breeze, and ran out to sea again in one desperate effort to reach Kadiak, the headquarters of the fur traders, before winter. Outside the shelter of the harbor, wind and seas met the ship. She was driven helpless as a chip in a whirlpool straight for the granite rocks of the shore, where she smashed to pieces like the broken staves of a dry water-barrel. Led by the indomitable Baranof, who seemed to meet the challenge of the very elements, the half-drowned crew crawled ashore only to be ordered to save the cargo now rolling up in the wave wash.

{320} When darkness settled over the sea on the last night of September, Baranof was in the same predicament as Bering—a castaway for the winter on a barren island. Instead of sinking under the redoubled blows of an adverse fate, the little Russian rebounded like a rubber ball. A messenger and some Indians were at once despatched in a skin boat to coast from island to island in an effort to get help from Kadiak. Meanwhile Baranof did not sit lamenting with folded hands; and well that he did not; for his messengers never reached Kadiak.

Holes were at once scooped out of the sand, and the caves roofed over with the remnants of the wreck. These underground huts on an island destitute of wood were warmer than surface cabins, and better withstood the terrible north winds that swept down from the Arctic with such force that for two months at a time the men could go outside only by crawling under shelter of the boulders. Ammunition was distributed to the fifty castaways; salmon bought from the Indians, whom Baranof's fair treatment won from the first; once a week, rye meal was given out for soup; and for the rest, the men had to depend on the eggs of sea-birds, that flocked over the precipitous shores in myriads, or on the sea-lions roaring till the surf shook on the rocky islets along the shore.

If there is one characteristic more than another that proves a man master of destiny, it is ability not only to meet misfortune but to turn it to advantage when it {321} comes. While waiting for the rescue that never came, Baranof studied the language of the Aleuts, sent his men among them to learn to hunt, rode out to sea in their frail skin boats lashed abreast to keep from swamping during storm, slept at night on the beach with no covering but the overturned canoes, and, sharing every hardship, set traps with his own hands. When the weather was too boisterous for hunting, he set his people boiling salt from sea-water to dry supplies of fish for the summer, or replenishing their ragged clothes by making coats of birds' skin. The last week before Easter, provisions were so low the whole crew were compelled to indulge in a Lenten fast; but on Easter Monday, behold a putrid whale thrown ashore by the storm! The fast was followed by a feast. The winds subsided, and hunters brought in sea-lions.

It was quite apparent now no help was coming from Kadiak. Baranof had three large boats made of skin and wreckage. One he left with the men, who were to guard the remnants of the cargo. A second he despatched with twenty-six men. In the third he himself embarked, now in a raging fever from the exposure of the winter. A year all but a month from the time he had left Asia, Baranof reached Three Saints, Kadiak, on June 27, 1791.

Things were black enough when Baranof landed at Kadiak. The settlement of Three Saints had been depending on the supplies of his wrecked ship; and {322} when he arrived, himself in need, discontent flared to open mutiny. Five different rival companies had demoralized the Indians by supplying them with liquor, and egging them on to raid other traders. Southward, toward Nootka, were hosts of foreign ships—Gray and Kendrick and Ingraham from Boston, Vancouver from England, Meares from East India, Quadra from New Spain, private ventures outfitted by Astor from New York. If Russia were to preserve her hunting-grounds, no time should be lost.

Baranof met the difficulties like a commander of guerilla warfare. Brigades were sent eastward to the fishing-ground of Cook's Inlet for supplies. Incipient mutiny was quelled by sending more hunters off with Ismyloff to explore new sea-otter fields in Prince William Sound. As for the foreign fur traders, he conceived the brilliant plan of buying food from them in exchange for Russian furs and of supplying them with brigades of Aleut Island hunters to scour the Pacific for sea-otter from Nootka and the Columbia to southern California. This would not only add to stores of Russian furs, but push Russian dominion southward, and keep other nations off the field.

That it was not all plain sailing on a summer day may be inferred from one incident. He had led out a brigade of several hundred canoes, Indians and Russians, to Nuchek Island, off Prince William Sound. Though he had tried to win the friendship of the coast Indians by gifts, it was necessary to steal from point {323} to point at night, and to hide at many places as he coasted the mainland. Throwing up some sort of rough barricade at Nuchek Island, he sent the most of his men off to fish and remained with only sixteen Aleuts and Russians. It was perfectly natural that the Alaskan Indians should resent the Aleuts intruding on the hunting-grounds of the main coast, one thousand miles from the Aleutian Islands. Besides, the mainland Indians had now learned unscrupulous brutality from foreign traders. Baranof knew his danger and never relaxed vigilance. Of the sixteen men, five always stood sentry at night.

The night of June 20 was pitch dark. Terrific seas were running, and a tempest raged through the woods of the mainland. For safety, Ismyloff's ship had scudded to the offing. Baranof had undressed, thrown himself down in his cabin, and was in the deep sleep of outdoor exhaustion, when above the howling of the gale, not five steps away, so close it was impossible to distinguish friend from foe in the darkness, arose the shrill war-cry of hostiles. Leaping to his feet, Baranof rushed out undressed. His shirt was torn to shreds by a shower of flint and copper-head arrows. In the dark, the Russians could only fire blindly. The panic-stricken Aleuts dashed for their canoes to escape to Ismyloff's ship. Ismyloff sent armed Russians through the surf wash and storm to Baranof's aid. Baranof kept his small cannon pounding hot shot where the shouts sounded till daylight. Of the sixteen men, two {324} Russians and nine Aleuts were dead. Of the men who came to his aid, fifteen were wounded. The corpses of twelve hostiles lay on the beach; and as gray dawn came over the tempestuous sea, six large war canoes vanished into the morning mist, a long trail of blood over the waves showing that the hostiles were carrying off their wounded. Well might Baranof write, "I will vanquish a cruel fate; or fall under its repeated blows." The most of men would have thought they had sufficient excuse to justify backing out of their difficulties. Baranof locked grapples with the worst that destiny could do; and never once let go. Sometimes the absolute futility of so much striving, so much hardship, so much peril, all for the sake of the crust of bread that represents mere existence, sent him down to black depths of rayless despondency, when he asked himself, was life worth while? But he never let go his grip, his sense of resistance, his impulse to fight the worst, the unshunnable obligation of being alive and going on with the game, succeed or fail. Such fits of despair might end in wild carousals, when he drank every Russian under the table, outshouted the loudest singer, and perhaps wound up by throwing the roomful of revellers out of doors. But he rose from the depths of debauch and despair, and went on with the game. That was the main point.

The terrible position to which loss of supplies had reduced the traders of Kadiak when his own vessel {325} was wrecked at Oonalaska on the way out, demonstrated to Baranof the need of more ships; so when orders came from his company in 1793 to construct a sailing boat on the timberless island of Kadiak without iron, without axes, without saw, without tar, without canvas, he was eager to attempt the impossible. Shields, an Englishman, in the employment of Russia, was to act as shipbuilder; and Baranof sent the men assigned for the work up to Sunday Harbor on the west side of Prince William Sound, where heavy forests would supply timber and the tide-rush help to launch the vessel from the skids. There were no saws in the settlement. Planks had to be hewn out of logs. Iron, there was none. The rusty remnants of old wrecks were gathered together for bolts and joints and axes. Spruce gum mixed with blubber oil took the place of oakum and tar below the water-line. Moss and clay were used as calking above water. For sail cloth, there was nothing but shreds and rags and tatters of canvas patched together so that each mast-arm looked like Joseph's coat of many colors. Seventy-nine feet from stem to stern, the crazy craft measured, of twenty-three feet beam, thirteen draught, one hundred tons, two decks, and three masts. All the winter of 1792-1793, just a year after Robert Gray, the American, had built his sloop down at Fort Defence off Vancouver Island, the Russian shipbuilding went on. Then in April, lest the poverty of the Russians should become known to foreign traders, Baranof sent Shields, the English {326} shipbuilder, off out of the way, on an otter-hunting venture. It was August of the next summer before the clumsy craft slipped from the skids into the rising tide. She was so badly ballasted that she bobbled like cork; and her sails so frail they flew to tatters in the gentlest wind; but Russia had accomplished her first ship in America. Bells were set ringing when the *Phoenix* was towed into the harbor of Kadiak; and when she reached Okhotsk laden with furs to the water-line in April of 1794, enthusiasm knew no bounds. Salvos of artillery thundered over her sails, and mass was chanted, and a polish of paint given to her piebald, rickety sides that transformed her into what the fur company proudly regarded as a frigate. Before the year was out, Baranof had his men at work on two more vessels. There was to be no more crippling of trade for lack of ships.

But a more serious matter than shipbuilding demanded Baranof's attention. Rival fur companies were on the ground. Did one party of traders establish a fort on Cook's Inlet? Forthwith came another to a point higher up the inlet, where

Indians could be intercepted. There followed warlike raids, the pillaging of each other's forts, the capture of each other's Indian hunters, the utter demoralization of the Indians by each fort forbidding the savages to trade at the other, the flogging and bludgeoning and butchering of those who disobeyed the order— and finally, the forcible abduction of whole villages of women and children to compel the alliance of the hunters. All Baranof's work to {327} pacify the hostiles of the mainland was being undone; and what complicated matters hopelessly for him was the fact that the shareholders of his own company were also shareholders in the rival ventures. Baranof wrote to Siberia for instructions, urging the amalgamation of all the companies in one; but instructions were so long in coming that the fur trade was being utterly bedevilled and the passions of the savages inflamed to a point of danger for every white man on the North Pacific. Affairs were at this pass when Konovalof, the dashing leader of the plunderers, planned to capture Baranof himself, and seize the shipyard at Sunday Harbor, on Prince William Sound. Baranof had one hundred and fifty fighting Russians in his brigades. Should he wait for the delayed instructions from Siberia? While he hesitated, some of the shipbuilders were ambushed in the woods, robbed, beaten, and left half dead. Baranof could not afford to wait. He had no more legal justification for his act than the plunderers had for theirs; but it was a case where a man must step outside law, or be exterminated. Rallying his men round him and taking no one into his confidence, the doughty little Russian sent a formal messenger to Konovalof, the bandit, at his redoubt on Cook's Inlet, pompously summoning him in the name of the governor of Siberia to appear and answer for his misdeeds. To the brigand, the summons was a bolt out of the blue. How was he to know not a word had come from the governor of Siberia, and the summons {328} was sheer bluff? He was so terrorized at the long hand of power reaching across the Pacific to clutch him back to perhaps branding or penal service in Siberia, that he did not even ask to see Baranof's documents. Coming post-haste, he offered explanations, excuses, frightened pleadings. Baranof would have none of him. He clapped the culprit and associates in irons, put them on Ismyloff's vessel, and despatched them for trial to Siberia. That he also seized the furs of his rivals for safe keeping, was a mere detail. The prisoners were, of course, discharged; for Baranof's conduct could no more bear scrutiny than their own; but it was one way to get rid of rivals; and the fur companies at war in the Canadian northwest practised the same method twenty years later.

The effect of the bandit outrages on the hostile Indians of the mainland was quickly evident. Baranof realized that if he was to hold the Pacific coast for his company, he must push his hunting brigades east and south toward New Spain. A convict colony, that was to be the nucleus of a second St. Petersburg, was planned to be built under the very shadow of Mount St. Elias. Shields, the Englishman employed by Russia, after bringing back two thousand sea-otter from Bering Bay in 1793, had pushed on down south-eastward to Norfolk Sound or the modern Sitka, where he loaded a second cargo of two thousand sea-otter. A dozen foreign traders had already coasted Alaskan shores, and southward of Norfolk Sound was a flotilla {329} of American fur traders, yearly encroaching closer and closer on the Russian field. All fear of rivalry among the Russians had been removed by the union of the different companies in 1799. Baranof pulled his forces together for the master stroke that was to establish Russian dominion on the Pacific. This was the removal of the capital of Russian America farther south.

On the second week of April, 1799, with two vessels, twenty-two Russians, and three hundred and fifty canoes of Aleut fur hunters, Baranof sailed from Prince William Sound for the southeast. Pause was made early in May opposite Kyak—Bering's old landfall—to hunt sea-otter. The sloops hung on the offing, the hunting brigades, led by Baranof in one of the big skin canoes, paddling for the surf wash and kelp fields of the boisterous, rocky coast, which sea-otter frequent in rough weather. Dangers of the hunt never deterred Baranof. The wilder the turmoil of spray and billows, the more sea-otter would be driven to refuge on the kelp fields. Cross tides like a whirlpool ran on this coast when whipped by the winds. Not a sound from the sea-otter hunters! Silently, like sea-birds glorying in the tempest, the canoes bounded from crest to crest of the rolling seas, always taking care not to be caught broadsides by the smashing combers, or swamped between waves in the churning seas. How it happened is not known, but somehow between wind and tide-rip, thirty of the canoes {330} that rode over a billow and swept down to the trough never came up. A flaw of wind had caught the mountain billows; the sixty hunters went under. From where he was, Baranof saw the disaster, saw the terror of the other two hundred men, saw the rising storm, and at a glance measured that it was farther back to the sloops than on towards the dangerous shore. The sea-otter hunt was forgotten in the impending catastrophe to the entire brigade. Signal and shout confused in the thunder of the surf ordered the men to paddle for their lives inshore. Night was coming on. The distance was longer than Baranof had thought, and it was dark before the brigades landed, and the men flung themselves down, totally exhausted, to sleep on the drenched sands.

Barely were the hunters asleep when the shout of Kolosh Indians from the forests behind told of ambush. The mainland hostiles resenting this invasion of their hunting-fields, had watched the storm drive the canoes to land. On one side was the tempest, on the other the forest thronged with warriors. The Aleuts lost their heads and dashed for hiding in the woods, only to find certain death. Baranof and the Russians with him fired off their muskets till all powder was used. Then they shouted in the Aleut dialect for the hunters to embark. The sea was the lesser danger. By morning the brigades had joined the sloops on the offing. Thirteen more canoes had been lost in the ambush.

{331} Such was the inauspicious introduction for Baranof to the founding of the new Russian fort at Sitka or Norfolk Sound. It was the end of May before the brigades glided into the sheltered, shadowy harbor, where Chirikoff's men had been lost fifty years before. A furious storm of snow and sleet raged over the harbor. When the storm cleared, impenetrable forests were seen to the water-line, and great trunks of trees swirled out to sea. On the ocean side to the west, Mount Edgecumbe towered up a dome of snow. Eastward were the bare heights of Verstovoi; and countless tiny islets gilded by the sun dotted the harbor. Baranof would have selected the site of the present Sitka, high, rocky and secure from attack, but the old Sitkan chief refused to sell it, bartering for glass beads and trinkets a site some miles north of the present town.

Half the men were set to hunting and fishing, half to chopping logs for the new fort built in the usual fashion, with high palisades, a main barracks a hundred feet long in the centre, three stories high, with trap-doors connecting each story, cabins and hutches all round the inside of the palisades. Lanterns hung at the masthead of the sloops to recall the brigades each night; for Captain Cleveland, a Boston trader anchored in the harbor, forewarned Baranof of the Indians' treacherous character, more dangerous now when demoralized by the rivalry of white traders, and in possession of the civilized man's weapons. Free distribution of liquor by unscrupulous sea-captains did not mend {332} matters. Cleveland reported that the savages had so often threatened to attack his ship that he no longer permitted them on board; concealing the small number of his crew by screens of hides round the decks, trading only at a wicket with cannon primed and muskets bristling through the hides above the taffrail. He warned Baranof's hunters not to be led off inland bear hunting, for the bear hunt might be a Sitkan Indian in decoy to trap the hunters into an ambush. Such a decoy had almost trapped Cleveland's crew, when other Indians were noticed in ambush. The new fort was christened Archangel.

All went well as long as Baranof was on the ground. Sea-otter were obtained for worthless trinkets. Sentries paraded the gateway; so Baranof sailed back to Kadiak. The Kolosh or Sitkan tribes had only bided their time. That sleepy summer day of June, 1802, when the slouchy Siberian convicts were off guard and Baranof two thousand miles away, the Indians fell on the fort and at one fell swoop wiped it out.[1] Up at Kadiak honors were showering on the little governor. Two decorations of nobility he had been given by 1804; but his grief over the loss of Sitka was inconsolable. "I will either die or restore the fort!" he vowed, and with the help of a Russian man-of-war sent round the world, he sailed that summer into Sitka Sound. The Indians scuttled their barricade erected on the site of the present Sitka. Here {333} the fort was rebuilt and renamed New Archangel—a fort worthy in its palmy days of Baranof's most daring ambitions. Sixty Russian officers and eight hundred white families lived within the walls, with a retinue of two or three thousand Indian otter hunters cabined along the beach. There was a shipyard. There was a foundry for the manufacture of the great brass bells sold for chapels in New Spain. There were archbishops, priests, deacons, schools. At the hot springs twenty miles away, hospitals and baths were built. A library and gallery of famous paintings were added to the fort, though Baranof complained it would have been wiser to have physicians for his men. For the rest of Baranof's rule, Sitka became the great rendezvous of vessels trading on the Pacific. Here Baranof held sway like a potentate, serving regal feasts to all visitors with the pomp of a little court, and the barbarity of a wassailing mediaeval lord.

But all this was not so much fireworks for display. Baranof had his motive. To the sea-captains who feasted with him and drank themselves torpid under his table, he proposed a plan—he would supply the Aleut hunters for them to hunt on shares as far south as southern California. Always, too, he was an eager buyer of their goods, giving them in exchange seal-skins from the Seal Islands. Boston vessels were the first to enter partnership with Baranof. Later came Astor's captains from New York, taking sealskins in trade for goods supplied to the Russians.

{334} How did Baranof, surrounded by hostile Indians, with no servants but Siberian convicts, hold his own single-handed in American wilds? Simply by the power of his fitness, by vigilance that never relaxed, by despotism that was by turns savage and gentle, but always paternal, by the fact that his brain and his brawn were always more than a match for the brain and brawn of all the men under him. To be sure, the liberal measure of seventy-nine lashes was laid on the back of any subordinate showing signs of mutiny, but that did not prevent many such attempts.

The most serious was in 1809. From the time that Benyowsky, the Polish adventurer, had sacked the garrison of Kamchatka, Siberian convicts serving in America dreamed of similar exploits. Peasants and officers, a score in number, all convicts from Siberia, had plotted to rise in New Archangel or Sitka, assassinate the governor, seize ships and provisions, and sailing to some of the South Sea Islands, set up an independent government. The signal was to be given when Naplavkof, an officer who was master plotter, happened to be on duty. On such good terms was the despot, Baranof, with his men, that the plot was betrayed to him from half a dozen sources. It did not trouble Baranof. He sent the betrayers a keg of brandy, bade one of them give a signal by breaking out in drunken song, and at the sound himself burst into the roomful of conspirators, sword in hand, {335} followed by half a hundred armed soldiers. The plotters were handcuffed and sent back to Siberia.

There was something inexcusably cruel in the termination of Baranof's services with the fur company. He was now over seventy years of age. He was tortured by rheumatism from the long years of exposure in a damp climate. Because he was not of noble birth, though he had received title of nobility, he was subject to insults at the hands of any petty martinet who came out as officer on the Russian vessels. Against these Baranof usually held his own at Sitka, but they carried back to St. Petersburg slanderous charges against his honesty. Twice he had asked to be allowed to resign. Twice successors had been sent from Russia; but one died on the way, and the other was shipwrecked. It was easy for malignant tongues to rouse suspicion that Baranof's desire to resign sprang from interested motives, perhaps from a wish to conceal his own peculations. Though Baranof had annually handled millions of dollars' worth of furs for the Russian Company, at a distance from oversight that might have defied detection in wrong-doing, it was afterwards proved that he had not misused or misappropriated one dime's worth of property; but who was to believe his honesty in the face of false charges?

In the fall of 1817 Lieutenant Hagemeister arrived at Sitka to audit the books of the company. Concealing from Baranof the fact that he was to be deposed, {336} Hagemeister spent a year investigating the records. Not a discrepancy was discovered. Baranof, with the opportunity to have made millions, was a poor man. Without explanation, Hagemeister then announced the fact—Baranof was to be retired. Between voluntarily retiring and being retired was all the difference between honor and insult. The news was a blow that crushed Baranof almost to senility. He was found doddering and constantly in tears. Again and again he bade good-by to his old comrades, comrades of revel with noble blood in their veins, comrades of the hunt, pure-blooded Indians, who loved him as a brother, comrades of his idleness, Indian children with whom he had frolicked—but he could not bear to tear himself from the land that was the child of his lifelong efforts. The blow had fallen when he was least able to bear it. His nerve was gone. Of all the Russian wreckages in this cruel new land, surely this wreck was the most pitiable—the maker deposed by the thing he had made, cast out by his child, driven to seek some hidden place where he might die out of sight. An old sea-captain offered him passage round the world to Russia, where his knowledge might still be of service. Service? That was the word! The old war-horse pricked up his ears! Baranof sailed in the fall of 1818. By spring the ship homeward-bound stopped at Batavia. There was some delay. Delay was not good for Baranof. He was ill, deadly ill, of that most deadly of all ailments, heartbreak, {337} consciousness that he was of no more use, what the Indians call "the long sickness of too much thinking." When the vessel put out to sea again, Baranof, too, put to sea, but it was to the boundless sea of eternity. He died on April 16, 1819, and was laid to rest in the arms of the great ocean that had cradled his hopes from the time he left Siberia.

To pass judgment on Baranof's life would be a piece of futility. His life, like the lives of all those Pacific coast adventurers, stands or falls by what it was, not what it meant to be; by what it did, not what it left undone; and what Baranof left was an empire half the size of Russia. That his country afterward lost that empire was no fault of his. Like all those Vikings of the North Pacific, he was essentially a man *who did things*, not a theorizer on how things ought to be done, not a slug battening on the things other men have done.

They were not anaemic, these old "sea voyagers" of the Pacific, daring death or devil, with the red blood of courage in their veins, and the red blood of a lawless manhood, too. They were not men of milk and water type, with little good and less bad. Neither their virtues nor their vices were lukewarm; but *they did things*, these men; added to the sum total of human effort, human knowledge, human progress. Sordid their motives may have been, sordid as the blacksmith's when he smashes his sledge on the anvil; but from the anvil of their hardships, from the clash of the {338} primordial warfare between the Spirit of the Elements and the Spirit of Man, struck out some sparks of the Divine. There was the courage as dauntless in the teeth of the gale as in the face of death. There was the yearning to know More, to seek it, to follow it over earth's ends, though the quest led to the abyss of a watery grave. What did they want, these fool fellows, following the rushlight of their own desires? That is just it. They didn't know what they sought, but they knew there was something just beyond to be sought, something new to be known; and because Man is Man, they set out on the quest of the unknown, chancing life and death for the sake of a little gain to human progress. It is the spirit of the heroic ages, and to that era belongs the history of the Vikings on the North Pacific.

[1] See Chapter XI.

{339}

INDEX

A

B

founds New Archangel (modern Sitka), 332-333; in old age deposed from governorship, 335-336; death of, 337.

Baranof Castle, Sitka, 301.

Barber, Captain, at Sitka, 310.

Barclay, English sea-captain, 224, 227, 254, 264, 272.

Barnes, sailor with Gray, 230.

Barrell, Joseph, 211, 215, 229, 241.

Bassof, otter hunter, 82-83.

Begg, cited, 290 n.

Behm, Major, 196, 208.

Behm Canal, 286.

Benyowsky, Mauritius, Polish exile to Kamchatka, 108-110; career of, at Bolcheresk, 113-122; escapes to sea on pirate cruise, 122; meets Ochotyn at Bering Island, 123-124; visits Alaska, 125; adventures of, in Luzon, Formosa, and China, 126-127; holds French commission in Madagascar, 137; returns to Europe, goes to Baltimore, and is sent on filibustering expedition to Madagascar, 127; death of, 127-128; authorities for, 128 n.

Berg, cited, 11 n., 22 n., 129, 295.

Bering, Anna, 8 n.

Bering, Jonas, 8 n.

Bering, Thomas, 22 n.

Bering, Unos, 22.

Bering, Vitus Ivanovich, birth and early history of, 8; commissioned by Peter the Great to explore waters between Russia and America, 8-10; first expedition of (1725-1730), 10-12; second expedition undertaken by, 12; difficulties of, with scientists about "Gamaland," 13-15, 19, 22, 24; arrival of expedition of, at Okhotsk, 16; start of, from Avacha Bay, Kamchatka (1741), 17; cruise of, in *St. Peter*, 22-45; landfall at Kyak Island, 26-27, 47 n.; Mt. St. Elias discovered by, 26; exploration of coast of Alaskan peninsula by, 28-36; forced to winter at Commander Islands, 35-36; death of, 54; summary of work of, 55-56, 61; conclusions of, rejected by scientists, 172-173; mentioned in connection with other explorers, 183, 184 n., 239, 263, 264; Cook verifies conclusions of, 189-194.

Bering Bay, 288.

Bering Island, 37-45, 97, 123-124, 300, 315.

Betshevin, Siberian merchant, 84, 87.

Bidarkas, fur hunters' boats, 67.

Billings, Joseph, 254, 258, 259-261.

D

E

F

G

Galiano, Don, 272-273.

Gama, John de, 6 n.

Gamaland, mythical continent, 6, 9, 168, 173; Bering's conclusion concerning non-existence of, 12, 18; on D'Isles' map, 19; Bering's second voyage in search of, 22-23; search for, relinquished, 24-25; Cook demolishes myth of, 181.

Garret, John, 141.

Glory of the South Seas, Spanish galleon, 155, 156, 157; captured by Drake, 158.

Glottoff, Stephen, 88, 96; Korovin rescued by, 104.

Gmelin, scientist, 14 n., 295 n.

Golden Hind, Drake renames the *Pelican* the, 150; cruise on the Pacific in, 151-165; end of, 166.

Gore, Cook's lieutenant, 190.

Gorelin, Russian sailor, 87, 91 n.

Gray, Robert, character of, 213; sent by Boston merchants on fur-trading voyage to the Pacific coast, 213-214; departure of, from Boston (October, 1787), 215-216; rounds Cape Horn and reaches Drake's "New Albion," 216-218; adventures of, in Tillamook Bay, 219-222; sails to Nootka, 222-223; meets Captains Meares and Douglas, 223-225; in spring explores Straits of Fuca, 227, 235; takes cargo of furs to China and returns to Boston (August, 1790), 228-229; leaves Boston on second voyage (September, 1790), 230; winters at Clayoquot (1791-1792), 232-234; builds sloop *Adventure*, 233, 234, 325; meets Vancouver expedition, 235, 268-270; discovers and names Columbia River (May, 1792), 236-238, 241, 268, 269; goes to China and returns to Boston (July, 1793), 238; death of, 238; place of, among discoverers, 238-240; authorities for, 240 n.; later mention of, 264, 272, 286, 322; Lieutenant Broughton's view of explorations of, 280.

Gray's Harbor, 236, 241.

Greenhow, cited, 241, 290, 295.

Guatalco, Drake stops at, 159.

Gulf of Georgia, 271.

Gvozdef, discoverer, 12 n.

H

I

208; Ledyard's encounters with, 251, 253, 258, 260-261; in service of Russian American Fur Company, under Baranof, 322, 323.

J

K

L

Lady Washington, the, Gray sails on, to Pacific coast, 213-219; Captain Kendrick in command of, 228; last mention of, 238.

Langsdorff, cited, 295.

La Salle, vii, 60.

Lauridsen, Peter, authority on Bering, 12 n., 61 n.

La Vérendrye, vii, 7, 19, 60, 177.

Ledyard, Dr., 243 n.

Ledyard, John, corporal of marines with Cook, 181-182, 195-196, 200, 203, 205, 247-252; authority for Cook's voyage, 209 n.; early career of, 242-244; authorities for life of, 243 n., 262 n.; student at Dartmouth College, 245; works his way to England, 245-246; experiences of, in London, 246-247; on return of Cook expedition sent to fight against United States, 252; returns to Groton and deserts from British navy, 252-253; borrows money, goes to Paris, and meets Paul Jones and Thomas Jefferson, 254-255; in England, 256; walks fourteen hundred miles from Stockholm around Baltic Sea to St. Petersburg, 257-258; accompanies Dr. Brown three thousand miles into Siberia, 258-259; joins Joseph Billings' expedition and reaches Lena River, 260; arrested as a French spy, carried back to St. Petersburg, and expelled from the country, 260-261; reaches London and is sent to discover source of Nile, 261-262; dies at Cairo, 262.

Lewis and Clark expedition, 60-61; John Ledyard's influence on, 242, 255, 262.

Lincoln, General, of Boston, 229.

Lisiansky, Captain, 295, 311, 313.

Lok, Michael, 275 n.

Lopez, Marcus, 216, 220; murder of, by Indians, 221.

Lynn Canal, Vancouver's survey of, 288.

M

Macao, Benyowsky in, 127, 128.

Macfie, *Vancouver Island* by, 295 n.

Mackenzie, Alexander, 219.

Madagascar, Benyowsky's adventures and death in, 127.

O

P

Q

Queen Charlotte Island, discovered, 227; Captain Kendrick at, 230-232.

R

S

T

U

V

W

Made in the USA
Las Vegas, NV
22 April 2022

47857005R00132